COOK

REAL

HAWAI'I

COOK

CLARKSON POTTER/PUBLISHERS NEW YORK

REAL HAWAI'I

SHELDON SIMEON WITH GARRETT SNYDER

FOR MY MOTHER JUANITA SIMEON,
WHO TAUGHT ME THE MOST.
YOUR WARMTH AND KINDNESS TO
OTHERS SHOWED ME THAT LIFE IS
SO MUCH BETTER WHEN YOU
GREET IT WITH A SMILE.

CONTENTS

INTRODUCTION

I'm local: L-O-C-A-L!
As brown as one dollar size 'opihi shell
I'm as local as the ume in your musubi
As one spaghetti plate lunch with side order kim chee
I'm as local as the gravy on the three scoop rice
As all the rainbow colors on da kine shave ice
                                    —Frank De Lima's Joke Book

What is the food of Hawai'i? *Ho boy*, that's one question I've been asked many times. I always have an answer, but every time it leaves my mouth I wonder if I captured the whole truth, in all its splendor and complexity.

Hawai'i has been home my entire life. I'm sure many people say this about where they grew up, but I believe there's no place on earth more beautiful than our islands, home to swaying palm trees, sugary white sand beaches, and impossibly green mountains streaked with waterfalls. The Hawaiian Islands form one of the most visited yet most remote archipelagos on earth, a tiny scattering of green surrounded by the blue vastness of the Pacific. We're the fiftieth state, but, as we joked in school, the guy who drew the map always stuck us way in the corner. About 1.5 million people live in Hawai'i, a number dwarfed by the 10 million who came as visitors last year. How does a place that has so long been defined by the outside world define itself? The answer is the reason why I set out to write this book.

After competing on two seasons of *Top Chef*, I've been extraordinarily fortunate to have a kind of national exposure. When I was younger, I saw these opportunities as a way to gain recognition and validation from the mainland, looking to restaurants in L.A. and New York for inspiration.

During my first season on the show, most people knew me as the chill Hawaiian guy. It took me a while to get across that I was not actually Hawaiian—as in native Hawaiian—but a third-generation Filipino *from* Hawai'i. Big difference. See, in Hawai'i we identify ourselves ethnically rather than geographically, which may tell you something about our cultural influences. On the mainland people might say "I'm a New Yorker," but here it's "Betty is second-gen Japanese Korean," or "Lyndon? He's Portuguese Chinese Hawaiian," and so on. More on that later. The Hawai'i-Hawaiian thing was the tip of the iceberg, though. On the show I

found myself answering lots of questions about where I was from. *Do you eat lots of Spam?* Yes. *Pineapple?* Sometimes. *Macadamia nuts?* Not as much as you think. *Is the poke really better there?* Yes, by a huge margin. *Do you drink mai tais?* Sure, but I like beer and Crown Royal better.

I came to realize that the Hawai'i I knew was often misunderstood on the mainland, shaped by years of ad campaigns with airline stewardesses handing out leis, ham and pineapple pizza, and big brown guys dancing with fire sticks. I mean, those do exist, but they're not the whole picture.

The warmth of home, what I missed most when I was away, was in things that guidebooks didn't explain to tourists, the deeper nuances that make our culture different from any other place on earth. Most of all that meant food. Hawai'i food, or what we call local food, tells a story of where we come from. It is embedded in every part of our language, our songs, our jokes. We celebrate it every chance we get. It doesn't just fill our bellies, it keeps us being who we are. If you didn't know the Hawai'i I knew, how could I share all of that with you in a plate of food?

For the last many years, that question has defined what I cook. It's not just about *ono grinds* (delicious food), it's about connecting what we love to eat with culture and community. A deeper meaning to the deliciousness, if you will. Eventually that pursuit led me to the cookbook that is in front of you. What better way to tell a story?

Before digging into local grinds, it's necessary to understand one concept that underpins the entire culture of Hawai'i. *Aloha* is a word you've no doubt seen plastered on coffee mugs and T-shirts at gift shops. You might even know it means both hello and goodbye. But the true meaning of the aloha spirit is something more profound: the extension of goodwill and grace with no expectation of reward, the purest expression of compassion, hospitality, and love. I don't think it's a coincidence that the concept of aloha originated in one of the most isolated places on earth, where by necessity people took care of each other and the land that fed them in order to survive. Aloha is demonstrated not just in words but in deeds, and the creating and giving of food for friends and strangers alike is one of the most essential acts of aloha in existence. Food makes family, families make food. There is no one without the other.

The family we talk about in Hawai'i can mean different things, as in your blood relatives but also your distant cousins, adopted relatives, in-laws, friends, and even neighbors, all encompassed in the Hawaiian word 'ohana. This notion of one big 'ohana suits the diversity found here, too, made up of a hodgepodge of cultures that arrived as immigrants from countries like China, Japan, Portugal, Korea, and the Philippines. You may have heard Hawai'i referred to as "the melting pot of the Pacific," but that's not entirely accurate, since it implies everything blended together into one homogenous stew. The reality is that Hawai'i is more of a salad bowl, or better yet a plate of chop suey: each ethnicity tossed together but still distinct. Growing up, we poked fun at each other's differences and quirks in a good-natured way, while also being aware and proud of those unique traits that made us who we are.

For a sociologist, this intermingling is fascinating. For a cook, it's delicious. Peek into a garage or house party on the weekend and count the number of cultures spread out on the table. Oxtail soup nestled next to kim chee dip with a side of fried wontons and fish cakes. Across the room the kids are fighting over the last piece of butter mochi. From afar this multicultural combination seems to have no rhyme or reason, but to us it just feels natural—the most organic form of fusion cuisine. It's a rich and intricate history playing out on the table. I'm not Korean, but I love to make kalbi. I'm not Chinese, but I love to make chow fun. Breaking bread together expanded our palates and created new combinations of flavors and ingredients. All those traditions running into each other is what makes our food so special. As locals say, *how lucky we live Hawai'i.*

But as much as I draw inspiration from local culture at large, my family heritage is equally important to how I cook. When my grandparents came to Hawai'i, their traditions came with them. Their recipes were based on memories from their relatively short time living in the Philippines, frozen in a

time capsule forever and passed down. Like many immigrant families, their food was frugal, came from the land, and was prepared with love. Most of all they were resourceful, re-creating what they'd grown up eating using what was around them. Eventually those nostalgic old traditions merged with the new traditions they were introduced to, creating a mash-up that was rooted in the past but distinct from anywhere else—Filipino through the lens of Hawai'i. I learned just as much from these hand-me-down lessons as I did from culinary school. As a chef I might cut the vegetables a little neater than Grandma and Grandpa did, but when it came to making sure everyone was nourished and well-fed, they were second to none.

Of the six major islands that make up Hawai'i—Kaua'i, Oahu, Moloka'i, Lāna'i, Maui, and Hawai'i (the Big Island)—the one I grew up on, the Big Island, is regarded as the most traditional in culture, the most laid-back, and certainly the one where the Hawaiian pidgin is the thickest. Here you've got perhaps the best growing climate in the world and fertile volcanic soil: banana trees and ti plants everywhere, taro and ginger you can pluck from the ground, and guavas and mangoes falling from the trees. Most everyone we knew either farmed, hunted, or fished. As kids, my brother and I would go up to the Hakalau Gulch and pick wild *pohole*, tender fiddlehead ferns. In school I'd skip class to go spearfishing with my buddies or spend the day down at the coast picking *'opihi* (limpets) or catching Samoan crabs. Or maybe one of my uncles would show up with a freshly butchered goat and we'd spend the afternoon at the house cleaning tripe. Those were the adventures you took for granted as a kid, but when you look back later you understand how unique and formative they were.

As big projects tend to do, writing a cookbook has helped me take a deeper look at my cooking career thus far, given that so much of it has flown past in a blur. It has helped me express in words what I love so much about our food, from the crunch of fresh *limu* (seaweed) gathered from the ocean to blocks of cut tuna gleaming like rubies at Suisan Fish Market. It's the smell of roasting chickens over kiawe wood, the first bite of sticky rice warm from the bento, and the soothing creaminess of chilled mac salad on a hot day. The recipes contained in this book are not just dishes I've served at my restaurants, they're foods that represent my culture and family, foods of great celebration and bounty, of poverty and humility. These are foods that capture the spirit of immigrants, both recent and long-settled, the foods of America. Though every local has their own traditions and perspectives, these are mine—one small fraction of what makes up the heart and soul of Hawai'i. In other words, this is local food. I hope you find as much joy and enlightenment in cooking these dishes for your 'ohana as I have for mine. Much *mahalos* (many thanks) for reading.

MY STORY

Here's what you need to know about me: I was born and raised on the Big Island. Both sides of my family come from the Philippines. My grandpa Urbano Simeon left his hometown of Laoag in Ilocos Norte when he was eighteen and came to Hawai'i as part of a wave of *sakadas*, or Filipino migrant workers, to work on the sugar plantations in the 1930s. Here, he met my grandma Felicisima, and they settled in the small company plantation town of Pepe'ekeo and had nine kids (my dad, Reinior Simeon, was the youngest son). Like most immigrant families, they didn't have much but they made ends meet, growing vegetables, raising chickens, fishing.

Our family lived on the outskirts of Hilo, a relatively sleepy town on the rocky windward (eastern) coast of the Big Island. Dad worked at a Hilo Coast sugar mill for twenty years, then spent another twenty-five years working for Hawai'i County. My mom, Juanita Janet "Joanne" Moreno, came here with her family from the Philippines (Santa Lucia in Ilocos Sur) in the 1970s and not long afterward she met my dad.

Both sides of my family tree were filled with amazing cooks. All of my uncles and aunts had their own dishes or recipes they were famous for and would cook for every family party, of which we had plenty. Our house had a long carport-slash-garage-slash-patio that was always packed with family and friends on the weekend. The Simeon house was known as the gathering spot (also the "gout house" because we served many rich foods). Dad was the designated cook of the community; before a big event like a wedding, graduation, or first birthday, he'd cook from sunup to sundown to feed upwards of three or four hundred people. He even welded together his own metal cookers to roast whole pigs and goats. As small kids we were taught to always help out, clean the table, wash dishes. If Uncle's beer was half full, you grab him another one before he even asks. Dad cooked for others so much our neighbors once reported us to the county because they thought he was running a bootleg catering business.

But Mom wasn't to be outdone either. She was always the life of the party and instilled a deep love and appreciation of food in me and my older brother, Jeremy, early on, much the way she had learned from her mother and grandmother. Mom was the one who also made us miki noodles when we were sick, or cooked up her famous pinakbet for dinner. When I was in grade school, though, my mom had her first stroke. Because of her health problems, in later years she wasn't able to drive and it became difficult for her to walk. Dad took on two jobs to support us, and Jeremy and I quickly learned to take care of ourselves. We lived frugally and Dad made sure that we never wasted a gallon of water or a single watt of electricity. Throughout it all, though, food and cooking were what kept us connected with each other.

Looking back now, it's not exactly surprising that both my brother and I ended up in culinary school after high school, since we'd both been butchering chickens since the first grade.

Going to culinary school on Oʻahu was the first time I was exposed to the world of serious chefs and restaurants, which seemed like a world away from the rustic, humble cooking we did in our backyards. I was hooked immediately. After I finished school, I ended up on Maui, where my then girlfriend and future wife, Janice, lived (we first met while working as interns at Disney World, but that's a whole other story). My first serious kitchen job, aside from when I was a pizza *artiste* at Pizza Hut, was working at a restaurant in Lahaina called Aloha Mixed Plate. I was a "prep cook," but 85 percent of the time I was the dishwasher. Maybe I'd cut up an onion here and there.

But slowly I worked my way to sous-chef. Even when I wasn't the best chef on the line, I made sure I was the hardest working. Someone call in sick the day of? Sheldon will take the shift. The job no one else wanted? Sheldon will handle it. I worked so much, one day my back gave out while reaching for a pan of chow mein and took almost a year to heal.

Around that same time was when my mom passed away. I felt guilty because I had spent so much of the last few years working, away from home, away from Hilo. That was also the same year that Janice and I got married and she became pregnant with our first kid (we have four now!). It was an emotional roller coaster to say the least, but food and family have kept me rooted throughout.

Eventually I got the chance to open my first restaurant, Star Noodle, a noodle shop in Lahaina that served food inspired by the local dishes I grew up with. Star Noodle turned out to be a hit among both locals and tourists, and the next year we started getting national recognition: James Beard Award nominations, and a nomination for *Food & Wine* "Best New Chef." Then the call came. I was scrubbing pots in the dish pit when our hostess told me someone from *Top Chef* was on the line. I packed my knives and my ʻukulele and headed off to the show.

The highlight of Season 10 for me was the "Restaurant Wars" segment, where we were tasked with creating our own restaurant concept and bringing it to life. My idea was one I'd been jotting down in a notebook for years: a restaurant called Urbano, named after my grandpa, that served contemporary Filipino food. I ended up winning the episode—and a Toyota Avalon, which I drive to this day!—but the part that stuck with me was seeing the judges react to my food. Here were the judges, iconic culinary figures, eating the humble

food I grew up on, sinigang soup and pork belly adobo, and being utterly blown away. It was a light-switch moment for my entire career.

Though I ended up being voted fan favorite, my season ended at the finale. It's a complicated tale, but the short version is that I was worried people would think I was a one-trick pony who could only cook Asian or Filipino food, not yet confident enough to realize that cooking from my own background was what had gotten me that far in the competition. I ended up creating dishes based on what I thought would impress others instead of doing what had gotten me to the finale in the first place, and the judges knew it right away. They sent me home. Still, I came back to Maui with my chin held high and a clearer idea of the food I wanted to cook. I was going to stay true to myself.

I opened a restaurant called Migrant. The name was based on the notion that everyone who came to Hawai'i from somewhere else was a "migrant," so the restaurant would celebrate the food of our grandparents and the cultures they brought here. On the menu there was stir-fried pancit, short rib ramen, lobster tempura, fried 'ahi belly, tocino with pickled onions. I guess you could say that it was a pretty wild collection of dishes considering the restaurant was in a fancy Wailea hotel, but I was learning to let go of what I thought people expected and cook what felt right to me.

The next restaurant I had was also the next step in the story of how I wanted to cook closer to, and for, the community. The story of Tin Roof begins with this old-school *okazuya* (Japanese deli) called Koko Ichiban Ya, which was tucked away in a big strip mall in Kahului between an island gift shop and a check-cashing store. Over several years and countless orders of katsu donburi—fried cutlet rice bowl—I became a regular at Koko. I got to know the Japanese family who had owned the place for twenty-five years: Mr. and Mrs. Komai and their two sons. I'd always joke with them that if they were ever thinking of moving on to give me a call first so I could take over the spot. A year before their lease renewal, Mr. Komai became ill. They pushed through that last year, but it was difficult for them to continue. One day out of the blue, as I was driving to work at Migrant, I got a phone call. On the other end of the line, in a Japanese accent, came the words, "Are you ready?"

Because of the legacy that Tin Roof inherited, it was important to me that the restaurant offer food that was affordable and accessible to everyone, most of all locals—simple, honest, delicious food that spoke to the community. Even though I was running an upscale restaurant, I dreamt about opening a plate lunch spot like the ones I used to eat at in Hilo. In fact, the name Tin Roof came from all the buildings with metal roofs on the Big Island, which gave off a comforting *tink-tink-tink* sound whenever it rained (which was all the time).

Janice and I poured in all our savings and emptied out our 401(k)s to open Tin Roof. It was a true mom-and-pop business. Just 538 square feet, and on opening day we had $200 left in the bank, $198 of which we then spent on a fire extinguisher we needed to pass inspections. With a mere $2 to our names, we served our first customer.

Right as Tin Roof was opening, I did something very crazy, possibly dumb. I agreed to appear on *Top Chef* for a second time (I know!). Another long story short, I ended up losing in the finale (again!) and being voted fan favorite (again!). Thankfully, when I came back to Maui, Tin Roof had not burst into flames while I was gone. From then on, I got to see Tin Roof grow into the place I imagined, a spot that fed the community and carried on local traditions. We could see how it impacted people's lives on a day-to-day basis, even if it was with something as simple as a pork belly bowl with mac salad. There was no better satisfaction.

After Tin Roof, I had the chance to open another upscale restaurant in Wailea called Lineage. For me it was a chance to show that although my cooking was born of these rustic traditions, it could also be presented in a refined, contemporary way—that authenticity and creativity wasn't an either/or proposition. Rather than focus on plate lunches like we did at Tin Roof, the concept at Lineage was to pay tribute to the special dishes you'd encounter at milestone celebrations: first birthdays, weddings, luaus, and such. There were boiled peanuts, fried noodles, smoked meat with guava jelly, cold ginger chicken, and my family's recipe for pork and peas. We even had a roving pupu cart (welded by my dad).

In the kitchen, we played around with local produce grown specifically for us and worked with some of the best foragers, farmers, and fishermen on the island. We pounded our own taro for poi and fermented it until it was tangy as sourdough, aged local fish for *bagoóng*, pickled and cured every tropical fruit and vegetable we could get our hands on. Our goal was to celebrate the old ways of Hawai'i by presenting them in a new context, peeling back layers of history. There was so much to explore just by looking backwards.

These days, although I still think of myself as a glorified line cook, I realize how unique the platform is that I've been given to tell the stories of the place where I grew up. Early on I was just a kid in the middle of the ocean cooking noodles and trying to get noticed by the outside world. Now I understand the responsibility that comes with the attention. Maybe all these opportunities were put in front of me for a larger reason. My grandpa came to Hawai'i in the hopes of making a better life for his family, and here I am two generations later, trying to do the same for mine, this time by sharing the Hawai'i I know with the world. But enough story already, like Auntie used to say: Go talk or come eat.

A BRIEF HISTORY OF HAWAI'I

To understand local food, you first have to understand the story of Hawai'i, which—in contrast to the beautiful scenery and heartwarming people here—can be downright ugly at times.

The earliest settlers to the islands were Polynesians who arrived some time during the first millennium AD. They called themselves *kānaka maoli*; they're who we know as native Hawaiians. Over the centuries, they created a rich food culture and carefully managed food system that allowed them to live off the land and sea, on a remote string of islands isolated in the middle of the Pacific Ocean. Though their kingdom no longer rules over Hawai'i, the influence of what the Hawaiians built is still felt among *kama'āina*—a Hawaiian word for non-native but lifelong residents—it means "child of the land." Because of Hawaiian culture, social concepts of aloha (unconditional love and compassion) and *pono* (fairness and righteousness) are instilled in children at an early age. The Hawaiians also created a strong fishing and farming culture, the legacy of which can be seen today through the containers of poke and poi found in every island grocery store. Even as non-natives, we sing Hawaiian songs and take part in dances and ceremonies. We eat Hawaiian dishes like kālua pig and laulau to mark big celebrations. That all these Hawaiian traditions survived and endured through so much oppression and hardship is a testament to how deep their roots go and how essential it is to preserve and honor them.

For around five hundred years or so—between the last of the Polynesian voyages and the arrival of Europeans—the Hawaiian people existed in isolation. This period saw the rise of intricate irrigation networks that channeled water down the valleys to feed crops, and the creation of a land management practice called *ahupua'a*, which divided the islands into parcels stretching from the oceanside (*makai*) to the mountainside (*mauka*), ensuring that each tribe could access the different microclimates for growing and harvesting. Fish and shellfish would be caught from coastal streams, shorelines, and the reefs beyond; lowland marshes were home to cultivated patches of *kalo* (taro) and other crops; ferns, fruits, and other vegetation were grown or gathered in the uplands. It was through this balance that the islands evolved as a self-sustaining food ecosystem, one that allowed the Hawaiian people to not only survive but thrive in harmony with the *'āina* (land).

But, as with many native and indigenous cultures across the world, the arrival of Western explorers changed things. The relationship originally brought trade, but soon gave way to disease, destruction, and colonization.

Three decades after Captain James Cook of Britain first made contact with Hawai'i in 1778, King Kamehameha I united all of Hawai'i—previously tribal factions who lived in relative peace—to form one Hawaiian empire, a reaction to the growing threat and influence of the outside world. Over the next few decades, native Hawaiian society began to evolve, banning a restrictive social *kapu* (taboo) system and adopting a Bill of Rights that established a constitutional monarchy and attempted to enact private land ownership as a way to distribute wealth between the royal class and the Hawaiian people. Around the same time, sugarcane and pineapple became extremely lucrative cash crops. The first commercial sugar plantation opened on Kaua'i in 1835. Not long after, production of sugar and pine-

apple in Hawai'i exploded; the exports fetched high prices on the mainland and across the globe. Eventually a group of American businessmen known as the Big Five came to dominate the market and established a vast system of plantations on the islands.

The Big Five became so wealthy and powerful, they functioned as a capitalist oligarchy in competition with the Hawaiian crown. The royal Hawaiian family, enriched by land ownership and trade, sought to modernize the empire by emulating European royalty, constructing the lavish and ornate 'Iolani Palace in 1882, which was equipped with electricity and telephones even before the White House. Meanwhile, the Big Five began to consolidate power, purchasing or outright seizing land and water rights from native Hawaiians and assembling foreign white militias to enforce their will.

In 1887, the American sugar barons effectively orchestrated a coup d'état against the Hawaiian throne, threatening King Kalākaua and his subjects with violence and forcing him to sign a "Bayonet Constitution" that stripped him of power. Five years later, they went further, imprisoning the Hawaiian queen Lili'uokalani and overthrowing the government outright. Grover Cleveland, then president, was so aghast at this seizure of a diplomatically recognized foreign country, he called it "a lawless occupation." That didn't stop his successor, William McKinley, from supporting the annexation of Hawai'i in 1898, which led to it becoming an official American territory two years later.

From the time when the Big Five first set up shop to when the islands became the fiftieth state in 1959, Hawai'i was for all intents and purposes a colony of America, with all the economic exploitation and oppression that entails. The plantation owners realized early on that exporting large amounts of labor- and resource-intensive crops like sugar and pineapple required a huge number of people who would work for cheap. At first they sought native Hawaiians to do the work, but most resisted the idea of laboring in the fields for meager wages, having supported their families through small-scale farming for generations. European-introduced diseases also took a lethal toll on the Hawaiians: A population estimated to be almost 700,000 pre-contact had shrunk to less than 100,000 by the 1850s.

As the plantations expanded, water and land were taken from Hawaiians, and plantation recruiters looked afar for workers, promising wealth and riches to impoverished people in countries like China and Japan. After signing exploitative multiyear contracts that put them in debt for their ship passage, those immigrant workers found themselves working brutal hours for scant pay. Many came in order to send money home to their families, others to start a new life. As worker contracts expired and xenophobic immigration laws were enacted on the mainland, the plantation owners enlisted new immigrant groups, who also dreamt that Hawai'i could provide a better life for their families, including Koreans, Portuguese, and Filipinos. Despite attempts by plantation bosses to break workers into castes by segregating them in ethnic camps, a sense of solidarity slowly but surely formed between these groups. Those who were able to leave the plantations started their own lives, opening businesses and shops and growing families, building a new community that interacted and shared food and talked story. While the identities of these immigrants remained intact—people still saw themselves as Japanese or Chinese or Filipino—eventually the customs of their homelands became memories that were retold and passed down, gradually remade by the local culture that was taking shape around them.

Early plantation life was crooked and cruel for countless reasons, but it also played a crucial role in how local food—and local language—emerged. Most important in that regard was the development of Hawaiian Pidgin English, a creole language that draws elements from Hawaiian, English, Chinese, Japanese, Portuguese, Filipino, and Korean and mashes them all together—a mixed-plate language, if you will. Not only did pidgin serve as a way for different ethnic groups to communicate on the islands, it provided shorthand ways to express knowledge of traditions and foods. Groups once divided by ethnicity were able to find common ground, most of all in what they ate day to day. The shared denomina-

tor of language sped up the process of many distinct cuisines melding together into one thing.

There is a widely held story of how local food formed: During breaks in the cane fields, all the different immigrant workers would sit around together and put their lunch in the middle, so that the Filipino guy developed a liking for kim chee and the Japanese guy tasted how delicious adobo was. It's a good story, but given the way that plantation workers were divided by ethnicity and their era of arrival, it's more likely that the local food developed *off* the plantations, where family-run shops and restaurant owners served dishes that not only catered to their own people, but created a hybrid mish-mash of all the cuisines on the island to reach as many customers as possible. That's how you came to see a Japanese-owned diner serving teriyaki bento, saimin noodles with char siu, kalbi, Portuguese sausage with eggs, beef stew, and pork katsu all on the same menu.

Much like pidgin is a mixed-plate language, local food is a mixed-plate cuisine, a changing amalgamation of the migrations that have shaped Hawai'i over the centuries. It is also more than the sum of its parts—over time, the way a Chinese cook may have made

chow fun noodles back in Canton evolved into something new and distinct, often affected by what ingredients were more readily available, or what the tastes of the immediate community were. The changes to traditional recipes and nostalgic homeland dishes might have been subtle and gradual, but they were there.

The living, breathing food culture of Hawai'i today is a direct product of its past. Each group of arrivals to the islands brought with them new plants, animals, ingredients, flavors, and dishes, incorporating them into what was already there. Though I'm not a historian (just a chef!), I've done my best, through my own personal experience, to put the stories and histories of these communities into context throughout the book. Though less prominently reflected in the recipes in these pages, there are also other immigrant groups that have influenced what local food is today—including Puerto Ricans, Pacific Islanders from Samoa and Guam, and, relatively recently, Vietnamese and Thai.

For a third-gen local like me, local food is just the way we eat. We might not always give thought to why hot dogs go with musubi or why mac salad goes with mochiko chicken—that was what we knew at plate lunch spots, birthday parties, local fairs, and picnics at the beach. But for my grandparents' generation, and for some of my dad's generation, too, the notion of taking pride in being local was hard won, formed over many years despite the challenges of poverty, oppression, and discrimination. During the 1970s—while Hawai'i was becoming known as an international tourist destination synonymous with pineapple, luaus, and hula dancing—a growing cultural renaissance and awareness movement on the islands led many locals to more deeply appreciate the richness of our shared history, opening the door to new rules and regulations that were intended to help preserve the legacy of Hawaiian culture.

These days, when someone asks me if I am Hawaiian, I'll explain that the term is respectfully reserved for those who are descendants of the original Hawaiians; but I am a child of this land. Although my 'ohana arrived here as immigrants, we—along with the natives Hawaiians—have taken up the mantle of aloha and pono that the first settlers passed down. No matter where my family came from originally, we're locals now.

How to Use This Book (FAQs)

What is the best way to serve the recipes in this book?

The easiest answer to that question would be *'ohana* (family) style. All of the dishes in this book are meant to be shared, and in general can be scaled up to serve as many friends and family as you like. As you'll see in the first chapter, you can even make an entire feast out of pupus (appetizers).

But I think it's also important to understand a style of eating that is near and dear to my own heart as well as many other locals: THE PLATE LUNCH. For diners, delis, drive-ins, lunch wagons, and other mom-and-pop joints, this is the format of choice. It usually includes two scoops (or more) rice, a scoop of creamy mac salad, and whatever main dish, or combination of main dishes, you choose, which could be anything from teriyaki beef to pork and peas to kalbi short ribs. If picking two or more main items, called a mixed plate, you generally want one that's soupy/saucy, e.g., beef stew, and one that's crispy-crunchy, e.g., chicken katsu. The concept of the mixed plate to me signals the abundance of culture and deliciousness that we are blessed with in Hawai'i. Where else in the world would you find garlic shrimp and pork adobo and teriyaki beef heaped onto a single plate?

The concept of the plate lunch is believed to have originated during the plantation era, when workers would bring *kau kau* (food) tins with them to the fields, eating white rice topped with whatever leftover meats and vegetables were available. Eventually the format spread to lunch wagons and small restaurants around the islands.

In this book, the main dishes (organized loosely by cooking method) can be eaten plate-lunch-style with rice and mac salad and maybe a pickle or vegetable. You can also mix and match with your favorite vegetables, sides, salads, and pickles from the rest of the book to make a well-rounded meal.

Why are certain words spelled differently? How do I pronounce them?

Not to get too bogged down in technicalities, but a few notes about romanization, orthography, and diacritical marks: You might find certain dishes spelled differently than you are accustomed to. For example, kim chee rather than kimchi, or kochujang rather than gochujang. These phonetic spellings are reflective of how the words were translated and romanized in Hawai'i, which generally predated common usage on the mainland.

If you see a ' mark in a word, that is known as an *'okina*, or glottal stop. It makes the sound like the hyphen between "uh-oh." You'll also see macron marks above vowels, like ō, called a *kahakō*, which indicates the vowel sound is long and stressed.

Why are there no recipes for kālua pig and poi?

This is a fair question. Kālua pig (roasted pork) and poi (pounded taro root) are two of the most iconic dishes in traditional Hawaiian cuisine. I've chosen not to include them in this book, because, frankly, I think such elemental dishes have to be experienced in Hawai'i to be fully understood and appreciated. There are many fine recipes out there that involve pork shoulder, salt, and liquid smoke, but ultimately, like making Texas barbecue brisket in the oven, I think they fall short of a kālua pig that has been wrapped in ti leaves and smoked and steamed inside an *imu* (underground oven). The same thinking applies to poi, a starchy fermented dipping paste whose delicate flavor is entirely dependent on the *kalo* (taro) root that it is made from. Much of the taro available on the mainland is completely different from what you find in Hawai'i. And likely the taro available on the mainland will not have the freshness required to make a quality savory-starchy-sour poi anyway. Instead, I would suggest ordering poi or *pa'i'ai* (concentrated taro paste) online from a reputable vendor, many of which exist across the United States. Even if you live in Hawai'i, I would recommend this, because food companies that produce real poi deserve all the support they can get. Check out www.alohaainapoico.com or tarobrand.com to order.

Where can I get the seafood you have in Hawai'i?

Given our position in the middle of the Pacific, encircled by powerful, nutrient-churning ocean currents, Hawaiian waters are home to a uniquely rich array of seafood, whether it's *'opihi* (limpets) that we pry off the rocky shorelines and eat raw with chili pepper water, or bright pink *kūmū* (goatfish) caught fishing near the reefs. There's a good reason why locals in Hawai'i eat three times as much fish as the rest of America. Some of the fish called for in this book, like yellowtail or 'ahi tuna, are commonly available on the mainland, but as a general rule it is better to use seafood that is available and recommended in your area rather than trying to track down the exact kinds we use in Hawai'i. Ideally this will lead you to picking fish that is fresh, local, and sustainable, which to me are the three most important factors when buying fish.

What's the easiest method to mince garlic/peel ginger/ chop scallions?

Since you'll be doing plenty of it when cooking from this book, here's the right way to peel and mince garlic: Place the clove on a flat surface and trim off the hard root with the tip of a chef's knife. Lay the side of your knife flat against it, blade edge away, and press down with your palm until the clove splits. Slip off the skin and chop or mince as needed.

For fresh ginger, never use a knife or a peeler; always use the side of a spoon, working in long strokes and using gentle pressure. This method wastes much less of the ginger.

For scallions, I trim the roots and use both the dark green tops and white parts unless specified. Chop them as finely or as coarsely as you prefer. Chopped scallions can also be placed in a zip-top plastic bag or sealable container (with as little air as possible) and stored in the freezer, which is a trick that many local families use. When you're in need of scallions, just take some out and let them thaw briefly before using.

When a recipe calls for ginger, garlic, or scallions to be crushed, use the butt of a knife or a wooden spoon to pound the ingredients until smashed and bruised, which will help the flavor release better while cooking or marinating.

Where should I source any hard-to-find ingredients?

Here's the good news about cooking local food: There's a solid chance you have most of the stuff you need already on hand. Most ingredients can be found in a well-stocked grocery store, with just a few items requiring a trip to your nearest Asian market. You can also turn to the Internet or online Hawai'i food retailers like snackhawaii.com or onlyfromhawaii.com. For these recipes, I've done my best to streamline ingredients lists (and offer substitutions where applicable) without sacrificing flavor. Flip to page 289 for a full guide to building out your pantry.

HEAVY PUPUS

Heavy pupus will be served. When you see those words printed on an invitation to a grad celebration, a birthday, or a good old-fashioned luau, you know to bring your appetite. *"Ho brah, dis gon be one good party, no?"*

Any self-respecting event in Hawai'i is going to involve pupus, of course, but *heavy* pupus is the top level: It means a spread of appetizers so bountiful and grand that you could graze like a gazelle on the vast savanna until completely stuffed. No need eat dinner first. I think we can all agree that a meal made completely of appetizers is the best kind of meal there is.

Although you might have seen it on the menu at an American Chinese restaurant, the word *pupu* is actually Hawaiian in origin. Initially it referred to seashells, but over time it came to mean small bites of food that could probably have fit on a seashell: hors d'oeuvres, appetizers, tapas, whatever you might call them. For locals, it implies a style of eating that is communal and never formal. "Go ahead, make plate," someone might say to you at a potluck.

The roots of pupu culture trace back to the Hawaiians, who were known to eat a communal variety of foods here and there rather than in distinct meals. That style of eating-slash-snacking eventually meshed with the island's many immigrant influences and the culture of *pa'u hana* (after work), a tradition of gathering over salty bites and drinks once a day's labor is finished. These days, when you go to any local festivity, you can bet that there will be two lines: one for the bar and one for the pupus.

Over the years, the Simeon household has played host to some epic pupu displays. People still talk about the food we served at my son Asher's first birthday, and that was over five years ago. But I understand why. Being asked to prepare pupus at a gathering is a high honor in local culture—even if the main courses are delicious, it's the pupus people will remember most. The size of the pupu line, after all, is how a party is often judged: There's something about seeing a forty-foot-long row of tables packed to the brim with lumpia, poke, teriyaki sticks, and everything in between that will bring a tear to even the toughest *moke*'s eyes.

The pupu genre is famously broad—how else could Honolulu's *Star-Advertiser* fill their cooking section every week?—but among the many possibilities are iconic dishes that you expect to see at every get-together or potluck (or at least the good ones), no matter how formal or informal. Those are the recipes you'll find in this chapter. Some are foods to share, some double as snacks. All of them represent my favorite way to eat and to cook. Think of it this way: You can have pupus without a party, but you can't have a party without pupus.

SHOYU DIP WITH SESAME CRUNCH

SERVES 4 TO 6

Mayo and shoyu. Shoyu and mayo. There is no kitchen in Hawai'i lacking these essentials, the building blocks of teriyaki and mac salad. I buy them in the gallon jugs they sell at Costco, if only because when raising four kids you can never *really* have too much.

It's not surprising that at some point a clever pupu connoisseur figured out that when you mix the right amount of shoyu with the right amount of mayo you end up with a tasty dip that grooves beautifully with many things, sort of like a homegrown spin on veggies and ranch dressing. At the Simeon house, we didn't even know what ranch was when we were little!

In the hierarchy of pupus, this is the most basic and elemental, but that's the appeal. My version is fancied up from what my uncles and aunties snacked on watching Laker games in our garage, but the salty-savory base is there, amplified with nutty sesame seeds and bright lemon zest. As for veggies, use whatever is in season and be creative. Shoyu mayo goes with everything.

1 cup mayonnaise

2 tablespoons shoyu (soy sauce)

2 teaspoons Lemon Olive Oil (page 278)

1½ teaspoons finely grated lemon zest (from 1 lemon)

3 teaspoons toasted sesame oil

Freshly ground black pepper

2 tablespoons roasted sesame seeds

1 tablespoon sugar

½ teaspoon kosher salt

2 pounds assorted vegetables (see Note), cut into 3-inch spears, for serving

In a small bowl, whisk together the mayonnaise, shoyu, lemon oil, lemon zest, and 2 teaspoons of the sesame oil. Season to taste with pepper and transfer the mixture to a serving bowl. Drizzle with the remaining 1 teaspoon sesame oil.

Heat a small nonstick skillet over medium heat. Add the sesame seeds, sugar, and salt. Cook, stirring constantly, until the sugar has melted and has caramelized around the sesame seeds, 2 to 3 minutes. Remove this from the pan to a plate, let cool, then crush it up and sprinkle over the dip. Serve with your assortment of vegetables.

NOTE: *Eat the dip with whatever vegetables are on hand—carrots, radishes, watercress, green beans, cabbage, celery, tomatoes, broccoli, cauliflower, asparagus, eggplant, squash, etc.—either raw, blanched, steamed, or roasted. Chill them before serving.*

KIM CHEE DIP

SERVES 4 TO 6

Hawai'i loves its kim chee (and yes, we spell it that way rather than kimchi). Jars of the briny fermented cabbage are a fridge staple here, and local grocery stores sell bottles of what's known as kim chee base: a concentrated sweet-spicy red sauce that you can pour over any salad or poke (think seaweed, tuna, squid) to turn it "kim chee style."

Kim chee also shows up as the star in kim chee dip, a common local dip that is usually served as a crowd-pleasing pupu. The basic components are chopped *won bok* (napa cabbage) kim chee, and a solid amount of cream cheese, which tames the punchy flavor and provides a distinct silkiness. The version at my restaurant is mostly traditional, with an extra touch of Parmesan and fried garlic for added savoriness. Depending on which brand you use (Halm's, Kohala, and High Max are popular here), you might consider increasing the sweetness of your kim chee slightly to match our local ones.

I tend to pair this dip with whatever chip is available at the corner gas station; I haven't found a bad combination yet. Try using it as a general spread, too: The iconic Hawai'i chef Sam Choy has one recipe where he slathers it on a steak sandwich.

8 ounces cream cheese, at room temperature
¼ cup sour cream
6 ounces cabbage kim chee, roughly chopped (about ¾ cup),
    with juice reserved
1 teaspoon sugar, plus more as needed
1 tablespoon grated Parmesan cheese
2 teaspoons fresh lemon juice
1 teaspoon kochugaru (Korean chili flakes), plus more to taste
Kosher salt
1 tablespoon Fried Garlic (page 283)
Wonton chips, crackers, Doritos (Cool Ranch preferred), Fritos, Tostitos,
    or any other available -*ito*, for serving

In a medium bowl, stir together the cream cheese and sour cream, adding kim chee juice as needed to achieve a smooth Velveeta-like texture. Fold in the chopped kim chee, sugar, Parmesan, lemon juice, and the kochugaru. Adjust the seasoning with salt and sugar to taste. Transfer the mixture to a serving bowl and top with the fried garlic and an extra sprinkle of kochugaru. Serve with chips.

KAMABOKO DIP

SERVES 2 TO 4

In Japanese, *kamaboko* means fish cake, generally. In Hawai'i though, the fish cake that we know as kamaboko is specific: big neon pink logs with a white center. Imagine a thick sausage made from mild white fish, and you're starting to get the picture. I fell in love with kamaboko early on, probably because on special occasions there would be a slice or two floating atop my favorite food in the world, saimin (more on that later). But the most efficient use for kamaboko? You already know: dip!

This dip is similar in a way to crab salad, only better because the bits of kamaboko bounce and squish pleasantly between your teeth. And it's fun to make. Shredding pink fish cake was like my arts and crafts time as a kid.

If you can only find imitation crab in your grocery store, that's fine. The charm of this version lies in the pops of umami provided by oyster sauce, sweet chili sauce, and powdered dashi, plus a showering of chopped scallion on top. With all those bold flavors dancing together, a classic, nonfussy butter cracker works best as a dipping vehicle here.

4 ounces cream cheese, at room temperature
¼ cup mayonnaise
2 tablespoons sour cream
¼ cup grated sweet onion
2 teaspoons Fried Garlic (page 283)
1 teaspoon Thai sweet chili sauce
1 teaspoon oyster sauce
½ teaspoon instant dashi powder (such as HonDashi)
1 (8-ounce) package kamaboko (fish cake) or imitation crab
Kosher salt and freshly ground black pepper
2 scallions, thinly sliced
Buttery crackers (such as Club or Ritz), for serving

In a medium bowl, stir together the cream cheese, mayonnaise, and sour cream until smooth. Stir in the onion, fried garlic, sweet chili sauce, oyster sauce, and dashi powder. Julienne or shred the kamaboko into 1-inch strips and fold it into the dip. Adjust the seasoning with salt and pepper to taste. Transfer to a serving bowl. Cover and refrigerate for at least 1 hour or up to overnight. Sprinkle with scallions and serve with buttery crackers.

BOILED PEANUTS WITH "OXTAIL SPICE"

SERVES 6 TO 8

Boiled peanuts. Just hearing the words makes my mouth water and the image of a cold beer pop into my head. No matter the occasion—a softball game, a potluck, a fishing trip, a day at the beach—there is a strong chance boiled peanuts will make an appearance. They're the quintessential *pa'u hana* (after work) snack. Back during what we call "small kid time," I would stack leftover shells on the table like they were stones and build peanut shell walls.

If you've ever eaten boiled peanuts in the South, the ones in Hawai'i are similar: raw peanuts cooked in salted water until buttery and soft. (I remember being driven around in production vans during *Top Chef: Charleston* and seeing peanut stands on the side of the road. I asked, but they wouldn't pull over!) The key difference in Hawai'i is that we season ours with star anise, which lends a subtle sweet-spicy aroma somewhere between pepper and licorice.

When I opened Lineage, I knew I wanted to turn the flavors of our boiled peanuts up to 11, so along with star anise, into the boiling pot went five-spice, cinnamon sticks, ginger, and orange zest, all seasonings traditionally used to make another local favorite, oxtail soup (see page 138).

Make sure you're using raw shell-on peanuts rather than the roasted kind. They can usually be found at Asian markets, or ordered online.

¾ cup Diamond Crystal (or 9 tablespoons Morton) kosher salt
2 teaspoons plus 2 tablespoons Chinese five-spice powder
2½ pounds raw unshelled peanuts
8 cinnamon sticks
¼ cup star anise pods
Zest of 1 large orange, cut in wide strips
10 bay leaves
2-inch piece fresh ginger, sliced and crushed

Fill a large pot with 4 quarts water and stir in ¼ cup of Diamond Crystal salt (or 3 tablespoons Morton) and 2 teaspoons of the five-spice. Add the peanuts, drop in a small plate or something to keep the peanuts submerged, and let soak overnight.

Drain the pot and refill with 8 quarts water. Add the remaining ½ cup salt and 2 tablespoons five-spice, cinnamon sticks, star anise, orange zest, bay leaves, and ginger and stir to combine. Bring the peanuts to a boil, then stir and reduce the heat to a simmer. Cover and simmer until the peanuts have a texture somewhere between a canned water chestnut and a tender boiled potato, 3 to 4 hours, replenishing the water as needed. Let cool to room temperature in the liquid before serving. Drain the peanuts and store in the fridge; keeps for up to 1 week.

"BUG JUICE" WITH PROSCIUTTO DUST

SERVES 4 TO 6

Imagine my confusion when I first learned, well into adulthood, that many people on the mainland know "bug juice" as a fruit punch they serve at summer camp.

On the Big Island, bug juice is a mix of vinegar, shoyu, and pepper into which you dip slices of tart, mouth-puckering green mango or green guava. Every island has a different name for this fruit dip, but in general it's a humble country snack that asks very little and makes you feel like a king if you're blessed with a mango tree in the yard.

My grandpa and his buddies from the sugar mill, most of whom, like him, came from the Philippines, would always dip their green mango into *bagoóng*, the potent Filipino fermented fish paste. For the less hard-core among us, bug juice scratched the same itch without being quite as intense: something sharp and salty to harmonize with the sweet-sour taste of unripe fruit. My modern contribution here is to up the saltiness and gaminess slightly with a sprinkle of cured ham ground into a powder, a sort of nod to prosciutto-wrapped melon.

1 cup apple cider vinegar
1 cup shoyu (soy sauce)
3 tablespoons light brown sugar
1 teaspoon freshly ground black pepper
2 tablespoons prosciutto dust (optional; recipe follows)
2 pounds sliced fruit (green mango, green papaya, melon,
     cucumber, jicama, etc.), for serving

In a shallow dish, combine the vinegar, shoyu, sugar, and pepper and whisk until the sugar is dissolved. Adjust the seasoning as desired with more of any of the above ingredients, then sprinkle the prosciutto dust over the top, if using. Serve with fruit as a dip.

PROSCIUTTO DUST

MAKES ABOUT ½ CUP

12 thin slices prosciutto

Preheat the oven to 350°F. Line a baking sheet with parchment paper.

Arrange the prosciutto in a single layer (no overlapping) on the baking sheet. Bake until golden brown and slightly shriveled, 15 to 20 minutes. Keep a close eye near the end since they can burn quickly.

Transfer to a rack to cool (they should crisp up as they sit), then pulverize into a fine powder using a rolling pin or spice grinder. Store in a sealable container.

PIPIKAULA

MAKES ABOUT 1 POUND

Cattle ranching on Hawai'i stretches back to the 1830s, when King Kamehameha III invited a group of Mexican *vaqueros* (cowboys) from California to come to the islands and train Hawaiian ranch hands on how to rope and work cattle. Those original ranch hands—many of whom were full-blooded Hawaiian and later married into Portuguese families—and their descendants became known as *paniolos*. As the cattle industry boomed for the next century or so, particularly on the Big Island, the hard-riding paniolo became an iconic figure in local culture.

One thing to know about paniolos—they loved chewing *pipikaula*, a sun-dried beef jerky meant to last through long rides. Even after most of the paniolos had hung up their saddles, the tradition of pipikaula continued. Living in Hilo, we were usually gifted some by friends; if you got invited to a party by a Portuguese 'ohana, particularly those with O.G. paniolo heritage, you knew you were hitting the pipikaula jackpot.

The secret to great pipikaula, in my experience, is to use quality beef (grass-fed is nice) and not overdry it in the oven. It should still retain some of its steak-like texture. I tend to keep seasoning minimal, though if you like heat, brush on some extra Kudeesh Sauce, a spicy chili paste and all-purpose hot sauce that we invented at Migrant—the name is a Portuguese exclamation that more or less means "hot damn!"

2 pounds flank steak
¼ cup Diamond Crystal (or 3 tablespoons Morton) kosher salt
2 teaspoons freshly ground black pepper
2 tablespoons shoyu (soy sauce)
1 tablespoon Kudeesh Sauce (recipe follows), or more to taste

Preheat the oven to 200°F.

Massage the flank steak enthusiastically with salt for several minutes. In a small bowl, combine the pepper, shoyu, and kudeesh sauce and coat the meat evenly.

Arrange the beef on a wire rack set in a sheet pan and bake for 5 hours. Once dried but tender (the inside should look medium to medium-well), slice the meat into thick strips and store in an airtight container. Keeps for weeks in the fridge.

KUDEESH SAUCE

MAKES ABOUT ¼ CUP

½ cup Hawaiian chilies, bird's eye chilies, or sliced red Fresno chilies (or any mix of spicy fresh chilies)

2 tablespoons apple cider vinegar

1 tablespoon sugar

2 teaspoons Diamond Crystal (or 1½ teaspoons Morton) kosher salt

In a blender or food processor, combine the chilies, vinegar, sugar, and salt and blend everything together for several minutes until a smooth sauce forms. Be careful not to breathe in any fumes when you open the container. Kudeesh can be used as an all-purpose hot sauce with fried noodles or rice. It will keep in the fridge indefinitely.

HURRICANE POPCORN

MAKES ABOUT 16 CUPS

Ask a local and they'll tell you: The Hawaiian movie theater experience is not complete without a big bag of hurricane popcorn. Hot buttery kernels, roasted sesame seeds, crispy roasted seaweed, and just the right kiss of sugar. Some concession stands sell their own, but no need for that: We always snuck in the furikake and *arare* (rice crackers) and made it ourselves.

Lucky for you, making hurricane popcorn from scratch is even easier than smuggling bootleg seasonings into the theater: pop, toss, and bake. If you can't find rice crackers (also called *kakimochi* or mochi crunch), go ahead and use your favorite cereal or crackers; just add another couple teaspoons of shoyu if you're substituting something that isn't salted.

¼ cup neutral oil

¼ cup sugar

½ cup unpopped popcorn kernels

4 tablespoons salted butter

1 tablespoon shoyu (soy sauce), plus more as needed

¼ cup Furikake (page 262)

1½ cups arare (rice crackers), pretzels, animal crackers, or breakfast cereal

Preheat the oven to 325°F.

In a 6-quart pot (if you don't have a pot that size, halve the recipe or make it in batches), heat the oil over medium heat. Once shimmering, stir in the sugar and popcorn and cover. Shake the pot constantly to keep the sugar from burning. The corn will start popping vigorously. Once the popping has slowed to once every 2 to 3 seconds, remove the pot from the heat and continue to shake for a few minutes until the popping has stopped. Pour into a very large bowl and allow to cool, stirring occasionally to break up any clumps.

In a small saucepan, melt the butter and add the shoyu and furikake. Add the rice crackers to the popped popcorn and pour the butter/shoyu/furikake mixture all over, tossing to coat. Transfer to a baking pan and bake until dry and crisp, 15 to 20 minutes, stirring once or twice. Keeps in a sealable container for up to 1 week.

SAKURA BOSHI
MAKES ABOUT 1 POUND

Part of the long and illustrious Hawaiian tradition of snacking on dried fish, *sakura boshi* is made from tuna that's been marinated teriyaki-style and dried in the oven until it develops a sweet, shiny lacquer (swapping in cola for the sugar in the teriyaki mixture is an old-timer's trick). Because of the familiar flavors in this marinade, sakura boshi is a great way to dip your toes into the severely underrated world of fish jerky, a special treat that I relished as a kid.

As you would when making poke, be sure to use very fresh fish for this, since the drying process will concentrate the fish's natural flavor.

1 cup shoyu (soy sauce)
1 cup Coca-Cola (preferably the kind sweetened with cane sugar)
1 tablespoon minced garlic
1 tablespoon grated fresh ginger
2 pounds 'ahi tuna (or other lean, meaty fish: marlin, swordfish, wahoo)
Neutral oil, for the roasting rack
2 tablespoons honey
1 tablespoon roasted sesame seeds

In a large bowl, stir together the shoyu, cola, garlic, and ginger. Cut the fish into strips 3 inches long, 1 inch wide, and ¼ inch thick. Add the fish to the marinade, stir, and let sit at room temperature for 2 hours.

Preheat the oven to its lowest setting. Or use a food dehydrator.

Rub a roasting rack with oil and set it in a sheet pan. Drain the marinade and transfer the strips to the rack. Place the rack in the oven but leave the door ajar (or use the dehydrator). Dry until no moist spots remain, flipping the fish halfway through. Drying times vary considerably, but expect between 3 and 6 hours.

Brush the fish on both sides with honey and dry for another 30 minutes to 1 hour, until the fish looks shiny. Sprinkle the fish with sesame seeds and allow to cool. Store in the fridge in a sealable container or zip-top plastic bag until you're ready to eat. Keeps in the fridge for up to 2 weeks.

CRISPY GAU GEE WITH SHOYU MUSTARD

MAKES 50 TO 60 GAU GEE: SERVES 6 TO 8

At Leung's Chop Suey House, a mom-and-pop Chinese spot on Kanoelehua Ave in Hilo, I was the kid who always asked for extra *gau gee* (fried wontons) on the family pupu platter. These days, if I'm feeling generous, I'll order a whole tray of gau gee to bring to the party. You know those crispy buggahs are the first thing to disappear on the pupu line.

But while I love these golden-brown pouches as takeout, I'm much happier when I spend the extra smidge of energy to fry them at home. Some recipes use fillings like Spam and kamaboko, but I prefer the traditional shumai filling like you'd find at Cantonese restaurants, a seasoned pork and shrimp mixture that is (somewhat confusingly) called "pork hash" by locals. The clincher here is the gau gee dipping sauce, which for me is a must: Chinese hot mustard cut with shoyu. (It's also great for dipping saimin noodles.) Whisk them together, then keep adding hot mustard until it makes your nose tickle.

Another tip: Uncooked gau gee can be frozen and used later. Try adding them to the simmering broth the next time you make Saimin (page 190).

GAU GEE
2 pounds ground pork
½ pound peeled large shrimp, finely minced
3 tablespoons minced fresh ginger
8 cloves garlic, minced
2 egg whites
¼ cup thinly sliced scallions
1 tablespoon light shoyu (soy sauce)
1 tablespoon oyster sauce
1 tablespoon fish sauce

2 teaspoons cornstarch
¼ teaspoon ground white pepper
1 (12-ounce) package wonton skins
1 egg
Neutral oil, for frying

DIPPING SAUCE
⅔ cup shoyu (soy sauce)
⅓ cup Chinese hot mustard, plus more to taste

For the gau gee: In a large bowl, combine the pork, shrimp, ginger, garlic, egg whites, scallions, 1 cup water, the light shoyu, oyster sauce, fish sauce, cornstarch, and white pepper and mix thoroughly. Test the filling by microwaving a small pinch until cooked. Taste it and adjust the seasoning as needed.

Place about 1 tablespoon of filling into each wonton skin. Beat the egg in a small bowl. Dip a finger into the egg and rub it halfway around the edge of the wonton skin, then fold it in half, pinching it shut to create a seal. Repeat until all the filling is used. Arrange the folded gau gee on a baking sheet until ready to fry.

Prepare a wire rack or line a baking sheet with paper towels. Fill a large, heavy-bottomed pot or Dutch oven with at least 2 inches of oil, making sure to leave a few inches of clearance from the top of the pot. Heat over medium-high heat until the oil reaches 350°F (use a thermometer), adjusting the heat as needed to maintain temperature. (Alternatively, drop a small pinch of wonton skin into the oil; if it immediately bubbles and sizzles, the oil is ready.)

Fry the gau gee in batches, making sure there is plenty of room for them to move in the oil, until golden in the center and dark brown near the edges, 2 to 3 minutes. Transfer to the wire rack or paper towels and let cool slightly.

For the dipping sauce: In a small bowl, mix the shoyu and mustard, adjusting the ratio to taste. Serve with the hot gau gee.

SPAM MUSUBI
MAKES 6

Perhaps you've heard somewhere that Hawai'i eats a lot of Spam. We love the stuff with the whole of our hearts, ever since it was introduced here during the rationing days of WWII. We eat more of it per capita than anyplace on earth besides Guam. Here's a haiku someone wrote on the Internet about Spam that sums up our (or at least my) collective feelings:

Can of metal, slick
soft center, so cool, moistening
I yearn for your salt

The porcine saltiness, the impossibly emulsified texture, the infinite shelf life—these are reasons why we add this humble king of canned luncheon meat to fried rice, saimin, wontons, or somen salad. We slice it up, we sauté it, we cook it with shoyu and sugar; we transform this gnarly industrial food scooped from a can into something beautiful and delicious.

No food allows Spam to shine brighter than musubi, a portable block of nori-wrapped rice that is sold at gas stations, corner shops, diners, gymnasiums, lunch wagons, and takeout counters of all stripes. You'll often see musubi stuffed with red hot dogs, mochiko chicken, egg omelets, or teriyaki, but the Spam-filled kind is easily the most popular.

There are many differing techniques for preparing and wrapping Spam musubi. Without getting too technical up top, here are a few of my basic guidelines: **1.** Cut your Spam thick so you can taste it (I prefer the reduced-sodium kind for its balanced taste). **2.** Sear then glaze the Spam with shoyu and sugar before wrapping. **3.** Make sure your rice is warm and your nori sheets are bone-dry. (And a musubi mold makes this easy, but you can use a Spam can. See Note.)

Neutral oil, for the skillet
1 (12-ounce) can 25% Less Sodium Spam,
  cut into 6 slices horizontally
¼ cup shoyu (soy sauce)
¼ cup sugar
2 tablespoons mirin
2 sheets sushi nori
4 cups cooked short-grain white rice, warm
2 teaspoons Furikake (page 262; optional)

NOTE: *Musubi maker molds, which are rectangular plastic boxes open on the top and bottom, are available for a few bucks online. If you don't have one, you can use the empty Spam can as a mold: Shape the rice into a block inside the can by firmly pressing it down with your fingers, then shake it from the can. Place the packed block of rice perpendicular to the nori strip and carefully wrap with the nori as directed.*

Lightly coat the bottom of a skillet with oil and heat over medium heat. Fry the Spam slices until browned and crispy, 2 to 3 minutes per side. Remove from the heat and set aside on paper towels to drain.

Wipe out any excess oil from the pan. Add the shoyu, sugar, and mirin and stir to combine. Bring to a boil, then reduce the heat to low, return the cooked Spam slices to the pan, and turn them to coat. Cook until a sticky glaze starts to form, about 1 minute. Remove the pan from the heat and let the Spam sit in the glaze until ready to use.

Toast the nori sheets by carefully waving them over a stove burner on low (this is easiest with gas; use tongs if needed) for 10 to 20 seconds until crisp and crackly, then cut each sheet into thirds lengthwise. (You can also toast them briefly in a hot oven, a minute or two, just until crisp.)

Prepare a bowl of warm water.

Lay a strip of nori on a clean surface. Moisten the lower half of the inside of a musubi mold (see Note) and place the mold perpendicular to the nori strip on the bottom third of the strip. Fill the mold with about ½ cup rice and press down

very firmly and evenly until the rice is packed ¾ inch high. Sprinkle the rice with furikake (if using). Top with a slice of Spam, making sure a little of the glaze carries over from the pan onto the rice. Pull off the mold and wrap the musubi tightly in the nori strip by rolling it away from you as you would a sushi roll. Seal the edge of the nori with a dab of warm water if necessary (the moisture in the warm rice should do most of the work). Wipe off the mold with warm water and repeat with the remaining Spam and rice. Serve immediately, or wrap in plastic wrap and save for later.

MUSU-BAE

During the filming of *Top Chef*, we contestants were given strict rules that we couldn't feed any of the crew on set. This might sound straight-forward, but if you saw how long these dedicated guys and ladies worked, you, too, would want to cook them something when messing around with food all day. So, during downtime on set, I would grab a can of Spam, some left-over rice, and some dried seaweed and crank out a dozen or so musubi, then quietly pass them out to the sound and camera crew on the low. Standing in front of the judge's table not sure if you were going to be eliminated was a terrifying feeling, but my strongest memory from those days wasn't the piercing gaze of Tom Colicchio. It was seeing, from the corner of my eye, one of the sound guys holding the boom mike, famished and exhausted, stealth-ily unwrapping his Spam musubi and taking a satisfied bite. That's aloha.

PAN SUSHI DYNAMITE

MAKES ONE 9-INCH SQUARE PAN; SERVES 4 TO 6

This easy-to-make potluck recipe is a sterling example of local ingenuity. Think of it as a sushi roll without the rolling, or in *haole* terms: sushi casserole.

The first time I remember having it was when my older brother, Jeremy, started dating Allison, who is now my sister-in-law. Allison's family is Japanese, so at parties they'd sometimes bring a big pan of vinegar-seasoned sushi rice layered with salmon, avocado, mushrooms, and pickled vegetables. It immediately captured me.

The variations for pan sushi are endless. Some line the pan with sheets of nori. Some alternate layers of rice and fillings, lasagna-style. My method leans simpler: a single layer of rice spread with spicy salmon "dynamite" and topped with scallions, avocado, and a sweet soy glaze, an ode to the flavor-bomb rolls found at American-style sushi bars.

If you're using canned salmon, broiling the dynamite mixture is optional, but I find it helps marry the ingredients in the sauce. As for the nori sheets, instead of layering them into the rice, I like to serve them on the side so they stay crisp. Scoop spoonfuls of pan sushi onto the dried seaweed and eat it like a hand roll or taco.

10 dried shiitake mushrooms

⅓ cup rice vinegar

¼ cup sugar

2 tablespoons mirin

1 teaspoon Diamond Crystal (or ½ teaspoon Morton) kosher salt

4 cups cooked white rice, warm

1 pound fresh salmon, diced, or 3 (5-ounce) cans salmon, drained and broken in flakes

1 cup mayonnaise

½ medium sweet onion, finely chopped

2 tablespoons shoyu (soy sauce)

1 tablespoon sambal oelek

1 tablespoon Thai sweet chili sauce

1 tablespoon oyster sauce

1 teaspoon toasted sesame oil

½ cup masago (capelin fish roe)

3 scallions, thinly sliced

2 medium avocados, thinly sliced

¼ cup Sweet Soy Glaze (recipe follows)

1 (1-ounce) package dried nori sheets, for serving (cut into 4-inch squares, if necessary)

In a small bowl, combine the mushrooms and warm water to cover. Let soak until soft, 10 to 15 minutes. Drain and squeeze out excess water. Cut off and discard any stems. Finely chop the caps and set aside.

In a small saucepan, combine the vinegar, sugar, mirin, and salt. Heat over medium-high heat, stirring until the salt is dissolved, then let cool slightly. In a bowl, pour the warm vinegar mixture over the rice evenly, using the back of a rice paddle or spatula to deflect the stream and spread it out. Mix thoroughly. Spread the rice evenly onto the bottom of a 9 x 9-inch baking pan (the rice should be about ¾ inch deep), gently but firmly using a paddle or spatula to compact the rice.

Adjust an oven rack to 6 inches from the broiler element and preheat the broiler.

(recipe continues)

Rinse out the rice bowl and use it to stir together the salmon, mayo, onion, shoyu, sambal, sweet chili sauce, oyster sauce, sesame oil, the rehydrated mushrooms, and masago until thoroughly combined. Spread the mixture evenly onto the rice, gently but firmly pressing down with a paddle or spatula. Broil until the top is lightly browned, 6 to 8 minutes. Remove the pan and let it cool slightly.

Top with the scallions and sliced avocado. Drizzle with sweet soy glaze. Cut the sushi into small squares and serve with dried sheets of nori on the side, for wrapping.

SWEET SOY GLAZE

MAKES A SCANT ½ CUP

¼ cup shoyu (soy sauce)
¼ cup sugar
2 teaspoons cornstarch

In a small saucepan, combine the shoyu and sugar and cook over medium-low heat until the sugar dissolves and starts to bubble. In a small bowl, stir the cornstarch together with 1 tablespoon water until dissolved, then stir it into the shoyu-sugar mixture. Continue cooking until the mixture is thick enough to coat the back of a spoon, 5 to 10 minutes. Let cool before using.

THE INFLUENCERS
KĀNAKA MAOLI (NATIVE HAWAIIANS)

When the first Polynesian explorers landed on Hawai'i, navigating across thousands of miles of the South Pacific in outrigger canoes, they found an uninhabited chain of islands that was staggeringly beautiful, utterly pristine, and rich in natural resources. But aside from fish, shellfish, *limu* (seaweed), and a handful of edible plants, there was little food to sustain their way of life. That changed as settlers arrived in waves from the Marquesas Islands and later Tahiti, bringing with them *pua'a* (pigs), *moa* (chickens), and various staple plants that had nourished them on their home islands, including *kalo* (taro), *kukui* (candlenut), *'ulu* (breadfruit), *'uala* (sweet potato), *ko* (sugarcane), *mai'a* (banana), *'awapuhi* (ginger), *pia* (arrowroot), and *niu* (coconut). These two dozen transplants, which thrived on fertile volcanic soil, formed the foundation of the traditional Hawaiian diet and are today referred to as the original "canoe crops."

The generous bounty of the land meant that native Hawaiian food was elemental in nature. The chief seasonings were simple: salt harvested from ocean water, dried and fresh seaweed—*limu*—and kukui nuts dug up from the ground. Taro root provided the main starch, roasted and pounded into a thick paste called *pa'i'ai* that was then blended with water to make poi. An everyday meal might be some dried 'ahi, a little limu on the side, and a bowl of fresh poi. For celebrations and ceremonies, the Hawaiians built *imu*—underground wood-fire ovens made from volcanic rock, sand, and banana and ti leaves. Since they sealed in moisture and concentrated natural flavor, the imu was suited for roasting whole pigs, tubers, and other large quantities of food, a tradition that many families, Hawaiian and otherwise, continue to honor during luau and other special occasions. Today you can find traditional Hawaiian dishes like kālua pig, laulau, lomi salmon, poi, and haupia available in one form or another at every local supermarket, though to be honest they rarely measure up to the kind cooked at home.

POKE: A PRIMER

In the past decade or so, the raw Hawaiian fish salad known as poke (POH-kay) has gone from a local favorite to a global obsession. As a chef who has spent his entire career spreading the gospel of local cooking, watching a dish that is so beloved in Hawai'i "go viral" has been heartening in some ways. But I also believe that the magic and charm of great poke is inseparable from Hawai'i itself. Poke done right tastes like home.

Native Hawaiians have been making poke from *i'a maka* (raw fish) long before Captain Cook landed in the islands in 1700s. Originally, Hawaiians would catch reef fish and scrape or slice the meat from the bones, seasoning the resulting bits with sea salt, fresh *limu* (seaweed), and *'inamona* (a condiment made from roasted and crushed *kukui,* or candlenuts). During the 1960s and '70s, when fishing vessels began to regularly trawl deeper waters around Hawai'i for larger fish like *'ahi* (yellowfin tuna) and *aku* (skipjack tuna), the poke that is more recognizable today—glistening cubes of 'ahi tossed with shoyu (replacing sea salt), raw onions (replacing seaweed), and sesame (replacing 'inamona)—became widely popular here.

These days, poke is an essential part of daily life in Hawai'i. It's found just about anywhere people gather. You'll see it at all types of restaurants, high and low, and sold from refrigerator cases at grocery stores and even liquor stores, many of which carry tray after tray of different flavors and styles. For me, there is no experience more pleasurable than sitting on the sand after a swim and cracking open a cooler filled with beers and fresh poke. I could enjoy that every day.

Here I've included two of my favorite recipes made with 'ahi, both meant to highlight the simplicity and vibrancy for which traditional poke is known. The first hews closer to what locals know as "Hawaiian style" poke, made using ogo seaweed and 'inamona (if you're on the mainland, these can be ordered online). The second is for a classic shoyu poke, arguably the most popular variety served in Hawai'i. With the second, I've included variations for a few other poke styles, including spicy mayo, wasabi, and kim chee. Whichever you choose, keep these general rules in mind while preparing poke.

Quality is king: As Sam Choy once said about poke, "Use the best fish your pocketbook can afford." That means seeking out sashimi-grade fish (fresh or frozen—great quality fish can be found frozen) from a reputable seafood vendor, or at the fish counter of an upscale grocery store. Japanese markets in particular are great. Don't be afraid to let the fishmonger know you're making poke; they can steer you in the right direction. If you're buying fresh, be sure to prepare the fish the same day to ensure the best flavor. Also, make sure you're using a well-sharpened knife to slice your fish (thank me later!).

Be flexible: While the most common protein used in poke is mild and meaty raw tuna (yellowtail, skipjack, bigeye, and albacore are all good options), it's not the only fish in the sea. Salmon is a popular option, as are swordfish, marlin, snapper, mackerel, and scallops. Also consider precooked options: octopus, squid, shrimp, fish cake, imitation crab, or firm tofu.

It's a balancing act: The best poke is harmonious in taste and texture. Keep this in mind as you mix and match seasonings and garnishes. Saltiness should never overwhelm, nor should strong flavors like kim chee or wasabi.

The lush flavor and texture of raw fish should be the star. Take care that the ingredients are uniformly chopped and evenly distributed. If you're using a paste or other thick sauce that doesn't immediately dissolve, mix together the liquid ingredients first before folding in the fish.

Now and later: Once prepared, poke can be eaten right away or left to marinate in the fridge for a few hours. Both methods have their charms. If you let your poke sit, the seasoning will absorb into the raw fish and become mellower; taste just before serving and add more salt if needed.

Rice or no?: Poke bowls (a scoop of poke over rice) are a common fixture at poke shops in Hawai'i and elsewhere, but that doesn't mean you have to eat your poke with a starch. Generally speaking, poke eaten by itself is considered a pupu (appetizer), while adding rice turns it into a light meal. Chilled poke over hot white rice with a sprinkle of furikake is a classic and delicious pairing, but you can also mix it up and try it with noodles, fresh greens, or a side of poi.

HAWAIIAN-STYLE 'AHI POKE

SERVES 4 TO 8

Made with crunchy fresh seaweed and roasted nuts, this style of poke takes its cues from how the dish was traditionally prepared by native Hawaiians.

2 pounds sashimi-grade 'ahi tuna, cut into
½-inch cubes
½ cup diced sweet onion
1 tablespoon flaky sea salt (such as Maldon)
or Hawaiian sea salt, plus more to taste
2 Hawaiian chili peppers or 1 bird's eye chili,
thinly sliced
¼ cup chopped ogo seaweed (optional; soaked in
water if dried)
2 tablespoons ground or finely chopped toasted
kukui (candlenuts) or macadamia nuts
¼ cup thinly sliced scallions

In a medium bowl, gently fold together the tuna, onion, salt, chilies, seaweed (if using), kukui, and scallions until thoroughly mixed. Adjust the seasoning with more salt to taste.

Serve immediately, or cover tightly and store in the fridge for up to a day. (If you plan on eating the poke later, taste again before serving and add salt if needed.)

SHOYU 'AHI POKE

SERVES 4 TO 8

This, the most prevalent style of poke today, is a study in balance: Nutty sesame is tempered by sharp raw onion, ginger and kochugaru add spice, and shoyu and oyster sauce provide salt and umami.

2 pounds sashimi-grade 'ahi tuna, cut into
 ½-inch cubes
½ cup diced sweet onion
2 tablespoons shoyu (soy sauce)
2 tablespoons oyster sauce
2 teaspoons minced fresh ginger
2 teaspoons toasted sesame oil
1 teaspoon kochugaru (Korean chili flakes) or
 sambal oelek
½ cup thinly sliced scallions
2 teaspoons roasted sesame seeds
Flaky sea salt or Hawaiian sea salt

In a medium bowl, gently fold together all the ingredients until thoroughly mixed. Taste and season with salt as needed.

Serve immediately, or cover tightly and store in the fridge for up to a day. (If you plan on eating the poke later, taste again before serving and add salt as needed.)

SPICY MAYO POKE
Omit the oyster sauce, ginger, and kochugaru. Add 3 tablespoons sriracha and ½ cup mayo (or to taste). Reduce the sesame oil to 1 teaspoon and the shoyu to 1 tablespoon. Omit the sesame seeds and add ⅓ cup masago (capelin fish roe).

WASABI POKE
Omit the oyster sauce and kochugaru. Add 4 teaspoons wasabi paste (or to taste) and a pinch of sugar. Increase the shoyu to ¼ cup. Replace the sesame seeds with 1 jalapeño pepper, seeded and minced.

KIM CHEE POKE
Omit the oyster sauce. Add ½ cup finely chopped kim chee, plus 1 tablespoon kim chee liquid, 1 teaspoon minced garlic, and a pinch of sugar.

53

WOK-FRIED POKE
SERVES 1 OR 2

This dish originated as a way to use leftover poke sitting in the fridge after a party, but it was local chef Sam Choy who elevated a down-home preparation into high art at his restaurants back in the '90s (go look up "fried poke" on YouTube if you want to see him in action).

Having soaked up the seasoning they were tossed in, the previous night's cubes of raw 'ahi are transformed into succulent flash-fried morsels when added to a hot pan. The idea here is to quickly sear the tuna in a small amount of oil so that the outside develops a smoky char and the interior stays rare. Since the fish won't taste as salty as when it was first mixed, glazing the fried poke in a splash more shoyu and sambal amps up the seasoning.

To stretch it into a meal, fried poke is almost always eaten with rice or poi. I like to garnish it with crisp raw vegetables as well, which restores some of the vibrancy of fresh poke.

Neutral oil, for searing
½ pound leftover poke, any kind
1 tablespoon sambal oelek
1 teaspoon shoyu (soy sauce), plus more to taste
1 tablespoon thinly sliced scallions
¼ avocado, thinly sliced (optional)
¼ medium tomato, thinly sliced into half-moons (optional)
¼ cucumber, peeled and thinly sliced into half-moons (optional)
Cooked rice or poi, for serving

Heat a skillet or wok over high heat and add enough oil to lightly coat the bottom. Once the oil begins to smoke, carefully slide in the leftover poke. Stir-fry for a few seconds to a minute, until the outside of the fish is seared but the inside is still raw. Add the sambal and shoyu, toss, and continue stir-frying a few more seconds until the liquid has evaporated. Remove from the heat and top with the scallions. Adjust the seasoning with more shoyu as needed. If desired, garnish with avocado, tomato, and cucumber. Serve with rice or poi.

GARDEN POKE

SERVES 2 TO 4

At Lineage, we had these cool rolling pupu carts that my dad welded together from scrap metal. The inspiration was that, like at our house, as soon as you sat down, you were already eating and drinking. I originally wanted to offer little bowls of poke off the carts, but apparently the health department frowns on raw fish circulating around an outdoor dining room in the tropics.

So, instead, we used all the wonderful produce we'd been getting from farmers on Maui and put it through the lens of traditional poke. The more we played around with the dish, the more we loved the idea of a poke that was completely vegan but also captured the spirit and soul of the original.

Any and all root vegetables work great for this dish. The key thing is to roast them long enough so they soften but don't turn mushy; you're roughly aiming for the texture of raw tuna, after all. Adding uncooked vegetables like shaved radish, onion, and cucumbers provides freshness and crunch. Snap peas would work well, too.

Here I like to use tamari instead of shoyu. It's made only from roasted soybeans instead of a blend of soy and wheat, and it has a robust earthiness that goes well with roasted vegetables.

2½ cups 1-inch cubes (about 1 pound) root or sturdy vegetables,
    such as sweet potato, taro, carrots, turnips, beets, parsnips, yuca, radishes
Olive oil
Kosher salt and freshly ground black pepper
¼ cup Tamari Dressing, plus more to taste (recipe follows)
½ cucumber, roughly diced
½ medium sweet onion, thinly sliced
2 or 3 small radishes, trimmed and thinly sliced
½ cup roughly chopped ogo seaweed (optional)
1 tablespoon finely chopped roasted macadamia nuts

Preheat the oven to 350°F.

In a bowl, coat the vegetables with a splash of olive oil and season to taste with salt and pepper. Lay out the vegetables in one layer on a baking sheet and bake until tender but slightly firm (think of the texture of raw tuna), 15 to 20 minutes.

Once the vegetables have cooled, transfer to a bowl and toss with the dressing. Let sit for a few minutes, then gently fold in the cucumber, onion, radishes, and seaweed (if using). Season with more dressing if needed. Top with the macadamia nuts and serve.

TAMARI DRESSING

MAKES ABOUT ½ CUP

½ cup tamari
1 teaspoon grated fresh ginger
1 teaspoon sambal oelek
1 teaspoon toasted sesame oil
2 Hawaiian chili peppers, thinly sliced, or red
   chili flakes to taste

In a small bowl, whisk together the tamari, ginger, sambal, sesame oil, and chilies. The dressing can be kept refrigerated for weeks.

JUMPING SHRIMP KINILAW

SERVES 4 TO 6

Having spent practically my entire life in Hawai'i, I sometimes think about how much courage and determination it took to do what my grandparents did when they immigrated here as teenagers. For my grandpa, coming to work on the sugar plantations meant the promise of a better life, yet it also meant giving up everything he knew from his home in Ilocos Norte.

But at the same time, I think about how the bounty of Hawai'i, especially on the tropical Big Island, felt at least a little familiar to their generation. Like in the Philippines, taro plants and papayas grew everywhere. The fishing was exceptional. You could hike up to mountain streams and catch the tiny mountain shrimp ('ōpae kala'ole) jumping in the water, then carry them back by the bucketful to make *kinilaw*, the distant Filipino cousin of ceviche.

This recipe is my re-creation of what I remember eating in my grandparents' yard, made with big, plump ocean shrimp instead of the krill-size "jumping shrimp" you get from freshwater, and with tart green apple instead of unripe mango or papaya. Adding heaps of raw ginger (I know it seems like a lot!) cures the shrimp much like lemon does in ceviche, but I find it does so without obscuring too much of the texture and taste. Consumed with a few beers, picking the heads off the shrimp and sucking the juices makes for a memorable *pulutan*, or Filipino drinking snack.

2 pounds large head-on, tail-on raw shrimp, body section peeled and deveined
1½ cups calamansi juice, or ½ cup orange juice plus 1 cup lime juice
¾ cup shoyu (soy sauce), plus more to taste
3 ounces fresh ginger, peeled and finely chopped (about ⅔ cup)
1 medium green apple, thinly sliced
½ large red onion, thinly sliced
6 Hawaiian chili peppers or 3 bird's eye chilies, thinly sliced
1 tablespoon minced garlic
Handful of cilantro sprigs

In a large bowl, combine the shrimp, calamansi juice, shoyu, ginger, apple, onion, chilies, and garlic and mix thoroughly. Cover and marinate for 2 to 4 hours in the fridge.

Season to taste with more shoyu and top with cilantro sprigs before serving.

SARDINE PUPU

SERVES 2 TO 4

Sardine night! On days when my dad didn't have time to cook dinner, usually after shuttling us to karate or volleyball practice or such, he'd bust open the cupboard and draw from our endless supply of canned sardines to make sardine pupus. We'd also eat it when we went camping at the Kapoho tide pools (before they got wiped out by lava flows). If you were really slick, you could fry the sardines over the fire without taking them out of the can.

Sardine pupus are a simple, prototypically Filipino treat: Splashes of shoyu and vinegar essentially qualify it as adobo, while a crucial glug of lemon oil on top adds complexity. My favorite part are the raw onions, which I first rinse under ice water until they turn glassy, a technique that softens their bite and brings out the sweetness. This dish makes for a primo snack, but you can also add two scoops of rice and turn it into a fast and economical meal.

2 (3.75-ounce) cans sardines in olive oil (the tomato sauce kind are good, too)
¼ medium sweet onion, thinly sliced into half-moons
2 cloves garlic, thinly sliced
Kochugaru (Korean chili flakes)
1 tablespoon shoyu (soy sauce)
1 tablespoon apple cider vinegar
¼ cup Basic or Simeon-Style Chili Pepper Water (page 265)
Freshly ground black pepper
2 teaspoons Lemon Olive Oil (page 278)

Carefully remove the sardines from the can, reserving the oil. Place the onion in a bowl and cover with ice. Rinse the onion under cold water, stirring, until the ice is melted. Drain the onion and lay them out to dry on paper towels.

Heat a medium skillet over medium-high heat. Pour in the sardine oil (or use a bit of neutral oil), add the garlic and kochugaru to taste, and sauté until lightly browned and fragrant. Add the sardines, keeping them as intact as possible. Deglaze with the shoyu and vinegar.

Once the liquid has evaporated, transfer the sardines to a plate and top with the onion and chili pepper water. Season to taste with black pepper and drizzle with the lemon oil. Serve immediately.

MISO TAKO

SERVES 4 TO 8

Spearfishing for *he'e* (octopus, or *tako* in Japanese) is a classic pastime all over Hawai'i. Of course, it's not for the faint of heart—it often involves traversing rocky reefs, free diving, and occasionally competing against rival sea life (a guy I know once fought off a twenty-foot tiger shark that tried to *cockaroach*—steal—his catch). When someone snags a fresh he'e, the best way to prepare it, in my opinion, is *miso tako*, a Japanese-inspired poke that pairs tender sliced octopus with a sweet and salty miso sauce.

More than octopus hunting, though, miso tako makes me think about KTA Super Stores (yes, plural) in Hilo, which is the best supermarket on Hawai'i and arguably the planet. It's a big warehouse where you can buy rubber boots, fifty-pound bags of rice, and freshly fried chicken all in one place—a righteous mash-up of Costco and Whole Foods without the corporate baggage.

Like any respectable grocery store in Hawai'i, KTA also has a refrigerated poke counter as long as a fishing trawler. Of all the kinds of poke in the case, the tray of miso tako is one of the largest, which shows just how much Hilo adores the stuff.

For this recipe, make sure you use white miso, which is milder in saltiness and has a more delicate flavor that brings out the sweetness of the octopus. You can find precooked octopus tentacles at most grocery stores, which is the easiest way to prepare this recipe. If you'd prefer to cook your own, look for cleaned and frozen octopus sold at seafood counters, which is actually preferable to fresh since the freezing process tenderizes the meat.

1 tablespoon mirin
2 tablespoons rice vinegar
1 tablespoon sake
3 tablespoons shiro (white) miso
1 tablespoon creamy peanut butter
1 teaspoon mustard powder
Juice of ½ lemon
Kosher salt
Sugar
Oven-Braised Octopus (recipe follows) or 1 pound precooked octopus tentacles,
    cut into ½-inch slices
1 cucumber, cut into ¾-inch chunks
¼ medium sweet onion, thinly sliced into half-moons
¼ cup thinly sliced scallions
1 teaspoon roasted sesame seeds

In a small saucepan, combine the mirin, vinegar, and sake and bring to a boil. Once the smell of alcohol has subsided (30 seconds to 1 minute), remove it from the heat and let cool. Whisk in the miso, peanut butter, mustard powder, and lemon juice. Taste and season with salt and sugar if needed.

(recipe continues)

In a medium bowl, toss the sliced octopus with the sauce. Let marinate for 1 to 2 hours.

In a bowl, toss the cucumber with a few pinches of salt and let it sit for 5 minutes. Drain the cucumber.

Toss the onion with the marinated octopus. Transfer the mixture to a plate and top with the cucumber, scallions, and sesame seeds. Refrigerate for at least 1 hour, or up to 1 day, before serving.

OVEN-BRAISED OCTOPUS

MAKES ABOUT 1 POUND

1 (3-pound) frozen octopus, thawed and cleaned
Kosher salt
2 tablespoons instant dashi powder
  (such as HonDashi)
1½ tablespoons shoyu (soy sauce)
½ tablespoon sugar
3-inch strip of dried kombu

Preheat the oven to 350°F.

Massage the octopus with salt to remove any slime. Rinse well.

In a Dutch oven or ovenproof pot, combine the dashi powder, shoyu, sugar, dried kombu, and 8 cups water. Stir until dissolved. Add the octopus, make sure it's submerged—add a plate or weight if necessary—and bring it to a simmer over medium heat.

Cover, transfer to the oven, and bake until the thickest part of the tentacles can be easily pierced with a knife, about 1 hour.

Remove the octopus from the pot and let it cool completely. Once cooled, separate the head from the tentacles, reserving the head for another use if desired. Cover and refrigerate the tentacles until ready to use.

BLISTERED SHISHITOS WITH FURIKAKE RANCH AND CRISPY QUINOA

SERVES 2 TO 4

I imagine many chefs have a dish like this, one that begins as a hastily assembled staff meal and somehow morphs into one of the most popular things they've ever served in a restaurant. Oh wait, is it just me?

It began with shishito peppers blistered in a screaming-hot pan, because who doesn't love shishitos? I took some cooked quinoa that was on the line and threw it in the fryer until it turned nutty and crunchy. I mixed some furikake and ranch together, because delicious plus delicious equals more delicious. The rest is history.

That dish first went on the menu at Migrant, which closed in 2016; people still request that I cook it for them to this day. But I'm fine with it, because it's still a combination of tastes and textures that I crave. In fact, I made it for the construction guys who poured the cement patio at my house just the other week. Furikake ranch forever.

4 tablespoons neutral oil
½ cup cooked quinoa
Kosher salt
1 pound shishito peppers
Garlic salt
½ lemon, cut into wedges
¾ cup ranch dressing
     (made from Hidden Valley ranch dressing mix)
3 tablespoons Furikake (page 262)

In a large skillet, heat 2 tablespoons of the oil over medium-high heat. When it's shimmering-hot, add the quinoa to the pan and spread evenly. Cook, stirring occasionally, until golden-brown and crisp, 5 to 15 minutes (depending on the quinoa's moisture content; freshly cooked quinoa will take longer). Drain the fried quinoa on paper towels and season with a pinch of kosher salt. Wipe the pan clean.

Add the remaining 2 tablespoons oil to the pan and place over high heat. Once the oil begins to smoke, add the shishitos. It's important that all the peppers touch the pan, so work in batches if necessary. Sear the peppers on all sides, turning occasionally, until they begin to blister and slightly char, about 4 minutes. Season to taste with garlic salt and a squeeze of lemon. Transfer to a plate and top with the fried quinoa.

In a small bowl, whisk together the ranch with 2 tablespoons of the furikake. Serve it alongside the shishitos. Sprinkle with the remaining 1 tablespoon furikake before serving.

MAUI FLYING SAUCERS

MAKES 8 SANDWICHES

Very few local dishes involve American cheese, which is somewhat surprising given our affection for canned meats and picnic condiments. One notable exception is the flying saucer, a molten-cheese-oozing grilled sandwich that you'll see sold at local fairs and Obon festivals (street fairs in honor of a Japanese Buddhist holiday) on the islands of Kaua'i and Maui.

Flying saucers can best be described as the glorious love child of a sloppy Joe and a grilled cheese: tomatoey beef goulash and Kraft Singles squished between two slices of white bread, then grill-pressed over an open fire until melty and toasty, using a special circular press contraption called a Toas-Tite.

I'd never actually tried a flying saucer before the Maui County Fair, but when I went for the first time I noticed that the flying saucer booths had by far the longest lines. The hype was deserved. At Lineage, I put the beefy toasted sandwich on the menu as a thank-you to my new home island and the Maui folks who had shown me so much aloha. Judging by how many we sold, I figure I might open a booth at next year's fair.

You can find Toas-Tite sandwich grills, which were invented in the 1940s, for sale online, but at $30 they're not exactly cheap (I splurged on like a dozen for the restaurant, yikes). Instead, trim the bread crust into a round and pan-fry the sandwich to achieve roughly the same effect.

2 tablespoons neutral oil
1 tablespoon minced garlic
½ teaspoon kochugaru (Korean chili flakes)
1 pound ground beef (80/20)
1 cup diced yellow onion
1 cup diced celery
½ cup diced carrots
2 tablespoons tomato paste

Half a (10.5-ounce) can condensed cream of
    mushroom soup
1 tablespoon Lawry's chili seasoning mix
Kosher salt and freshly ground black pepper
Salted butter, at room temperature
16 slices white bread, crusts removed and
    trimmed into rounds
16 slices American cheese

In a large skillet, heat the oil over medium heat. Add the garlic and kochugaru and cook until the garlic starts to brown, 30 seconds to 1 minute. Add the beef and cook until browned, then stir in the onion, celery, and carrots. Cook, stirring occasionally, until the onion and carrots soften and smell sweet, 12 to 15 minutes. Stir in the tomato paste. Stir in the mushroom soup and seasoning mix. Reduce the heat to low and simmer for a few minutes until fully incorporated. Season to taste with salt and black pepper. Transfer the meat mixture to a bowl and rinse and dry the skillet.

Preheat the oven to warm, or 200°F.

Heat the skillet over medium heat. Butter one side of each slice of bread. Place 2 slices of bread, butter-side down, in the skillet and top each with 1 slice of cheese. Spoon ¼ cup of the meat mixture onto one piece of bread and top it with the other. Cook, squishing the sandwich down gently but firmly with a spatula, until the bread is well browned on both sides and the cheese is gooey, 2 to 3 minutes per side. Repeat with the remaining sandwiches, keeping the finished ones warm in the oven until ready to serve.

THE INFLUENCERS
HAOLES (WESTERNERS)

Captain James Cook, a British explorer who mapped large swaths of the Pacific in the name of the Royal Navy, landed at Waimea Bay on Kaua'i in 1778. He and his crew were the first Europeans to set foot in Hawai'i, which were later dubbed the Sandwich Isles in honor of the Earl of Sandwich. The native Hawaiians referred to them as *haole*, a word that meant foreigner, but in modern times has become a catch-all term for white people.

Other European explorers and sailors began to arrive soon after Cook. Cattle were introduced in 1793, thriving in the grassy valleys of Maui and the Big Island and eventually becoming part of native Hawaiian cuisine. Two decades later, Don Francisco de Paula Marín, a Spanish horticulturalist and advisor to King Kamehameha I, introduced the cultivation of chili peppers, pineapple, coffee, citrus, potatoes, tomatoes, cabbage, and other New World staples of the Americas to the islands.

By the 1820s, Americans had begun to arrive, too, in the form of Protestant missionaries from New England, whalers and sailors from the Pacific Northwest, and East Coast businessmen interested in lucrative sugarcane crops. With them came a taste for corned beef, potatoes, beans, salted salmon, hardtack, bread, and cakes.

At the start of the twentieth century, Hawai'i became home to a substantial number of military bases, which housed soldiers from the mainland who brought a taste for Midwestern Americana dishes like chicken and dumplings, beef stew, and goulash. Later, food rationing during WWII turned shelf-stable food items like canned soup, Spam, Vienna sausages, and evaporated milk into fixtures of the local pantry.

CASCARON WITH CHICKEN LIVER MOUSSE AND GUAVA JELLY

SERVES 8 TO 10

A few years ago, after thumbing through issues of *Food & Wine,* I noticed a significant number of famous chefs in America all had chicken liver mousse on their menus, usually paired with some type of pastry or bread that was linked to their local area. I started to get a little jealous. I loved chicken liver mousse as much as the rest of them. What would my regional riff be?

Inspiration struck after a visit to a grocery store and deli near Tin Roof that happens to sell my favorite Filipino dessert, *cascaron* (fried coconut mochi balls). The seamless flavor combo of velvety liver mousse with salty furikake, guava jelly, and coconut-mochi fritters felt like it was meant to be; that it was so effortlessly *of Hawai'i* made it that much sweeter.

1 (16-ounce) box mochiko (sweet rice flour)
1 cup unsweetened flaked coconut
2 tablespoons sugar
2 cups full-fat coconut milk
Neutral oil, for deep-frying
½ cup guava jelly
Chicken Liver Mousse (recipe follows), for serving (see Note)
2 tablespoons Furikake (page 262), for serving

In a medium bowl, stir together the mochiko, coconut flakes, sugar, and coconut milk until a dough has formed and there are no lumps. Use your hands to roll into balls the size of golf balls (about 2 tablespoons) and place on a plate until ready to fry.

Prepare a wire rack or line a baking sheet with paper towels. Fill a large, heavy-bottomed pot or Dutch oven with at least 2 inches of oil, making sure to leave a few inches of clearance from the top of the pot. Heat over medium-high heat until the oil reaches 350°F (use a thermometer), adjusting the heat as needed to maintain temperature. (Alternatively, drop a small pinch of dough into the oil; if it immediately bubbles and sizzles, the oil is ready.)

Fry the balls in batches, making sure there is plenty of room for them to move in the oil, until golden-brown and crispy, 4 to 5 minutes (check the interior for doneness: it should be chewy and elastic all the way through). Transfer the cascaron to the wire rack or paper towels and let cool slightly.

Spoon the guava jelly into a medium-tipped pastry bag or a plastic sandwich bag with one corner cut off. Once the cascaron are cool enough to handle, use a paring knife to cut a slit into the middle of each. Pipe slightly less than 1 teaspoon of guava jelly into each.

(recipe continues)

Transfer the cascaron to a serving plate. Spread the chicken liver mousse onto the plate and sprinkle with the furikake. Serve immediately while the cascaron are warm.

NOTE: *If you've already prepared the chicken liver mousse, remove it from the fridge and let it come to room temperature for about 1 hour before serving.*

CHICKEN LIVER MOUSSE

MAKES ABOUT 4 CUPS

1 pound chicken livers
Garlic salt
Freshly ground black pepper
4 tablespoons salted butter
1 small sweet onion, grated
1 tablespoon shiro (white) miso
¼ cup whiskey or brandy
Tabasco sauce
1 cup full-fat coconut milk

Clean the livers of any hard bits with a sharp knife. Rinse them and pat very dry with paper towels. Season them with garlic salt and pepper.

In a large skillet, heat the butter over medium heat until sizzling. Add the chicken livers and cook on both sides until opaque, then stir in the onion and miso. Continue cooking until the livers are firm but still pink in the center, about 2 minutes per side. Add the whiskey and a few shakes of Tabasco and cook until the liquid has evaporated.

Transfer the mixture immediately to a blender, pour in the coconut milk, and blend on medium speed until completely smooth. Adjust the seasoning with garlic salt if needed.

Pour the mixture into ramekins or a serving dish. Cover with plastic wrap, lightly pressing the wrap to the surface of the mousse so that it doesn't oxidize. Refrigerate until set, 1 to 2 hours. This can be made a day in advance if desired.

BISCUIT MANAPUA

MAKES 20 MANAPUA

Manapua is a food with roots in old Hawai'i. Originally brought to the islands by Chinese immigrants, these steamed pork buns are the local equivalent of *char siu bao*. The story goes that vendors would carry them around hanging from long poles, selling them to passersby on the streets. Among Hawaiians they supposedly became known as *mea 'ono pua'a*, a phrase that loosely translates as "delicious pork thing."

Affordable, portable, and large enough to silence any between-meal hunger pangs, fluffy manapua filled with sweet red pork have remained as popular as ever. Most of the bakeries and delis famous for manapua are located in Oahu's Chinatown (which is near the airport), making them a popular *omiyage* (souvenir gift) item to bring to family and friends when traveling between the neighbor islands.

I love a good manapua, but I also have memories of our fridge being packed with at least two weeks' worth after an uncle or auntie visited Oahu. I ate 'em until I got sick! Better now to satisfy my manapua cravings a little at a time. Rather than making *bao* dough from scratch, this recipe swaps in refrigerated biscuit dough, a common shortcut among time-crunched locals that allows them to make smaller batches more often. Make sure you use regular biscuits rather than jumbo size or extra flaky; they produce the closest results when steaming. This recipe has you make your own char siu, but you could also look for precooked char siu pork at the store (check the freezer section).

½ cup chicken broth
1 tablespoon all-purpose flour
2 teaspoons sugar, plus more for sprinkling
1 tablespoon shoyu (soy sauce), plus more for dipping
1 teaspoon toasted sesame oil
2 teaspoons cornstarch
½ pound Easy Char Siu (page 286), small-diced
¼ cup chopped scallions
Kosher salt
2 (7.5-ounce/10-count) tubes refrigerated buttermilk biscuit dough
Neutral oil, for greasing
Chinese hot mustard, for dipping

In a medium saucepan, stir together the broth, flour, sugar, shoyu, and sesame oil. Bring to a boil. Meanwhile, in a small bowl, whisk together the cornstarch and 2 teaspoons water. Add to the broth and simmer until thickened, about 1 minute. Remove from the heat and stir in the char siu and scallions. Taste and season with salt if needed.

Fill a steamer pan halfway with water and bring it to a boil. (The manapua can also be baked; see Note.) Line the steamer tray with parchment paper (or cabbage leaves), leaving a few holes exposed for steam circulation.

Grease a baking sheet.

Separate the biscuits. Sprinkle a pinch of sugar on a clean work surface to help keep the dough from sticking. Flatten a biscuit into a 4-inch round. Place about 2 tablespoons of filling in the center and pinch to close, forming a ball. Place it seam-side down on the greased baking sheet. Repeat with the remaining biscuits and filling.

Working in batches, steam the manapua until the dough has doubled in size and is no longer wet or sticky to the touch, 15 to 18 minutes. Turn off the heat and wait for the steam to subside before lifting off the lid. Remove the steamer tray and transfer the buns to a wire rack to cool.

Serve warm with a dipping sauce of Chinese hot mustard and shoyu (mixed to taste). Store any leftovers in a sealable container and refrigerate for up to 5 days. To reheat, wrap manapua in a damp paper towel and microwave for 30 to 45 seconds.

NOTE: *To bake the manapua, preheat the oven to 350°F. Arrange the buns on a greased baking sheet and bake for 15 to 20 minutes until golden-brown.*

THE INFLUENCERS
THE CHINESE COMMUNITY

To feed a growing demand in the sugarcane fields, plantation owners in Hawai'i originally turned to China for contract labor. The first ships in 1852 brought workers from Canton (now known as Guangzhou) in the southern Chinese province of Guangdong. By 1884, Hawai'i was home to more than 25,000 Chinese immigrants, many of whom had arrived on five-year work contracts. About one-third returned to China after their time was up, but the majority stayed, bringing their families from overseas and opening businesses or raising vegetables, poultry, or rice, the latter of which had emerged as the island's chief staple crop due to demand from Chinese workers. A wave of newly opened Chinese shops manufactured or imported ingredients from back home, including fresh noodles, salted bean paste, and preserved fruits like li hing mui. In Honolulu, a growing Chinatown district—one of the oldest in the United States—gave rise to restaurants and bakeries that served Cantonese dishes like manapua (opposite) filled with char siu pork, chow fun (see page 202), and fried rice (see page 195).

HIBACHI STYLING

Some call it grilling, some call it barbecue, some call it cooking out. Here in Hawai'i we call it hibachi.

The name originally referred to a traditional style of Japanese charcoal-powered grill, but locally it has come to mean any kind of cooking done over fire or hot embers, also known in Hawaiian as *pūlehu*.

As you might expect from a state renowned for its gorgeous weather, locals love to grill just about everything here, high and low: hot dogs to rib eyes, pork ribs to rack of lamb, whole fish to fresh shrimp. More than anything, hibachi is an excuse to gather. Along with rice cookers, humongous coolers, pop-up canopies, and games of Portuguese Horseshoe, at least one dome-shaped Weber grill is required gear for a true Hawaiian party outdoors.

Around Hilo, my dad was known as an expert welder and expert cook, which meant he was versed in both constructing grills and using them. I knew grilling as a full-day activity, one that yielded plenty of food to fill the stomachs of our whole 'ohana. If we could get local kiawe wood, the island equivalent of mesquite, we'd cook with that, but if not we'd pick up bags of Kingsford at KTA. I learned it was crucial to have pupus on hand as soon as you lit the hibachi—it's much easier to be patient with the huli huli chicken when you've got boiled peanuts and poke to take the edge off growling stomachs.

These days, I do most of my grilling in my backyard, on an old Weber, up in the hills of Wailuku looking down onto Kahului Bay. Though I'll cook for large gatherings of friends here and there, I'm just as often searing a couple steaks to feed the wife and kids. The recipes in this chapter draw from both traditions, with some befitting big Sunday shindigs and others tailored for weeknight meals. Either way, hibachi cooking brings people together and provides an excuse to relax, unwind, and talk story.

SHOYU SUGAR STEAK

SERVES 6 TO 8

I like to think of shoyu and sugar as the mother sauce of local cuisine. Mixed together in sweet and salty balance, "shoyu sugar" forms the foundation for a number of dishes, from Chicken Hekka (page 172) to Okinawa Pig's Feet (page 153). The combination makes sense on a cultural level as much as on a culinary one: Sugarcane was the economic lifeblood of Hawai'i for generations, while shoyu is the one seasoning we use in Hawai'i more than any other.

The idea for this recipe came about when I faced a very specific conundrum. I love the simplicity of grilling a thick steak on my backyard grill. But if I wanted to season it with shoyu sugar, I'd have to marinate it, which would change the texture of the meat. Brushing the steak with shoyu sugar while on the grill didn't work great either, since the liquid drips off without imparting much flavor.

The solution I came up with was a take on Japanese *tare*, a basting sauce thickened with brown rice that's been toasted and pulverized. The rice powder adds a pleasant nuttiness, but more important, it helps the shoyu sugar cling to the steak, so you end up with a gorgeous caramelized crust.

With this method, any steak at least ¾ inch thick will work, including the usual rib eye, New York strip, T-bone, top sirloin, flank steak, etc. My favorite cut to use, however, is boneless chuck roast (aka "the poor man's rib eye"), a piece of meat that comes from the shoulder and is most often used for braising or roasting, thus making it a more frugal option (my dad would always pick it up on sale at Foodland). It's not as tender as a filet mignon, but if you prefer a beefier-tasting steak, its robust flavor and satisfying chew make it an appealing option.

Use any leftover slices of steak to make Chop Steak (page 111) the next day, or try steak sandwiches topped with Kim Chee Dip (page 32) and watercress.

3 pounds boneless chuck roast or steaks of choice, cut about 1 inch thick
Garlic salt
½ cup raw brown rice or barley (see Note)
1 cup mirin
½ cup sake
1 cup shoyu (soy sauce)
½ cup loosely packed light brown sugar
2 tablespoons apple cider vinegar
6 cloves garlic, crushed and peeled
6 scallions, cut into thirds and crushed
2-inch piece fresh ginger, sliced and crushed
Oil, for the grill
Freshly ground black pepper

Sprinkle the steaks generously with garlic salt. Place on a plate and let stand for 40 minutes at room temperature.

(recipe continues)

Place the rice in a spice grinder and pulse until finely ground.

In a dry saucepan, toast the rice powder over medium-high heat, stirring constantly, until caramel-colored and fragrant, about 5 minutes.

Reduce the heat to medium-low, add the mirin and sake, and bring to a boil, stirring to loosen any browned bits from the bottom of the pan. Once boiling, add the shoyu, brown sugar, vinegar, garlic, scallions, and ginger and simmer very gently until the mixture is thickened and slightly reduced, about 15 minutes. Use a slotted spoon to remove the aromatics (or pour the mixture through a sieve into a bowl, discarding the solids).

Prepare a grill for high indirect heat (for a charcoal grill, push the coals to one side; for a gas grill, leave one or two burners off). Using tongs, oil the grates of the grill with an oiled rag or paper towels. Sprinkle the steaks generously with pepper and place on the grates on the indirect heat side. Cover the grill and cook until a thermometer inserted into the thickest portion registers 105°F, 20 to 25 minutes, flipping the steaks and checking the internal temperature every 5 minutes or so.

Move the steaks over direct heat, brush liberally with the sauce, and grill, flipping every 30 seconds to 1 minute, brushing each time with more sauce, until a nice charred glaze has developed and the internal temperature registers 125°F (for medium-rare) or to desired degree of doneness.

Transfer the steaks to a cutting board and let rest at least 10 minutes. Carve into thick slices and serve immediately with the remaining sauce.

NOTE: *if you don't have a spice grinder to grind the grain, substitute ⅓ cup Cream of Wheat or Cream of Rice hot cereal.*

THE INFLUENCERS
THE KOREAN COMMUNITY

The first large group of Korean workers came in 1903, three years after the United States passed a law that outlawed contract labor in American territories. Mainly from rural villages or southern port cities, the 7,000 Koreans who arrived were a mix of men, women, and children. Since many weren't locked in to long contracts at the sugar plantations like other immigrant groups, they promptly ditched their field jobs and opened local businesses, farms, and markets. Dishes like Local-Style Kalbi (page 82) and spicy kim chee (see page 269) quickly found widespread popularity in the islands due to their relative closeness to the Japanese and Chinese influences that already dominated local food.

LOCAL-STYLE KALBI

SERVES 6 TO 8

I've learned the secret to world-beating kalbi is a lengthy marinating time, two or three full days at least. Anyone who says you can do them quicker is selling you snake oil. Soaking the thinly sliced ribs in shoyu and sugar for that long helps the beef become cured and almost candied. That way when the ribs hit a hot grill, they retain their succulence and develop their signature caramelized and charred crust.

High heat is crucial when grilling kalbi, but since there's plenty of sugar and sesame oil in the marinade, watch them closely on the grill so they don't burn or flare up. They'll be fully cooked in a matter of minutes. If you're having a hard time finding the correct style of short ribs, ask your butcher for bone-in short ribs cut in half crosswise. Short of that, you can also cut long strips of boneless short rib in ½-inch-thick pieces.

5 pounds short ribs, cut across the bones into ½-inch-wide slices (flanken-style)

3 cups shoyu (soy sauce)

3 cups sugar

½ cup toasted sesame oil

1 tablespoon sambal oelek

10 scallions, cut into thirds and crushed

3-inch piece fresh ginger, sliced and crushed

12 cloves garlic, crushed and peeled

2 tablespoons plus 1 teaspoon roasted sesame seeds

Oil, for the grill

Shaved green cabbage or "Bottom of the Plate Lunch" Salad (page 214; see Note), for serving

Cooked white rice, for serving

Kim chee or other pickles (pages 266–269), for serving

Rinse the ribs to wash away any bone fragments, pat dry, and place them in a wide shallow bowl or large zip-top plastic bags. In another bowl, whisk together the shoyu, sugar, sesame oil, sambal, scallions, ginger, garlic, and 2 tablespoons of the sesame seeds. Pour the marinade over the short ribs and mix well. Cover and refrigerate for 2 to 3 days, stirring and mixing every 12 hours or so.

An hour or so before grilling, remove the ribs from the fridge and let them come toward room temperature, stirring once in a while to let the meat in the middle of the pile warm up in the air.

Preheat a grill to hot. Using tongs, oil the grates of the grill with an oiled rag or paper towels. Once the grill is very hot, remove the ribs from the marinade, letting the excess drip off, and place directly onto the grill. Be careful of any flare-ups. Grill for 3 to 4 minutes per side, until nicely browned but juicy. (This can also be done using a broiler on high heat, but if you're doing that, really make sure the ribs aren't soaking in marinade when you put them on a sheet pan. Make sure to open windows and turn on exhaust fans to clear away any resulting smoke.)

Transfer the cooked ribs to a sheet pan. Let rest for 10 minutes, then drain off any meat drippings and reserve for the "Bottom of the Plate Lunch" Salad or to pour over rice, if desired.

Sprinkle the short ribs with the remaining 1 teaspoon sesame seeds. Serve with rice, pickles, and either shaved cabbage or the "Bottom of the Plate Lunch" Salad.

NOTE: *This kalbi recipe is a main component in Bottom of the Plate Lunch, a dish I served at Migrant that took all the components of a traditional plate lunch and mixed 'em together in different ways. These ribs are spectacular on their own, too, of course—just figured I'd let you know in case you wanted the full experience.*

CALL ME MR. KALBI

My first real restaurant job (not including when I worked at Pizza Hut) was at a place called Aloha Mixed Plate, which had been open since the '90s. I had just enrolled in Maui Community College when the restaurant hired me as prep cook and dishwasher. You should have seen this place: It was a big patio covered in deck umbrellas that was a rock's throw away from the beach along Front Street. The menu was local-style food that both tourists and Maui folks went nuts for: heaping portions of teriyaki beef, katsu, mahi mahi, shrimp. Everything was served on paper plates.

The food we cooked at Aloha Mixed Plate was right up my alley. I'd been eating mixed plates—two or more main dishes with rice and mac salad—since small kid time. If forced to choose, I'd pick the same main dish as most of our customers, a dish that every serious plate lunch spot has on their menu: cross-cut grilled kalbi short ribs. The kalbi in Hawai'i, sweeter and more boldly seasoned than what you might find in Seoul, evolved here over the years, going from a special-occasion food eaten mainly by Koreans to a ubiquitous treat adored and relished by locals of all stripes—a classic immigrant success story. It was also the most premium plate item. Every shrewd establishment had a note on their combo menu that read: KALBI +$2.50.

After a few years at Aloha Mixed Plate, I had grilled more kalbi than most people would in a lifetime. I'm talking hundreds of pounds a day. Tourism was booming in Lahaina and we were so busy we could barely keep up with the crowds. On a standard night, we might serve 700 plates of food with 2½ cooks working the line (the ½ guy was a dishwasher who would run between the dish pit and the prep station when we were getting crushed). Then there was the kitchen itself, an old 1960s concrete brick building that couldn't have been larger than a trailer home. There were no windows and during serving it felt like the surface of the sun. I remember one of my former cooking in-structors stopped by once and used his infra-red thermometer to measure the temperature in the kitchen: 120°F!!!

After we'd finish dinner service, completely exhausted and wiped out, we'd get to eat our staff meal: anything off the menu for free. For me, it was always kalbi—best kalbi ever, we had there. I wouldn't just get three or four ribs (a standard order), but like ten charred hunks piled over a mountain of rice and mac salad with extra shaved cabbage. Every night that's what I took home. The other chefs and I would sit at the empty patio tables, half-delirious, feasting and drinking out of big paper cups filled with Coke and whiskey. Then we'd go home, get up the next morning (or afternoon), and do it all over again.

TERI BEEF STICKS

SERVES 4

The classic companion to a bowl of Saimin (page 190), teriyaki beef sticks are a staple at any local diner, plate lunch spot, county fair, or church carnival. At home, the smartest way to prepare these juicy flavor bombs is to do the bulk of the work the day before. Mix together six ingredients to marinate the beef, then boil a portion of it to make a finishing sauce that will be used later.

These sticks can be done over a hot grill or under the broiler, but keep a close eye since the thin strips of meat will cook in a short amount of time. I like to eat these as a side with any fried rice or noodle dish, but you can also turn them into a full meal by adding some good old steamed rice and a salad or pickles.

1½ cups sugar
1½ cups shoyu (soy sauce)
⅓ cup sake or dry sherry
4 scallions, roughly chopped, green and white parts
    kept separate
4 cloves garlic, crushed and peeled
2-inch piece fresh ginger, sliced and crushed
1½ pounds flank or skirt steak, thinly sliced crosswise into
    1-inch-wide strips

In a large bowl, whisk together the sugar, shoyu, sake, scallion whites, garlic, and ginger. Transfer 1 cup of the marinade to a small saucepan. Add the beef to the remaining marinade, cover, and refrigerate for at least 4 hours, or overnight.

Bring the saucepan of marinade to a boil. Reduce the heat and simmer until the sauce has thickened slightly, about 8 minutes. Remove from the heat and set aside (or store in the fridge).

An hour before you're ready to grill, soak bamboo skewers in warm water. Remove the beef from the fridge and let it come to room temperature. Thread the beef onto the skewers, shaking off any excess marinade, and place on a baking sheet or plate.

Preheat a grill to medium-hot (or preheat a broiler to high). Grill or broil the skewers, basting with the reserved reduced sauce, until cooked through and slightly charred, 2 to 3 minutes per side. Transfer to a serving platter and garnish with the scallion greens before serving.

CHICKEN BAR-B-QUE*

SERVES 2 TO 4

*Big Islanders have a habit of reversing certain words and phrases, especially with food. We call it chicken barbecue; other islands call it barbecue chicken. Same for "ice shave" vs. "shave ice" and "broccoli beef" vs. "beef broccoli."

Known to most mainlanders as teriyaki chicken, the flavors of this Japanese-rooted dish are deeply ingrained in the local palate. Stroll through any state park or beach on the weekends and you'll be hit by the smell, an intoxicating smoky aroma wafting from the portable hibachis set up at picnics and family reunions.

As popular as this style of sweet-salty grilled chicken is, though, it's also one of those straightforward-seeming dishes that often falls short of its delicious potential: the meat dry or overcooked, not marinated long enough, the skin burnt. You truly hate to see it.

Done properly, the first step is to rub the chicken thighs (always chicken thighs) with salty seasonings first, which gives them a head start penetrating the meat (sugar can slow the absorption of salt in a marinade). When you're ready to light the grill, pull the chicken from the fridge and let it come to room temperature, which, along with indirect heat, will ensure the thighs finish cooking before the outside burns. Finally, use thighs with the skin attached. Even if you're not a skin fiend, the outer layer of fat insulates the dark meat, keeping it moist and forming a rendered crust that holds the teriyaki sauce.

NOTE: *This recipe can be used to make another popular local dish, shoyu chicken, in which the thighs are braised instead of grilled. Try make: Once you've dry-brined the chicken in the garlic salt, add it to a pot along with the remaining ingredients and cover with water or stock. Stir to combine. Bring to a boil, then reduce the heat and simmer until the chicken is tender. Thicken the sauce with a cornstarch slurry if desired and serve over rice.*

2 pounds boneless, skin-on chicken thighs

2 teaspoons garlic salt

2 teaspoons ground turmeric

1 teaspoon freshly ground black pepper

8 scallions, white and green parts separated, greens roughly chopped

1 cup shoyu (soy sauce)

1 cup sugar

1 tablespoon toasted sesame oil

4 cloves garlic, crushed and peeled

2-inch piece fresh ginger, sliced and crushed

Oil, for the grill

Place the chicken in a large shallow bowl or heavy-duty zip-top plastic bag and rub evenly with the garlic salt, turmeric, and pepper. Marinate for 30 minutes to 1 hour in the fridge.

Using the butt of a knife, crush the white parts of the scallions and add to a small saucepan along with the shoyu, sugar, sesame oil, garlic, and ginger. Cook over medium-low heat until the sugar is dissolved and the sauce has slightly thickened, about 5 minutes. Let cool.

Measure out ½ cup of the sauce for basting on the grill. Pour the remainder over the chicken and marinate the chicken for another 2 to 3 hours in the fridge, or overnight, mixing once or twice.

COOK REAL HAWAI'I

One hour before you're ready to cook, remove the chicken from the fridge and let it come to room temperature.

Prepare a grill for high indirect heat (for a charcoal grill, push the coals to one side; for a gas grill, leave one or two burners off). Using tongs, oil the grates of the grill with an oiled rag or paper towels. When the grill is hot, set the chicken skin-side down on the direct heat side of the grill. Once the chicken has some grill marks and releases easily from the grates, 2 to 3 minutes, move over indirect heat, still skin-side down, and cook, turning often and basting with the reserved sauce, until the juices run clear or a thermometer inserted into the thickest part of the thigh registers 160°F, another 8 to 10 minutes. The chicken should spend about three-quarters of its grilling time skin-side down, which will create a nice charred crust. If the skin is browning too quickly, move it farther away from the heat source. Transfer to a serving platter (or cutting board) and let rest 10 minutes. Garnish with the scallion greens and serve.

STUFFED UHU WITH LAP CHEONG

SERVES 2 TO 4

Uhu is the Hawaiian word for parrotfish, a colorful fish with a prominent sharp beak (hence the name) that it uses to munch on algae-coated coral. Since they live around reefs, uhu are a prime target for local spearfishers.

Although I was never the best at diving, I always had friends who would supply me with fish because they knew I'd make something *ono* (delicious) with it. Stuffed uhu—filled with a mixture of mayo, sliced veggies, sausage, and aromatics—was the ultimate preparation. The fish's flaky fillets are tender and sweet, which perfectly balances the savory fillings. You can use whatever produce is sitting in the fridge (mushrooms, onions, tomatoes, celery, zucchini) plus some type of fatty cured meat (here I use lap cheong, a dried Chinese sausage, but Portuguese Sausage [page 284] or Smoke Meat [page 100] are excellent, too). Once the uhu is stuffed and rubbed with seasoned mayo, it's wrapped in ti leaves (or banana leaves) and heavy-duty aluminum foil, sealing in the moisture so the fish steams and cooks evenly. Some locals say uhu is best grilled, which adds a subtle smokiness, but others prefer to bake the whole thing in the oven. My feeling is that you can't go wrong either way.

1 cup mayonnaise

1 tablespoon plus 1 teaspoon shoyu (soy sauce)

1 tablespoon oyster sauce

2 teaspoons sambal oelek

Grated zest of 1 lemon

1 lemon, halved

Garlic salt

Freshly ground black pepper

Ti leaves (see page 294) or banana leaves, for wrapping

1 whole fish (see Note), 3 to 4 pounds, scaled and cleaned

2 cloves garlic, thinly sliced

1-inch piece fresh ginger, peeled and julienned

4 ounces lap cheong (Chinese sausage), thinly sliced (about ⅔ cup)

4 dried shiitake mushrooms, soaked in warm water to soften, stems discarded, caps roughly diced

½ cup diced tomato

¼ medium sweet or yellow onion, thinly sliced

2 scallions, thinly sliced

Cilantro sprigs, for serving

Preheat a grill or an oven to 375°F.

In a small bowl, whisk together the mayo, shoyu, oyster sauce, sambal, lemon zest, and lemon juice from ½ lemon. Season to taste with garlic salt and pepper and set aside.

On your work surface, place overlapping sheets of heavy-duty aluminum foil so that you can fit the fish on them with enough room to bring the sheets together in a tent above the fish. Line the foil with ti leaves. Arrange the fish in the center. Using a paring knife, cut four or five long slits on each side of the fish, deep enough to reach the bone. Season the outside generously with garlic salt and pepper.

Stuff the sliced garlic and ginger into the slits of the fish, dividing evenly. Coat each side of the fish with a large spoonful of the mayo mixture, decorating the top side with a few slices of sausage. Stir together the remaining mayo mixture with the remaining sausage, the mushrooms, tomato, onion, and scallions and spread it inside the fish's cavity. To enclose the fish, bring the leaves and the long sides of the foil together to form a triangular tent and fold the seal over itself twice, then flatten and tightly roll in the short sides.

Grill the foil-wrapped fish over medium heat for 20 minutes on each side (or bake for 30 to 40 minutes). Listen for the sound of the mayo bubbling and sizzling before unwrapping to check the fish for doneness (the flesh should yield easily when poked with a chopstick). Squeeze the remaining ½ lemon over the top and garnish with cilantro before serving.

NOTE: *Parrotfish can be tough to find on the mainland (check Asian markets), but this recipe works just as well with any firm, flaky whole fish such as sea bass, snapper, tilapia, branzino, or trout.*

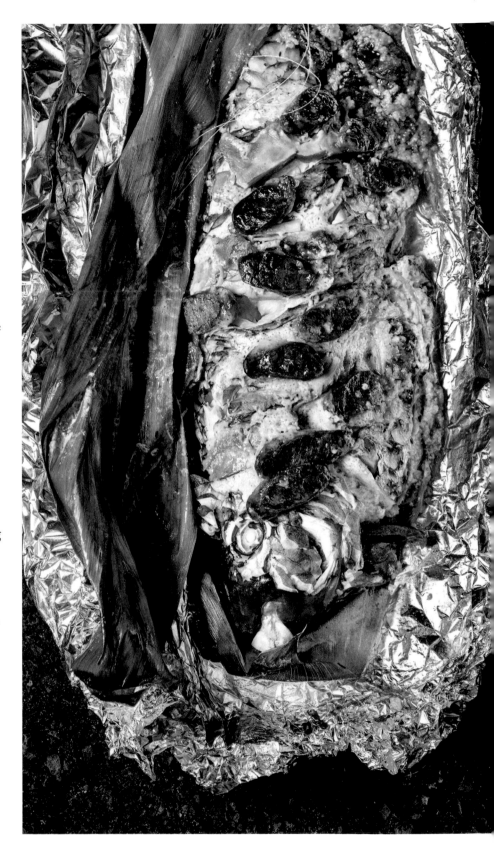

TAILGATE-STYLE LOMI SQUID

SERVES 2 TO 4

When I was growing up, every local family we knew had one of those little charcoal hibachis that could fit in the back of a pickup. This was a handy thing, because it meant that no matter where you were, or what the occasion—football game at Hilo High, race at the Kamehameha Canoe Club, rodeo at the Pana'ewa Stampede—you were never without the ability to light the grill and cook up what was in the cooler.

For us, an important virtue of any grilled food was how fast it could be prepared, because that meant how soon we could be eating it. *Ika* (squid) was a top contender because it only took a couple minutes—seconds, even—before the meat turned plump and tender.

Although you can find ika in local waters, there's not as much interest in catching them these days, at least directly. During the 1920s, Okinawan squid fishermen in Hilo figured out that the giant 'ahi tuna were eating squid off their hooks (squid are like candy for big fish) and invented a technique called *ika shibi* that used bait to attract the squid, which in turn drew in the 'ahi. Smart guys.

If I'm lucky, a buddy might hook me up with Hawaiian squid now and then, but most of the time when I'm craving this recipe I head to the store and pick out a big flattened squid from the freezer case. Look for whole cleaned ones that are around 1 pound each, which you can find at Asian markets. They're tasty, affordable, and easy to prepare. Octopus tentacles are a great alternative, too.

The technique here is to *lomi* (massage) the squid with garlic salt just before grilling so as to tenderize it. From there it's as simple as cutting it up and tossing the warm slices with raw onion, tomato, hot sauce, and tangy chili pepper water. Juicy grilled squid and a cold drink—good times.

½ medium sweet onion, diced
½ cup diced tomato
Garlic salt
Freshly ground black pepper
2 pounds large whole squid (or squid tubes), cleaned
2 tablespoons neutral oil
Tabasco sauce and/or Basic or Simeon-Style Chili Pepper Water (page 265)
2 scallions, thinly sliced
2 teaspoons Lemon Olive Oil (page 278)

In a small bowl, combine the onion and tomato and season to taste with garlic salt and black pepper.

Preheat a grill to medium-high heat. Pat the squid dry with paper towels. In a large bowl, coat the squid with the oil. Season liberally with garlic salt and massage into the squid for a minute or two until seasoned all over.

(recipe continues)

Grill the squid quickly, turning once, until opaque but tender, 1 to 2 minutes per side. Be careful not to overcook. Remove from the grill and, when cool enough to handle, separate the head from the tentacles; remove the plastic-like quill from inside the head, if necessary. Slice the head lengthwise and grill the interior for another 1 to 2 minutes. Slice the body into ½ × 2-inch pieces and cut the tentacles in half. Transfer to a serving plate.

Spoon the tomato-onion salad over the squid and season to taste with splashes of Tabasco and/or chili pepper water. Top with scallions and lemon olive oil before serving.

HULI HULI CHICKEN

SERVES 2 TO 4

Huli means "turn" in Hawaiian, a reference to the special rotating grills used to cook this local style of rotisserie chicken. Huli huli, so the legend goes, was created by an enterprising poultry farmer named Ernest Morgad in 1955. In the decades since, it has become a favorite here, often sold at school fundraisers and stands that set up along the highway. During one fundraiser for my high school volleyball team, my dad's guys built a huge contraption made from chicken wire and rebar: The chickens were sandwiched between the wire and cooked over a huge hibachi pit filled with kiawe wood, which sent up billows of sweet-smelling smoke that perfumed the air for miles.

Recipes for huli huli chicken vary, but most tend to use a general teriyaki marinade with the addition of ketchup or pineapple for tanginess. When I put huli huli chicken on the menu at Lineage, the idea was to combine those homey roadside flavors with how classic roast chicken is often presented at fancy restaurants. I start by coating the chicken in *shio koji*, a paste for marinating or seasoning made from fermented rice malt and salt, which has the dual effect of tenderizing the bird and unlocking a whole universe of savoriness. (Ready-to-use shio koji paste or marinade is available at most Japanese and Asian markets, or can be ordered online.)

The second step, which can be done ahead of time, is to create a sweet-tangy glaze to brush on the chicken, since the real secret of huli huli is not only the turning, but the repeated shellacking of glaze that keeps the chicken succulent. To mimic the effect of a rotating spit, create two zones of low heat and high heat on your grill and flip the bird between the zones, basting it often to create a glistening browned crust. Also, using a spatchcocked chicken will help the meat cook evenly.

1 whole chicken (3 to 4 pounds), spatchcocked (see Note)
½ cup shio koji paste
3 cups chicken stock
8 tablespoons (1 stick) salted butter
2 tablespoons oyster sauce
¼ cup pineapple juice
¼ cup packed light brown sugar

4 ounces ginger, sliced and crushed
6 cloves garlic, crushed and peeled
2 tablespoons toasted sesame oil
12 scallions, white and green parts separated, greens roughly chopped
1 tablespoon cornstarch
Garlic salt
Oil, for the grill

Place the chicken on a large sheet pan and rub all over with the shio koji. Cover loosely with parchment paper and refrigerate overnight.

In a saucepan, combine the chicken stock, butter, oyster sauce, pineapple juice, brown sugar, ginger, garlic, and sesame oil. Crush the white parts of the scallions with the butt of a knife and add those, too. Bring this to a boil, then reduce the heat and simmer for 30 minutes, stirring occasionally, or until the liquid has reduced by about half. Remove the ginger, scallions, and garlic using a slotted spoon or sieve.

(recipe continues)

In a small bowl, mix the cornstarch with 2 tablespoons water to make a slurry. Stir it into the sauce and increase the heat to bring back to a boil before removing from the heat.

An hour before you're ready to cook, remove the chicken from the fridge and let it come to room temperature.

When you're ready to cook the chicken, rinse off the shio koji and pat the chicken dry with a paper towel. Season the chicken lightly and evenly with garlic salt.

Preheat a grill to medium-hot. Using tongs, oil the grates of the grill with an oiled rag or paper towels. Set up the grill for two-zone cooking: If using coals, push them off to one side of the grill so you have direct and indirect heat. If using gas, reduce the heat to low on one side of the grill.

Place the chicken, breast-side up, on the cooler side of the grill. Cover and grill for 10 minutes. Uncover, brush the chicken with sauce, cover, and grill another 10 minutes. Uncover, glaze the chicken again, then flip the chicken breast-side down onto the hotter part of the grill. Cook over direct heat, uncovered, until the skin begins to brown and char slightly, about 10 minutes, then brush with sauce and flip the chicken breast-side up, still over direct heat. Brush the breasts with sauce and continue cooking the chicken over direct heat until the juices run clear or a thermometer inserted into the breast reads 160°F (plan for about 40 minutes total cook time). Remove the chicken from the grill and let rest for 15 minutes.

Meanwhile, bring any remaining sauce to a boil (if the sauce is broken, don't worry, it will emulsify when it boils). Remove from the heat and let cool slightly. Slice the chicken and serve topped with some more sauce and the chopped scallion greens.

> **NOTE:** *The easiest way to spatchcock a chicken is to have your butcher do it. Otherwise, use a sharp pair of kitchen shears to cut along both sides of the chicken's backbone (spine), separating it from the ribs. With the backbone removed, turn the bird over so the breast is facing up. Splay out the legs and breasts until they lie flat and give the bird a firm press in the center of the breast; you may hear a crack, and it should lie flat on its own.*

CHARRED FISH SINIGANG (HANGOVER SOUP)

SERVES 4

My late Uncle Frank—aka Francisco, my dad's second oldest brother—was famous in the Simeon family for his boldly seasoned cooking. Uncle Frank worked his whole life in construction and his hands showed it. He was the guy who was five-foot-five and 125 pounds but would haul around 100-pound bags of cement. After he retired, he'd start his morning with a cup of black coffee, then switch straight to vodka. When he'd drink, he'd cook, and vice versa.

The foods that old Uncle Frank championed were the ones with slap-you-in-the-mouth flavor: He'd sneak extra-bitter beef bile into our tripe stew, and load up the Chicken Papaya soup (page 147) with heaps of bitter melon. He loved the "manly" Filipino dishes, the ones that were supposed to put hair on your chest.

After a long night of drinking, when all the adults were rubbing their foreheads and us kids were screaming for Breakfast Fried Rice (page 195), Uncle Frank would bring the zombies back to life by throwing together his twist on Ilocano *sinigang*, a savory fish soup zapped with enough citric acid and sour tamarind to make you sit up straight.

Uncle Frank's trick involved grilling a whole fish until the outside was blackened in spots, then removing the tender fillets and throwing the charred skin, bones, and head into the stockpot. The smoky scraps provided a balancing touch of bitterness, a crucial flavor in Filipino cooking and one that was beloved by Uncle Frank in particular. Bright and acidic and improved with fresh tomatoes and aromatics, this deeply flavored soup has the power to hit every corner of your taste buds.

For this recipe, I use tamarind concentrate (sometimes labeled tamarind paste), a sour and slightly sweet dark-brownish paste that gives sinigang its signature tartness. It can be found at any Asian grocery store, but keep in mind that brands will vary in their potency and sweet-sour balance, so you might need to adjust the amount called for to taste.

Neutral oil

1 whole fish (see Note), 2 to 3 pounds, scaled and cleaned

2 bay leaves

2 teaspoons instant dashi powder (such as HonDashi)

3 tablespoons tamarind concentrate, or to taste

1 tablespoon fish sauce, plus more to taste

½ red onion, thinly sliced

2-inch piece fresh ginger, peeled and thinly sliced

1 cup halved cherry tomatoes

Freshly ground black pepper

Lemon Olive Oil (page 278)

¼ cup chopped cilantro, for garnish

1 lemon, quartered, for garnish

Preheat a grill to hot (or preheat a broiler to high). Using tongs, oil the grates of the grill with an oiled rag or paper towels.

Brush the fish lightly with oil and grill, turning often, until the fish is cooked through and the skin is charred and burnt in places, 15 to 20 minutes. Transfer to a sheet pan and let cool. Use a fork to remove the charred skin and separate the fillets from the bones, setting the fillets aside.

Place the charred skin, bones, and fish head in a soup pot along with the bay leaves and cover with 4 cups water. Bring to a boil, then reduce to a simmer and cook until the broth is cloudy and all the bits of flesh have loosened, 30 to 40 minutes.

Strain the broth and return it to the pot. Stir in the dashi powder, tamarind concentrate, fish sauce, onion, ginger, and tomatoes and simmer until the tomatoes are soft and the onion is translucent, about 10 minutes.

Divide the reserved fish fillets among four bowls and ladle the soup over the top. Season to taste with more fish sauce, black pepper, and lemon olive oil. Garnish with the cilantro and serve with lemon wedges.

NOTE: *Any type of fish will work for this recipe, though firm, white-fleshed fish like rockfish, branzino, tilapia, sea bream, catfish, cod, or trout are good picks if you're on the mainland.*

SMOKE MEAT WITH GUAVA JELLY AND BROCCOLINI

SERVES 4 TO 6

Got that shoyu, sugar, ginger, garlic, chili peppa watah
'Cause the boys just came back with one big freakin' pua'a
—Ka'ikena Scanlan, "Smoke All Day"

A humble country food at heart, "smoke meat" is a Big Island tradition that goes back many generations, rooted in paniolo ranchers and Hawaiian *pua'a* (wild pig) hunters who elevated traditional preservation methods like curing, drying, and smoking into an art form.

I grew up eating bags and bags of the stuff—strips of pork marinated in shoyu and sugar for a few days, then cooked over hot kiawe smoke until they took on the texture of candied bacon. Pig hunting is a major pastime on the Big Island, so often the kind we ate was made from wild boar. (Particularly delicious were the ones that had gotten fat gorging on the fallen macadamia nuts and guavas.) The Simeons weren't much of a hunting family, but my dad was known around Hilo for his mean smoke meat recipe, which meant we were useful people to know when you were figuring out what to do with 150 pounds of feral pork.

Most of the time, the rich luxurious flavor of smoke meat needs no embellishment. We'd eat it as a pupu or with a scoop of rice, or pan-fried with onions and a spoonful of sweet guava jelly (a classic pairing). But as the bag in the freezer got low, we'd start to stretch our supply: smoke meat with potatoes, smoke meat with cabbage, et cetera. When I opened Lineage, I wanted to create a dish that built upon the Simeon tradition of making each morsel count. As we cycled through the seasons on Maui and experimented with different produce, the kitchen found a winning combination: sprouting broccoli, or broccolini, which offered a nice snap when sautéed and whose leaves soaked up the meat juices, plus lychee fruits, which provided a sweetness and brightness that went well with guava jelly.

My recommendation would be to break this recipe into two parts: Make a large batch of smoke meat as a weekend project, then stash it in the fridge or freezer to use as needed. *(Ho, da stuff last forevah!* my dad might say.) That way when you're ready to make the stir-fry, you'll have a quick meal that can be cobbled together with no muss or fuss.

2 tablespoons neutral oil
1 pound Smoke Meat (recipe follows), cut into ¼-inch slices
1 tablespoon oyster sauce
4 ounces broccolini or broccoli rabe

½ medium red onion, sliced into half-moons
1 heaping tablespoon guava jelly
6 ounces canned lychees in syrup, drained and halved
Cooked rice, for serving

In a large skillet or wok, heat the oil over medium-high heat. When the oil is shimmering-hot, add the smoke meat and stir-fry until seared on the edges, less than a minute. Add the oyster sauce, broccolini, and onion and continue stir-frying until the vegetables are wilted. Add the guava jelly and lychees and toss, cooking briefly until any moisture has evaporated. Serve with rice.

(recipe continues)

SMOKE MEAT

MAKES ABOUT 4 POUNDS

6 pounds pork butt (shoulder), cut into
   1½ × 1½ × 8-inch strips
3 cups shoyu (soy sauce)
3 cups sugar
4-inch piece fresh ginger, sliced and crushed
10 cloves garlic, crushed and peeled
10 scallions, cut into thirds and crushed
1 cup Basic or Simeon-Style Chili Pepper Water
   (page 265) or 3 tablespoons sambal oelek
Kiawe or mesquite wood chips, soaked

Place the pork in a wide shallow bowl or large zip-top plastic bags. In another bowl, whisk together the shoyu, sugar, ginger, garlic, scallions, and chili pepper water. Pour the marinade over the pork and mix well. Cover and refrigerate for 2 to 3 days, stirring and mixing every 12 hours or so.

When ready to smoke, remove the pork from marinade and thread onto wooden skewers. (Reserve the marinade for brushing, if desired.)

Preheat a smoker to 225°F with the soaked wood chips. If using a gas grill, prepare the grill for medium-low indirect heat, leaving one or two burners off. Place the soaked wood chips in a smoker box and set over direct heat. If using a charcoal grill, push the coals to one side and place a pile of soaked wood chips next to them. Cover and open a vent as far as possible from the direct heat so the smoke is drawn over the meat as it escapes; if the temperature reads between 210° and 230°F coming out of the vent, you're in good shape. Adjust the heat as needed.

Place the skewers in the smoker or over indirect heat, leaving a small gap between each piece to allow smoke to circulate. Cover and smoke, replenishing the wood chips (or charcoal) as needed, for 3 to 4 hours, until the pork is cooked through and has developed a jerky-like texture on the outside. After an hour or so, you can brush the skewers with the reserved marinade, if desired.

Remove the pork from the smoker and pull out the skewers. If not using immediately, smoke meat can be stored in the fridge in a sealable container for up to 2 weeks, or in the freezer indefinitely.

PORK BELLY DINAKDAKAN

SERVES 6 TO 8

Among my Filipino 'ohana, the go-to hibachi recipe was usually *dinakdakan,* a downhome Ilocano dish of assorted pig parts grilled and chopped, then tossed with onions and chilies. I'd say Filipinos are world champs when it comes to grilling fatty bits of pork.

Here I'm using commonly available pork belly; after the belly slices are cured in shoyu and vinegar, they're slowly grilled over indirect and direct heat to render out the fat and help them get crispy. It's important not to rush this step, since you'll want to avoid any flare-ups that risk turning that succulent pig candy into burnt rubber.

Once the belly is finished cooking, the pork gets cut into bite-size chunks and tossed in a salty and sour vinaigrette flavored with fresh ginger—more or less a crispy meat salad. A few handfuls of flash-grilled shishito peppers add green contrast.

Back in the day, dinakdakan was often mixed with cooked pig brain, which turned into a creamy sauce when tossed. Don't worry—most locals now use mayo for the same effect, but some cooks in my family prefer just to leave it out altogether. I can attest that it's tasty either way.

As with many dishes in this chapter, dinakdakan is great as a pupu or as a main course with rice.

4 pounds skinless pork belly, cut into ¾-inch-thick slices
Garlic salt
Freshly ground black pepper
3 cups apple cider vinegar
2 cups shoyu (soy sauce)
15 cloves garlic, crushed and peeled
8 bay leaves
8 Hawaiian chili peppers or 4 bird's eye chilies, thinly sliced
1 large red onion, sliced
Oil, for the grill
6 ounces shishito peppers
2 tablespoons minced fresh ginger
½ cup mayo (optional)
2 tablespoons fish sauce, or to taste

Season the pork belly slices generously with garlic salt and black pepper. In a bowl, whisk together the vinegar, shoyu, garlic, bay leaves, half the chilies, and half the red onion. Measure out 1 cup of the sauce and set aside. Transfer the pork belly to a container or zip-top plastic bag and cover with the remaining sauce. Marinate the pork for at least 3 hours at room temperature, or overnight in the fridge.

An hour before you're ready to cook, remove the pork belly from the fridge and let it come to room temperature, stirring occasionally to let the cold meat in the middle warm up in the air.

(recipe continues)

Prepare a grill for high indirect heat (for a charcoal grill, push the coals to one side; for a gas grill, leave one or two burners off). Using tongs, oil the grates of the grill with an oiled rag or paper towels.

Remove the pork belly from the marinade, shaking off the excess. Place it on the indirect heat side, cover, and cook for 20 minutes, flipping and rotating halfway through. Uncover and place the pork belly over direct heat, grilling until charred and crispy on both sides, 10 to 15 minutes. If the pork belly starts to flare up, move back over indirect heat and cook, covered, for another 5 minutes or so before moving it back to direct heat again. Transfer the pork belly to a cutting board and let rest 10 minutes.

While the pork is resting, grill the shishito peppers over direct heat until blistered and charred, about 5 minutes.

Slice the pork belly into bite-size pieces (about 1 inch wide). Place them in a large bowl and toss with the reserved sauce, ginger, mayo (if using), and the remaining red onion and chilies. Gently fold in the shishito peppers. Add the fish sauce and season to taste with black pepper. Serve immediately.

FRY ACTION

When I went to culinary school, and then when I got my first line cook job, I always gravitated to the sauté station. It was fast, it was fun, and you had to be organized or you were going down. I liked the challenge, plus it was much different from the way we cooked at home. Frying oil wasn't cheap, and I joked with my dad that he's the stingiest guy in Hilo when it comes to deep-frying (he still argues with me about it: *Eh! Why you wasting so much oil?*). When we'd eat breakfast at my grandparents' house, the funky oil used to fry pork the previous night was crisping up that morning's banana fritters. Nothing went to waste. It was a world away from the excess and abundance of the restaurant world, where you're never more than an arm's length away from a squeeze bottle of grapeseed oil. I guess that's why I've always been fascinated by stir-frying, pan-frying, deep-frying, and all shades in between, techniques that have a long local history thanks to immigrant Chinese cooks known for their wok skills.

The importance of that style of cooking became even clearer to me when Janice and I opened Tin Roof, our rice bowl spot located in a semi-industrial strip mall off Dairy Road in Kahului. Before we took over, the tiny space had been a Japanese bento spot called Koko Ichiban Ya, which for the last twenty-five years had served tempura and *katsu donburi* (rice bowls) to blue-collar workers nearby. When the owners were ready to retire and looking for a new tenant, their son approached us. It felt like fate.

I knew I wanted to cater to the same community that depended on Koko Ichiban Ya's affordable lunches, so we took inspiration from *kau kau* tins, the cross-cultural meat-over-rice meal for immigrant workers laboring in the plantation fields (*kau kau* means "to eat" in Hawaiian pidgin). The fact that most of our customers didn't have long breaks meant our food had to be ready fast and carry out well. If we could crank out five hundred bowls (plus sandwiches and salads and all that) in four hours of business, that was a win.

Although most dishes in this chapter are what is known in the chef world as "quick pick-ups," a few involve longer roasts, braises, or marinades before they're fried. The key to these dishes—or any stir-fried, pan-fried, or deep-fried dish—is to get everything laid out ahead of time so you'll be prepared once the oil is hot. (Local tip: Check the temperature by dipping the tip of a wooden chopstick in the pot. If it bubbles, the oil is good to go.) Generally speaking, this practice of front-loading your kitchen work is known as *mise en place*, a French phrase that means "everything in its place," or put into pidgin terms, *da kine make ready*. Do that and *kau kau* time will be waiting for you, not the other way around.

GARLIC SHRIMP

SERVES 4

Local-style garlic shrimp got its start in the early 1990s on the North Shore of Oahu when a truck called Giovanni's started serving plates of shrimp sautéed in garlicky butter. It was straightforward, delicious, and smart: The nearby coastal towns of Hale'iwa and Kahuku were home to aquaculture farms, which sold their fresh shrimp to the trucks.

But as it often goes in Hawai'i, Giovanni's became so popular that it spawned other shrimp trucks hustling for business along the Kamehameha Highway. Soon the dish spread to the neighboring islands, and before long garlic shrimp was edging out poke as the dish that mainland visitors most obsessed over.

When I opened Tin Roof in 2016, I put garlic shrimp on the menu because I knew it would be an immediate hit. But what made me happy was to see that the dish resonated with Maui folks as much as it did vacationers.

The biggest thing I'll say about this recipe, aside from its clutch use of locally beloved Lawry's seasoning salt, is the importance of adding lemon juice to the pan, instead of just before serving. This extra acidity allows you to increase the amount of butter and garlic you can use without overwhelming the dish. *Mo' garlic, mo' butter, mo' bettah.*

1½ pounds large shrimp, shell on
3 tablespoons all-purpose flour
1 teaspoon Lawry's seasoning salt
2 tablespoons neutral oil
7 tablespoons salted butter, cut into chunks
10 cloves garlic, minced
¼ cup white wine
2 tablespoons fresh lemon juice
½ teaspoon garlic salt, plus more to taste

FOR SERVING
Cooked rice
Salt-Pickled Cabbage (page 266)
   or watercress
Lemon wedges

Using kitchen shears or a paring knife, cut down the back of each shrimp shell and remove the vein, stopping at the tail. This will make the shrimp easier to peel later on, if you prefer to remove the shells (I prefer to eat them!). For now, leave the shells on since they'll soak up flavor and help protect the shrimp from overcooking.

In a medium bowl, toss the shrimp with the flour and seasoning salt. Heat a large skillet over medium-high heat and add the oil. When the oil is shimmering-hot, add the shrimp and cook for about a minute on each side (use tongs to flip the shrimp more efficiently).

Reduce the heat to medium and add 2 tablespoons of the butter and the garlic and toss to coat the shrimp. Cook until the garlic is fragrant, about 1 minute. Deglaze the pan with the wine, lemon juice, and ¼ cup water. Bring the sauce to a boil, then remove it from the heat and stir in the remaining 5 tablespoons butter until melted. Season with the garlic salt, adding more to taste if needed.

Serve over rice with pickled cabbage and lemon wedges.

TIN ROOF PORK BELLY

SERVES 12

In 2009, when I was working as a chef for Aloha Mixed Plate's restaurant group, I got tapped for a new assignment: launch my first restaurant, a concept called Star Noodle.

Back then, Dave Chang's Momofuku Noodle Bar was the coolest restaurant in America. Being savvy restaurateurs, my bosses wanted me to open Maui's version of Momofuku Noodle Bar, which ended up being a very good business plan.

First, they sent me on a mission to slurp ramen and eat pork buns at all the hot places in SF and NYC. I pored over cookbooks and studied every dish on Dave's menu. I guess you could say imitation is the sincerest form of flattery.

With marching orders in hand, I was beyond stoked to build the menu. I had a million ideas running through my head, mash-ups of local foods with foods that were trending on the mainland: tonkatsu saimin, udon bowls, yakitori, and, of course, pork belly steamed buns, which were all but lifted directly from the Momofuku playbook, complete with pickled cucumbers and hoisin sauce.

Star Noodle was a smash hit almost immediately and the more exposure the restaurant got, the more confident I became in my dishes. Slowly but surely, I started to personalize those copycat buns little by little. After roasting the pork belly until tender I started deep-frying it, too, in classic Filipino style, so it became crispy and golden brown. Bay leaf and black peppercorns, traditional Filipino seasonings, went into the curing salt. I brushed on Mang Tomas, a tangy Filipino dipping sauce, instead of hoisin, and swapped in a chopped tomato and raw onion relish sloshed with patís (fish sauce) for the pickled cucumbers. Eventually, once I opened Migrant and then Tin Roof, I ditched the steamed buns altogether for a side of garlic rice.

I loved the combination of tastes and textures in this dish so much that I've served it at every one of my restaurants. Technically, it's similar to Ilocano *bagnet* or *lechon kawali* (Filipino fried pork belly), though I hesitated to call it that because (a) nobody besides Filipinos knew what bagnet or lechon kawali was then, and (b) there was a good chance that some Filipinos might be ticked off that it didn't resemble what their mom made. So I just made it my own thing.

For me, this is still one of the ultimate pork dishes, a fireworks display of perfectly cooked crispy goodness. If you don't feel like setting up a pot for frying, the pork belly can be served after it's roasted and glazed in the oven. It will still be delicious. But getting the pork belly crispy by deep-frying is what takes it to the next level.

½ cup Diamond Crystal (or ⅓ cup Morton)
   kosher salt
½ cup sugar
2 tablespoons freshly ground black pepper
8 cloves garlic, minced
4 bay leaves, minced
4-pound piece skinless pork belly
¼ cup shoyu (soy sauce)
¼ cup apple cider vinegar
Neutral oil, for deep-frying

FOR SERVING
Garlic Rice (page 293)
Mang Tomas All-Purpose Sauce
Tomato-Onion Lomi (recipe follows), for serving
Soft-boiled eggs, halved

In a bowl, combine the salt, sugar, pepper, garlic, and bay leaves. Rub this mixture all over the pork belly thoroughly, then place the pork on a wire rack set in a sheet pan and let cure overnight in the fridge, or up to 2 days.

Preheat the oven to 275°F.

Rinse the pork belly to wash off the cure and pat it dry. Place it on a wire rack set in a sheet pan or roasting pan, with a shallow layer of water added to the bottom. (You can use the same rack and sheet pan as the one you used to cure it, but be sure to rinse them off first.) Roast, uncovered, until the pork is tender and yields easily to a pair of tongs or a paring knife, 2 to 2½ hours.

With the pork still in the oven, increase the temperature to 425°F. In a small bowl, combine the shoyu and vinegar and baste the pork every few minutes, until the exterior has developed a deep brown glaze, 10 to 15 minutes (add a little more water to the sheet pan if needed). Remove the pork from the oven and let it rest for 20 minutes. When the pork is cool enough to handle, transfer to a cutting board and slice the pork into ¾-inch-thick slices, then cut the slices into 2-inch pieces. You can serve it now, or . . .

Prepare a wire rack or line a baking sheet with paper towels. Fill a large, heavy-bottomed pot or deep skillet with at least 2 inches of oil, making sure to leave a few inches of clearance from the pot's rim. Heat over medium-high heat until the oil reaches 350°F (use a thermometer), adjusting the heat as needed to maintain this temperature.

Fry the pork pieces in batches, until deep golden brown, about 5 minutes, turning every so often to brown evenly. Remove and let cool on the rack or paper towels.

Serve over garlic rice topped with Mang Tomas sauce, tomato-onion lomi, and soft-boiled eggs.

TOMATO-ONION LOMI (PINOY DE GALLO)

MAKES ABOUT 2½ CUPS

3 medium plum tomatoes, chopped
1 medium sweet white onion, chopped
2 scallions, finely chopped
2 tablespoons apple cider vinegar
1 tablespoon fish sauce
1 tablespoon neutral oil
Kosher salt and freshly ground black pepper

In a medium bowl, combine the tomatoes, onion, scallions, vinegar, fish sauce, and oil and toss thoroughly to coat. Season to taste with salt and pepper. Serve immediately.

CHOP STEAK

SERVES 4

The chop steak I knew at home was the product of practicality. Whenever we had steak left over from a hibachi party, we'd fry the slices in a ripping-hot pan with aromatics, lots of onions, and oyster sauce to turn it into a brand-new meal. Making chop steak with fresh steak rather than leftover was borderline unconscionable in our household.

That wasn't the case everywhere. Broadly speaking, you'll see chop steak as an option at many plate lunch spots, but in my opinion the only places that make it right are chop steak specialists, of which each island has maybe one or two left (it broke my heart when Kitada's, Maui's chop steak house in the upcountry town of Makawao, closed a couple years ago).

At Tin Roof, to honor the nostalgia of leftovers, we make our chop steak by searing the meat first, which gives it a smoky *wok hei* (breath of the wok) flavor that is hard to achieve once other ingredients are added to the pan. After that, the steak goes into the freezer for a quick chill, which will keep it from overcooking later. Done correctly, the onions and garlic will have turned just tender by the time the steak is perfectly medium inside.

Though not strictly required, I like to serve my chop steak with a bright and aromatic ginger-scallion relish, which acts like a signal boost for the ingredients in the stir-fry.

1½ pounds sirloin or flat iron steak
Kosher salt and freshly ground black pepper
2 tablespoons plus ¼ cup neutral oil
10 cloves garlic, halved or roughly sliced
2-inch piece fresh ginger, peeled and thinly sliced
4 tablespoons oyster sauce
1 large yellow onion, thinly sliced from stem to root
6 scallions, cut into 2-inch sections
⅓ cup Ginger-Scallion Relish (page 143)
Cooked rice or Fried Garlic Noodles (page 196), for serving
Salt-Pickled Cabbage (page 266), for serving

Pat the steak dry with paper towels and season on both sides with salt and pepper. Heat a skillet over medium-high heat and swirl in 2 tablespoons of the oil. When the oil is smoking-hot, sear the steak for 2 minutes on each side and remove it from the pan (the inside will still be rare). Wrap the steak in foil or parchment paper and chill in the freezer until completely cooled, for 15 to 20 minutes. Wipe the skillet clean.

Once the steak has chilled, cut into 1-inch-thick slices. Heat the same skillet over high heat and swirl in the remaining ¼ cup oil. Once the oil is smoking-hot, add the garlic, ginger, and steak slices. Stir-fry for about a minute until the garlic is fragrant, then add the oyster sauce and toss to coat. Add the onion and scallions and cook until the onions are just tender but not soft, about 2 minutes; the steak should be about medium at this point.

Transfer to a serving plate and top with ginger-scallion relish. Serve over rice or garlic noodles with pickled cabbage on the side.

MOCHIKO FRIED CHICKEN

SERVES 4 TO 6

Mochiko chicken is Hawai'i's own style of fried chicken, distinct for its use of *mochiko* (sweet rice flour) in the batter, which lends a pleasant bouncy chew in addition to that classic fried chicken crunch. Depending on who's cooking (and what recipe they're using), local mochiko chicken can draw influence from Japanese *karaage*, Korean *dak kang jung*, and even a little from Southern fried chicken.

At Tin Roof, the mochiko chicken is far and away the most popular item on our menu. On a solid day, we'll go through *three hundred pounds* of chicken thighs in the four hours we are open for lunch. Not bad for a place that's only five hundred square feet.

I've been eating mochiko chicken since small kid time, but it wasn't until I started cooking professionally that I got serious about cracking the code. Early on, I served a stripped-down version like what locals bring to parties and potlucks, similar to my recipe for Nori Chicken (page 118). But over time, hints and tips I picked up from that #friedchickenlife began to snowball. I started adding a dab of kochujang paste after eating some delicious spicy Korean wings. I started adding eggs to the batter after an auntie in Lahaina told me, "You should add eggs." I started glazing the chicken with a sweet miso sauce because I recalled a takeout spot on Oahu I went to often doing that (this was during my brief stint as the world's laziest stock boy at Party City).

Eventually, all these revelations came together to form the maximalist, ultimate, supreme version you see here, drizzled with two finishing sauces and showered with fried garlic, furikake, and mochi crunch. There are simpler mochiko recipes out there, but none of them offers the whole epic package like this one.

Last thing: Most people think the important part of fried chicken is the dredging process (get that flour into every nook and cranny), but equally crucial is letting your chicken drain on a wire rack (preferred) or paper towels after it's fried. Air circulation is what helps create that loud shattering crust.

¾ cup mochiko (sweet rice flour)
¼ cup plus ¾ cup cornstarch
½ teaspoon Diamond Crystal (or a good pinch of Morton) kosher salt
2 tablespoons sugar
2 large eggs
2 tablespoons shoyu (soy sauce)
2 tablespoons minced fresh ginger
2 tablespoons sake
2 tablespoons kochujang (Korean chili paste)
2 pounds boneless, skin-on chicken thighs
Neutral oil, for deep-frying
¾ cup all-purpose flour
2 teaspoons garlic salt

FOR SERVING
Cooked rice
Kochujang Aioli (recipe follows)
Su-Miso Sauce (recipe follows)
¼ cup Furikake (page 262)
½ cup arare (rice crackers), crushed into bite-size pieces
2 tablespoons Fried Garlic (page 283)
Chopped scallions
Salt-Pickled Cabbage (page 266)

(recipe continues)

In a medium bowl, whisk together the mochiko, ¼ cup of the cornstarch, the salt, and sugar. In a small bowl, whisk together the eggs, shoyu, ginger, sake, kochujang, and 2 tablespoons water. Stir this into the dry ingredients until mixed, then add the chicken and toss thoroughly with your hands to coat. Cover and marinate for at least 4 hours (overnight is best).

When you're ready to fry, remove the marinated chicken from the fridge.

Prepare a wire rack or line a baking sheet with paper towels. Fill a large, heavy-bottomed pot or deep skillet with at least 2 inches of oil, making sure to leave a few inches of clearance from the pot's rim. Heat over medium-high heat until the oil reaches 350°F (use a thermometer), adjusting the heat as needed to maintain temperature.

While the oil is heating, in a medium bowl, whisk together the flour, garlic salt, and remaining ¾ cup cornstarch. Remove the chicken from the marinade, letting any excess batter drip off, and dredge thoroughly in the flour mixture, taking your time and making sure every wet spot is coated and absorbed. Shake off any excess flour and transfer the chicken to a plate.

Working in batches so as not to crowd the pot, fry the thighs until deep golden brown, 5 to 6 minutes, turning halfway through. Remove and let cool on the wire rack or paper towels.

When ready to serve, cut the chicken lengthwise and then crosswise into bite-size pieces. Place the chicken over a bed of rice and drizzle with the kochujang aioli and su-miso sauce. In a small bowl, toss the furikake, rice crackers, and fried garlic together and sprinkle over the chicken. Top with scallions. Serve immediately with salt-pickled cabbage on the side.

KOCHUJANG AIOLI

MAKES ABOUT ½ CUP

1 tablespoon kochujang (Korean chili paste)
1 teaspoon sugar
1 clove garlic, grated
½ cup mayonnaise

In a small bowl, whisk together the kochujang, sugar, garlic, and mayonnaise with a teaspoon of water until incorporated.

SU-MISO SAUCE

MAKES ABOUT ½ CUP

1 tablespoon sake
¼ cup mirin
¼ cup sugar
1 tablespoon white (shiro) miso

In a small saucepan, stir together the sake, mirin, and sugar. Bring to a boil, cooking until the smell of alcohol goes away and the sauce starts to thicken, 1 to 2 minutes. Remove from the heat and whisk in the miso until dissolved. Let cool before using.

CRISPY PATA

SERVES 8 TO 10

A classic Filipino party dish, "crispy pata" is the knuckle and hock of a pig made, as the name suggests, crispy. But since that portion of the pig has lots of cartilage and bones and connective bits, it first must be braised until tender, then air-dried so that the skin puffs up when baptized in hot oil. Making crispy pata takes a fair amount of work, I'm not going to lie to you. So why does anyone bother? Because when done right, it is arguably the most glorious expression of fried pork in the universe (sorry, carnitas): chewy, crispy, juicy, moist, crunchy, and intensely rich all at once.

At Lineage, making the crispy pata was an involved, multistep process for our small kitchen staff, but it's always worthwhile to see the finished product land on the table—watching guests carve off hunks of succulent meat, wrapping it in lettuce leaves and herbs, dipping it in pools of tangy sauce. There was also something subversive about standing over a pata bubbling in the fryer, looking out Lineage's kitchen window at the Louis Vuitton store in the Shops of Wailea outdoor mall across the way. I mean, we were getting people to order fried pig's knuckle in a luxury resort town. That tickled me.

This method for crispy pata is somewhere between what we do at Lineage and what's usually done at home. The most crucial step here is to let the pork dry in the fridge overnight before frying (a rub of baking soda helps draw out the moisture), which will give the skin the texture of pork rinds once fried.

For serving, lettuces and fresh herbs offer a lovely contrast to the fatty meat when deployed as wraps. I've included a couple common Filipino sauces for dipping, but anything that offers some combination of sour-salt-sugar will work, too.

1 whole skin-on pork leg, hock or shank, including knuckle (3 to 5 pounds)
2 (12-ounce) cans lemon-lime soda
12 cloves garlic, crushed and peeled
1 tablespoon black peppercorns
5 bay leaves
¼ cup Diamond Crystal (or ⅓ cup Morton) kosher salt
2 teaspoons baking soda
Distilled white vinegar

2 tablespoons fish sauce
All-purpose flour or cornstarch
Oil, for frying (at least 4 cups)

FOR SERVING
Romaine lettuce leaves, for wrapping
Handful of cilantro and basil sprigs
Finádenné (page 279)
Mang Tomas All-Purpose Sauce
Banana ketchup

In a large, deep pot, combine the pork, soda, garlic, peppercorns, bay leaves, salt, and water to just cover. Bring to a boil, skimming any scum that accumulates on top. Reduce the heat, cover, and simmer until the meat is tender and can be easily pierced by a fork, but not falling apart, for 1½ to 2 hours. Check on it every half hour or so; if the liquid drops below the pork, add more water as needed.

(recipe continues)

Drain the pork and discard the liquid and aromatics. In a small bowl, stir together the baking soda with 2 tablespoons water and rub this all over the pork. Place the pork on a wire rack over a baking sheet and allow to dry, uncovered, in the refrigerator, for at least 12 hours.

Remove the pork from the fridge and rinse thoroughly with vinegar to remove any residual baking soda. Pat dry, then coat the skin with the fish sauce and dust lightly with flour, shaking off any excess. Let sit at room temperature while you prepare the frying oil.

Set a wire rack over a baking sheet. Fill a large, deep heavy-bottomed pot with enough oil to come halfway up the pork during deep-frying (about 4 cups), making sure to leave at least a few inches of clearance from the pot's rim. Heat over medium-high heat until the oil reaches 350°F (use a thermometer), adjusting the heat as needed to maintain temperature.

Gently add the pork and fry, turning as needed, until golden on all sides, 15 to 20 minutes. To reduce oil splatter, you can cover the pot with a lid, but leave it slightly askew so steam is able to escape. Remove the pork from the pot with tongs and drain for a minute on the wire rack.

Optional: To achieve extra-crispy, bubbly skin, use your fingertips to flick small amounts of water (about a teaspoon or two at a time) into the hot oil during the last few minutes of frying. This will agitate the oil and help the skin crackle and puff up, but it should be done sparingly and with caution, as the hot oil can boil over and become extremely flammable if too much water is added. Only do this if you have a very deep pot with a lot of clearance between the oil and the top of the pot.

Serve hot with lettuce, herbs, and dipping sauces.

NORI CHICKEN

SERVES 6 TO 8

The humbler, homespun cousin of Tin Roof's fully loaded Mochiko Fried Chicken (page 112), this basic fried chicken is more in line with what you find at family gatherings and at old-school Japanese delis called *okazuya*. One of my favorites is at Hilo Lunch Shop, a small family-run okazuya not far from my dad's house. Their nori chicken, pieces of crispy thigh coated in a light crust, is so addicting, I can put two dozen of those bad boys away in one sitting.

The beauty of this style is its simplicity: just a three-ingredient marinade and a quick dredge in cornstarch and *mochiko* (sweet rice flour). The kicker is a strip of dried nori wrapped around the center of each chicken piece, a traditional touch that adds an earthy flavor and a bonus level of crunch.

½ cup shoyu (soy sauce)
3 tablespoons sugar
3 tablespoons sake
2 pounds boneless, skinless chicken thighs, cut into 1 × 2-inch strips
4 scallions, cut into thirds and crushed
Oil, for frying
¼ cup cornstarch
¼ cup mochiko (sweet rice flour)
4 sheets nori, cut into 1-inch-wide strips

In a small bowl, whisk together the shoyu, sugar, and sake. Place the chicken and the scallions in a wide shallow dish or zip-top plastic bag, add the shoyu mixture, and marinate for at least 4 hours in the fridge (overnight is best).

Prepare a wire rack or line a baking sheet with paper towels. Fill a large, heavy-bottomed pot or deep skillet with at least 2 inches of oil, making sure to leave a few inches of clearance from the pot's rim. Heat over medium-high heat until the oil reaches 350°F (use a thermometer), adjusting the heat as needed to maintain temperature.

While the oil is heating, drain the chicken from the marinade, shaking off any excess. Combine the cornstarch and mochiko in a shallow bowl and coat the chicken thoroughly, shaking off any excess, then wrap a strip of nori around the center of each piece (dab a little of the marinade on the nori to help it stick) and transfer to a plate.

Working in batches so as not to crowd the pan, fry the chicken until deep golden brown, 5 to 6 minutes, turning every so often to brown evenly. Remove and let cool on the wire rack or paper towels. Serve immediately.

"POCHO" STEAMED CLAMS WITH PORTUGUESE SAUSAGE

SERVES 2 TO 4

It's impossible to overstate how much the previous generation of local chefs—people like Sam Choy, Alan Wong, Roy Yamaguchi, and Bev Gannon—paved the way for the cooking I do now. Although I never had a chance to work for them directly (aside from brief internships in culinary school), these were the chefs I looked up to in school and whose restaurants I saved up to eat at when I was a line cook. Many of them have kept their restaurants going strong, feeding their community, for over three decades now.

All of them—along with many others—were part of what is known as Hawai'i Regional Cuisine (HRC), a culinary movement that started in the 1990s. HRC played a huge role in raising the profile of our cuisine on the international stage, and without their attention and awards, restaurants like mine probably wouldn't exist. The movement championed locally produced ingredients foremost, whether it was goat cheese from Surfing Goat Dairy in Kula or littleneck clams raised off Kaua'i.

As with any movement, HRC sometimes veered over the top (macadamia nut–crusted mahi mahi with mango salsa, pickled asparagus, and soy-ginger gastrique), but at its best it was focused on using the finest ingredients in a way that honored the 'āina—the land.

This simple sautéed clam dish, often called "Pocho" (Portuguese) style clams, is one of my favorite things to eat at home and a perfect example of that HRC mentality. Clams aren't native to Hawai'i, but there's a growing industry of aquafarmers raising them here as a way to lessen dependence on imported seafood. Sweet and briny, plump littleneck clams are a perfect match for the smokiness and spice of Portuguese sausage, especially when cooked down with a glug of sake, salted butter, and lots of aromatics and fresh herbs. It's delicious on its own or with a side of rice or freshly baked Portuguese Sweet Rolls (page 256).

4 tablespoons (½ stick) salted butter
½ medium red or green bell pepper, minced
6 cloves garlic, minced
1 cup minced or crumbled Portuguese Sausage
  (page 284)
2 pounds littleneck or Manila clams

1 teaspoon minced fresh ginger
1 cup sake or dry white wine
½ lemon
Cilantro sprigs
Thai basil leaves, torn in half

In a large, deep skillet or Dutch oven, melt 2 tablespoons of the butter over medium-high heat. When it's foamed, add the bell pepper, garlic, and sausage and sauté until the garlic is fragrant, about 1 minute. Add the clams and ginger and deglaze with the sake. Cover the pan and let steam until the clams open, 3 or 4 minutes. If there are stubborn clams, either take out the opened ones and keep cooking the unopened ones, or toss them if they take too long. Squeeze the lemon over the clams and stir in the remaining 2 tablespoons butter. Garnish with the cilantro and basil before serving.

EGGPLANT "JUN BOY"

SERVES 4 TO 6

Back in the day, my grandparents owned a two-acre guava farm just north of Hilo. On weekends during guava season, my brother, my cousin, and I would be enlisted to help pick fruit. Help was a loose term. If we spent six hours at the farm, we did maybe forty-five minutes of actual picking. The rest was messing around, throwing guavas, generally being little punks.

In our kid minds, the focus was always on what was for lunch, which my grandma cooked out of the farm's small shack with a rusted metal roof and moss-covered tables. There was no electricity and no gas, so we'd start a fire using guava branches as fuel. My favorite was cooking eggplant picked from the garden, roasted until it was soft and sweet. Sometimes we'd eat it with just raw tomato, but if we were lucky, Grandma would bring a couple of eggs along and turn the tender eggplant into *tortang talong*, a browned Filipino-style omelet that we doused in shoyu and hot sauce and ate with plenny rice.

Later, I started to connect tortang with a local Korean dish I loved called *meat jun*, essentially marinated beef bulgogi dipped into beaten egg and fried. My mash-up of the two dishes fortifies the tortang with seasoned ground beef, a sort of eggplant jun. Filipinos love giving nicknames, so for any son named after their dad, "Junior" becomes "Jun Boy." That's how Eggplant "Jun Boy," my hapa Filipino-Korean son, was born.

Rather than a thin delicate coating, you'll want the eggplant here to absorb as much of the egg as possible to make it a proper omelet. Also, don't be afraid to use a spatula to squish the eggplant into the pan: Crispy browned edges are your friend.

4 medium Chinese or Japanese eggplants
½ cup shoyu (soy sauce)
½ cup sugar
1 tablespoon toasted sesame oil
3 cloves garlic, minced
Freshly ground black pepper
Neutral oil
1 pound ground pork or beef
6 large eggs, beaten
Kosher salt

FOR SERVING

Jun Boy Dipping Sauce (recipe follows)
Sesame Bean Sprouts (optional; page 270)
Cooked rice

Preheat the oven to 375°F.

Use a fork to pierce the skin of the eggplants a few times (this will help steam escape), then place them on a baking sheet. Bake until the eggplants are soft throughout and can be easily pierced by a fork, 35 to 45 minutes. Transfer the hot eggplants to a bowl and cover tightly with plastic wrap (or place inside a zip-top plastic bag) and let steam for 5 minutes, or until cool enough to handle. Peel the skin off the eggplants and discard; use a spatula to press the eggplants flat, squishing them to about ½ inch thick. Set aside.

(recipe continues)

In a small bowl, whisk together the shoyu, sugar, sesame oil, garlic, and a pinch of black pepper.

In a large skillet, heat 2 tablespoons oil over medium heat until shimmering-hot. Add the ground pork and stir-fry until browned and mostly cooked, 3 to 4 minutes. Pour the shoyu mixture into the pan and continue stir-frying until most of the liquid has evaporated, another 1 to 2 minutes. Transfer the cooked meat to a bowl and wipe out the skillet.

In a shallow dish or pan, combine the eggs with a generous pinch of salt and pepper.

Prepare a wire rack or line a baking sheet with paper towels. In the same skillet, heat ¼ cup of oil over medium-high heat until shimmering-hot. One at a time, dip both sides of the flattened eggplant in the eggs, coating as much as possible, and quickly place in the hot pan. Spread one-quarter of the pork mixture over the top of the eggplant, then pour a few more spoonfuls of egg over the top. Carefully flip the eggplant after 3 to 4 minutes, when the bottom is nice and golden brown. Cook for another 3 to 4 minutes on the other side, using the spatula to press the eggplant into the pan and to "seal" the pork to the egg and eggplant. Transfer to the wire rack or paper towels to drain. Repeat with the remaining eggplants, replenishing the oil in the pan as needed.

Serve immediately with dipping sauce, bean sprouts (if desired), and rice.

JUN BOY DIPPING SAUCE

MAKES ABOUT ½ CUP

¼ cup fresh lemon juice
1 teaspoon shoyu (soy sauce)
2 tablespoons thinly sliced scallions
1 tablespoon sriracha or sambal oelek
Kosher salt and freshly ground black pepper

In a small bowl, stir together the lemon juice, shoyu, scallions, and sriracha. Season to taste with salt and pepper and serve.

CRISPY BLACK BEAN BUTTERFISH

SERVES 4

One of the few local foods I didn't grow up eating was black bean sauce. For some reason, my dad hated the stuff and his unofficial *kapu* (ban) extended to us. But at some point, as these things go, I tried it at a local spot and had a moment of awakening. Sharp, pungent, and bittersweet—the mysterious salted and fermented Chinese black bean hooked me instantly.

One of the things they don't tell you about *Top Chef* is that each contestant is allowed to bring a kit of ten tools and ten pantry items from home, sort of like your own secret arsenal. Along with instant dashi powder, premium oyster sauce, and lemon olive oil (all things deployed in this book), I brought a jar of black bean sauce, which fit right in with my slayer lineup of umami boosters.

In Hawai'i, black bean sauce is often paired with freshly made *look fun* (rolled rice noodles) or with steamed or fried seafood. In this case, I'm using black cod, a rich and succulent fish known locally as butterfish (sea bass, salmon, or another flaky fish can also work). Just dredge it in starch, pan-fry it until golden and crunchy, then serve it with blanched bok choy and the black bean sauce. Instant winner.

The jars of black bean sauce you see in the Asian section of grocery stores are actually very solid, but I still think making your own sauce is worthwhile. A bag of Chinese salted black beans, which will basically last you forever, can be found at any Asian market or online.

2 tablespoons Chinese salted black beans

2 tablespoons Shaoxing wine or dry sherry

Kosher salt

2 tablespoons neutral oil, plus more for pan-frying

3 cloves garlic, minced

1 tablespoon minced fresh ginger

3 scallions, thinly sliced, white and green parts kept separate

2 teaspoons sugar

2 teaspoons shoyu (soy sauce)

2 tablespoons oyster sauce

1 teaspoon sambal oelek

1 cup clam juice or chicken stock

1 tablespoon cornstarch, plus more for dredging

1 tablespoon salted butter

4 skin-on black cod or sablefish fillets (6 ounces each), ½ to 1 inch thick

¾ pound baby bok choy (2 or 3 heads), root ends trimmed and leaves separated

FOR SERVING

Cilantro sprigs (optional)

Cooked rice or Fried Garlic Noodles (page 196)

In a small bowl, soak the black beans in the Shaoxing wine along with 2 tablespoons warm water for 10 minutes to soften. Mash together with a fork and set aside.

Bring a large pot of well-salted water to a boil for the bok choy.

Meanwhile, in a saucepan, heat the 2 tablespoons oil over medium-high heat until shimmering-hot. Add the garlic, ginger, and scallion whites and stir-fry until fragrant and lightly browned, about 1 minute. Add the sugar, shoyu, oyster sauce, sambal, and black beans and cook for another 1 or 2 minutes, stirring. Add the clam juice and bring to a boil before reducing to a

(recipe continues)

simmer. Whisk the cornstarch with 1 tablespoon water to form a slurry, then stir it into the sauce mixture, and bring it back to a boil to thicken. Stir in the butter and scallion greens and remove from the heat.

Season the fish on both sides with salt. Dredge the fish pieces in as much cornstarch as they will hold, making sure to coat any wet spots completely.

Prepare a wire rack or line a baking sheet with paper towels. In a large skillet, heat ¼ inch of oil over high heat until shimmering-hot. Working in batches if necessary, add the fish skin-side down and cook until browned and crispy, about 4 minutes per side. Transfer the cooked fish to the wire rack or bed of paper towels to drain.

Add the bok choy to the boiling water and cook until bright green and slightly tender at the stems (they should still be crisp), 1 to 2 minutes. Drain and rinse briefly in cold water, then drain again and squeeze out liquid.

Transfer the bok choy to a serving plate and cover with black bean sauce, reserving a few spoonfuls to drizzle over the fish. Add the fish to the plate and top with the remaining sauce, garnishing with a sprig or two of cilantro, if desired. Serve with rice or noodles.

THE INFLUENCERS
THE JAPANESE COMMUNITY

As Chinese workers began to move off the plantations in the 1860s, Japanese immigrants were recruited to take their place, starting in 1868 but becoming widespread in 1885, when the Japanese government okayed a trade deal that exported cheap labor in return for cheap rice. In total, between 1885 and 1924, around 180,000 Japanese workers came to Hawai'i. Many came from poverty-stricken regions in southwest Japan like Hiroshima and Fukuoka, and later from the rural, southernmost prefecture of Okinawa (many Okinawan descendants refer to themselves as Okinawan, distinct from other Japanese). About half of the original Japanese immigrants returned home when their contracts were finished. The rest followed the path of the Chinese before them, opening small shops that made tofu or mochi, breweries that produced sake and shoyu, or small farms that grew vegetables like daikon and kabocha squash. By the 1930s, Japanese cuisine had become the most dominant influence on local food, showing up in favorites like katsu (see opposite), sashimi, udon, teriyaki sticks (see page 85), and shave ice. There's even strong evidence that the concept of the plate lunch or *kau kau* tin was originally based on Japanese bentos.

COOK REAL HAWAI'I

CAULIFLOWER KATSU CURRY

SERVES 4 TO 6

I'll be honest, I started out dubious about this dish. At Lineage, we were getting these gorgeous shipments of yellow and purple cauliflower from Ryan Earehart at Oko'a Farms. The best cauliflower you ever tasted. I took a poll among my sous-chefs about what to do with them and they came up with one idea in unison: *katsu*. Say what?

In my mind, proper katsu was panko-crusted chicken or pork, a classic plate lunch item that every local has strong opinions on how it should be done. Why mess with the formula?

Thankfully, my team didn't let me spoil their fun. I quickly discovered that katsu cauliflower was magical: The crunchy coating contrasted beautifully with the tender inside, and the entire dish could easily be made vegan, which in pork-heavy Hawai'i is no small feat.

And then there was the icing on the cake: a warm and velvety curry sauce ladled over the top. In Hawai'i, the pairing of slightly sweet Japanese-style curry with crispy katsu is an iconic comfort combo, appealing to our deep obsessions with anything fried or smothered in gravy. Most Japanese curry these days is made with a prepackaged sauce base (my favorite is S&B Hot Golden Curry), which can then be tweaked and doctored up with any number of additions. Here I use grated apple, but whenever my staff at Lineage makes curry for staff meal, they'll mix in anything sweet: frozen mango bars, squares of dark chocolate, yogurt, raisins, coffee milk, etc. The same flexibility goes for vegetables. The basic carrots, onions, and potatoes can be swapped for whatever vegetables are on hand: sweet potato, green beans, mushrooms, peppers, etc.

To balance the richness of the curry, I garnish it with bright and crunchy *beni shōga* (red pickled ginger), also labeled *kizami shōga*, a sharp and refreshing Japanese condiment that can be found in the refrigerated section of most Asian markets.

CURRY
2 tablespoons neutral oil
1 large yellow onion, diced
3 cloves garlic, minced
2 teaspoons minced fresh ginger
1 Fuji apple, peeled and grated
1 large carrot, peeled and diced
2 celery stalks, diced
3 cups vegetable stock
Half a (7.8-ounce) box S&B Golden Curry
    sauce mix
Shoyu (soy sauce)

CAULIFLOWER KATSU
2 medium heads cauliflower, cut into
    ¾-inch-thick steaks
Garlic salt
Freshly ground black pepper
1 cup all-purpose flour
3 eggs, beaten (or 2 tablespoons vegan mayo)
3 cups panko bread crumbs
Neutral oil, for deep-frying

FOR SERVING
2 tablespoons beni shōga
Cooked rice

For the curry: In a large pot, heat the oil over medium heat. Add the onion, garlic, and ginger and cook, stirring occasionally, until the onion is softened and golden, about 10 minutes. Add the apple, carrot, and celery and cook for a few minutes, until slightly softened. Add the vegetable

(recipe continues)

stock and bring to a boil. Remove the pot from the heat and break the curry mix into pieces, adding them to the pot and stirring until they completely dissolve. Simmer for 5 minutes more, stirring constantly, or until your desired curry thickness is reached. Season with shoyu to taste.

For the cauliflower katsu: Season the cauliflower steaks generously on both sides with garlic salt and black pepper. Place the flour, eggs, and panko into three separate shallow dishes or plates. (If substituting vegan mayo, thin it out with an equal amount of water and use in place of the eggs.) Coat the cauliflower in the flour, shaking off any excess. Next, dip in the egg (or thinned mayo), allowing any excess to drip off, then press into the panko, coating both sides thoroughly. Set the breaded cauliflower on a plate or wire rack.

Prepare a wire rack or line a baking sheet with paper towels. Fill a large, heavy-bottomed pot or deep skillet with at least 2 inches of oil, making sure to leave a few inches of clearance from the pot's rim. Heat over high heat until the oil reaches 350°F (use a thermometer), adjusting the heat as needed to maintain temperature.

Fry the cauliflower steaks individually, or in batches, until golden and crispy, 3 to 4 minutes on each side. Be careful when flipping: Use tongs to lift the cauliflower and gently place it back into the oil. Transfer the cauliflower to the wire rack or paper towels to cool. Season to taste with garlic salt. Let cool slightly.

To serve, carefully slice the cauliflower steaks into strips and top with curry. Garnish with beni shōga and serve with rice.

NOTE: *If you'd rather make traditional chicken or pork katsu (I feel ya), swap the cauliflower steaks for boneless, skinless chicken thighs or ½-inch-thick pork cutlets, coating and frying as directed. Serve with curry if desired, or mix together a basic katsu sauce (recipe follows) for dipping.*

KATSU SAUCE

MAKES ABOUT 1 CUP

¼ cup ketchup
2 tablespoons Worcestershire sauce
¼ cup sugar
3 dashes of Tabasco sauce, or to taste
Garlic salt
Ground white pepper
2 teaspoons cornstarch

In a saucepan, combine ½ cup water, the ketchup, Worcestershire sauce, sugar, Tabasco, and garlic salt and white pepper to taste. Bring to a boil. In a small bowl, stir together the cornstarch and 2 teaspoons water until dissolved. Stir this into the sauce and cook until thickened. Remove the sauce from the heat and let cool before serving. Store in the fridge in a sealable container for up to 1 week.

COCONUT SHRIMP

SERVES 4 TO 6

I know what you're going to say. *This doesn't look like the coconut shrimp we had on Maui???!!!* And you're right, it doesn't. Nobody knows better than me what that kind of coconut shrimp looks like, since during my years cooking at Aloha Mixed Plate, I fried up thousands upon thousands of those suckers. Yes, shredded coconut and fried shrimp is delicious, but to this day I won't order it just on principle. I'm still traumatized. And if you think I had it bad, spare a thought for Auntie Lovey, who was our veteran prep cook: Every day, she'd have to bread two thousand shrimp in under three hours.

But beyond my culinary PTSD, there is another reason why I'm jaded. For the most part, locals don't eat coconut shrimp. It's pure haole bait. Going to Hawai'i to eat coconut shrimp would be like bragging about all the California rolls you ate in Tokyo.

But rather than be a hater, I try to be constructive with such opinions. So I thought back to the shrimp dishes that, to me, symbolized celebration and indulgence. My mind went back to special occasions, when my family would go to Sun Sun Lau, a bygone Chinese restaurant in Hilo, and order honey-walnut shrimp. The shrimp were flash-fried in cornstarch, and then covered in a sweet, condensed-milk-and-mayonnaise-based sauce and served with crunchy honey walnuts. Broke. The. Mouth.

So that's how we got here: coconut shrimp reimagined as honey-walnut shrimp. Instead of sweetened condensed milk, I reduce coconut milk down to a creamy sauce, and rather than candied walnuts I use oven-baked candied coconut chips, a crispy snack that you'll find sold in local gift shops (easy to make it yourself, though). Even better than Leung's, I daresay. Let's get coconut shrimp 2.0 trending and maybe, just maybe, unseat the original.

⅓ cup mayonnaise
¼ cup Sweetened Condensed Coconut Milk (recipe follows)
2 teaspoons fresh lemon juice
Kosher salt
Ground white pepper
2 egg whites
¾ cup chilled club soda or seltzer water
2 cups mochiko (sweet rice flour)

¼ cup cornstarch or tapioca starch
1½ pounds peeled and deveined large shrimp, rinsed
Neutral oil, for deep-frying
2 tablespoons Coconut Candy (page 280)
2 teaspoons Fried Garlic (page 283)
1 tablespoon thinly sliced scallions
Cooked rice or Fried Garlic Noodles (page 196), for serving

In a small bowl, whisk together the mayo, condensed coconut milk, lemon juice, and salt and white pepper to taste. Set the sauce aside.

In a large bowl, whisk together the egg whites, club soda, 1 cup of the mochiko, the cornstarch, 1 teaspoon salt, and ½ teaspoon white pepper. Let stand for 5 to 10 minutes so the flour can hydrate. Place the shrimp on a baking sheet and pat dry with paper towels.

(recipe continues)

Meanwhile, prepare a wire rack or line a baking sheet with paper towels. Fill a large, heavy-bottomed pot or deep skillet with at least 2 inches of oil, making sure to leave a few inches of clearance from the pot's rim. Heat over high heat until the oil reaches 350°F (use a thermometer), adjusting the heat as needed to maintain temperature.

Place the remaining 1 cup mochiko in a shallow dish or pan and coat the shrimp, shaking off any excess, then dip into the batter, letting the excess drip off. Once the oil is ready, fry the shrimp in batches until they turn pink and the coating is golden, about 3 minutes. Transfer to the wire rack or paper towels and let cool slightly.

In a medium bowl, toss the warm shrimp with ½ cup of the reserved sauce, adding more if needed to evenly coat (but not drown) the shrimp. Spoon any remaining sauce onto a plate and top with the shrimp. Garnish with the coconut candy, fried garlic, and scallions. Serve with rice or garlic noodles.

COOK REAL HAWAI'I

SWEETENED CONDENSED COCONUT MILK

MAKES ABOUT ¾ CUP

1 (13.5-ounce) can full-fat coconut milk
½ cup sugar

In a small saucepan, bring the coconut milk to a boil over medium-high heat and whisk in the sugar. Reduce the heat to a gentle simmer and cook, stirring often, until the mixture is thickened and reduced by half, 30 to 40 minutes. Let cool before using. Leftovers can be stored in the fridge for up to 1 week.

SIM SIMMER

Slow and methodical, that was the Simeon way of cooking. When I came back home from culinary school, my dad would scold me for turning up the flame even a little. *Everything high heat with you!* He never rushed. He flowed. It was all a gentle simmer.

My dad wasn't alone in that way. Many of the cherished dishes from my childhood, cooked by uncles and aunties, were things that bubbled away on the stovetop for hours while us *hanabada* (snot-nosed) kids pedaled bikes or snacked on mangoes and boiled peanuts. Many of Hawai'i's most deeply held foods, whether it's shoyu chicken or oxtail soup or beef stew, are the ones where a surplus of time is a crucial ingredient.

Through my years of home cooking, I came to understand the technical reasons for why slow-cooked food tastes so good. The long exposure to mellow heat breaks down foods over time, coaxing out flavors and melding them together. But through my time spent in professional kitchens and on cooking shows, I also saw that the brownish braises and gravy-rich stews—not unlike the Filipino foods I grew up eating—weren't always the dishes that got shine at fancy restaurants and in gorgeous food magazines. Delicious, sure, but not exactly pretty.

Maybe you didn't see it on TV, but there were plenty of moments in my career when I doubted whether the local food I loved was good to enough to be considered "high cuisine." As chefs we all want to cook dishes that are personal, but doing so means it feels like it's not just your food that's being judged. Also on the table are who you are and where you came from.

The peak of those doubts came during the finale of my first season on *Top Chef*, when I became obsessed with the kind of food I thought "serious chefs" made instead of doing what was authentic to me . . . and what had gotten me to the finale in the first place. Overthinking 101. That's what got me sent home.

It wasn't an easy lesson to learn. But I guess if it wasn't for that moment, I might not have grasped how afternoons spent babysitting bubbling pots in the family garage shaped who I am. "Be true to yourself" might be a giant cliché, but that doesn't make it any less accurate.

I had a friend who used to call me Sim Simma (who's got the keyz to the Bimma, *VROOM!*), which was a random nickname that stuck. Simeon. Sim Simma. Simmer? Maybe that's a stretch. But when I think about our family's cooking, on some level I picture those simmered homespun meals filled with deep and memorable flavors. Soup and stew and rice were always what kept us fed.

I'll leave you with two golden rules for Simeon-style cooking. First: The magic happens in the pot, don't rush it. Second: No matter how good the stew is now, it will always taste better the next day.

BEEF SHANK À LA OXTAIL SOUP

SERVES 6 TO 8

A cook who recognized a bargain, my dad was known to follow the rise and fall of butcher prices like a business tycoon does the stock market. This was especially true when it came to offal, or the "off-cuts." Walking past the meat counter at Foodland, he might elbow me and jut his chin: *Eh, look how much they stay charging for oxtail now!*

Going back to the plantation days in Hawai'i, there is a tradition of local cooks taking the humblest cuts of meat or fish—often what the earliest immigrants could afford—and making it into something captivating. There are plenty of examples, but one that has gained a serious following over the years is oxtail soup, a beefy, brothy soup flavored with Chinese-rooted ingredients like star anise, dried chilies, and orange peel.

On the Filipino side, a similar dish—and one of my favorites—is beef *lauya*, a simple soup made with beef shank, fish sauce, and cooked cabbage. Like oxtail, shank is an affordable cut that has a good amount of gelatinous connective tissue, which gives the broth a deep flavor and richness. Since beef shank is both easier to find in the store and meatier, I actually prefer it when making oxtail soup (as sacrilegious as that sounds) out of pure convenience. This recipe draws from both soup traditions and I believe is the better for it.

Anyway, here's the kicker: Serve the hot soup with a flavor-boosting ginger relish enhanced with raw peanuts. This can be made in advance and refrigerated until ready.

5 pounds beef shanks, cut into 1½-inch-thick medallions

1 tablespoon Diamond Crystal (or 2 teaspoons Morton) kosher salt

1 teaspoon ground white pepper

1 tablespoon minced fresh ginger plus 2-inch piece of ginger, peeled and thinly sliced

10 dried shiitake mushrooms

2 tablespoons neutral oil

¼ cup Shaoxing wine, dry sherry, or whiskey

4 quarts beef stock or water

4 wide strips orange zest (use a vegetable peeler)

6 whole star anise

6 dried Chinese red chilies

½ cup raw peanuts

6 ounces bok choy or mustard greens, trimmed and cut crosswise into 3-inch pieces

1 teaspoon fish sauce, plus more to taste

1 bunch cilantro, roughly chopped, for garnish

Peanut-Ginger Relish (recipe follows)

Place the beef shanks in a shallow pan or plate and coat evenly on all sides with the salt, white pepper, and minced ginger. Let sit for 1 hour, either in the fridge or at room temperature.

Meanwhile, place the dried shiitakes in a bowl and cover with 1 cup hot water to soften them slightly (just enough so they can be easily cut). Reserving the soaking water, drain the softened mushrooms. Cut off and discard any stems and cut the caps into slices.

In a large, heavy pot, heat the oil over high heat until shimmering-hot. Add the beef shanks along with the sliced ginger and sear until the shanks are browned on all sides, about 4 minutes per side. Deglaze the pot with the Shaoxing wine, scraping up any browned bits that have formed.

(recipe continues)

Once the wine has reduced slightly, add the stock, reserved mushroom soaking liquid, sliced mushrooms, orange zest, star anise, chilies, and peanuts. Bring to a boil (skim off any foam that accumulates on the surface), then reduce the heat and simmer until the meat is tender and pulling from the bone, 2 to 2½ hours.

Add the bok choy and simmer until tender, 5 more minutes. Season with fish sauce before serving. Garnish bowls with cilantro and serve with peanut-ginger relish.

PEANUT-GINGER RELISH

MAKES ABOUT 1 CUP

¼ cup finely chopped raw peanuts
¼ cup minced fresh ginger
1 cup thinly sliced scallions (about 1 bunch)
¼ cup neutral oil
Kosher salt

Place the peanuts, ginger, and scallions in a heatproof bowl. In a small saucepan, heat the oil over high heat until shimmering-hot. Slowly pour the hot oil into the bowl and stir until incorporated. Let cool for 30 minutes, then season with salt to taste.

COLD GINGER CHICKEN

SERVES 4 TO 6

Cold ginger chicken is my jam. Back when I was living at my auntie's house on Oahu and going to culinary school, there was a Chinese deli I'd frequent, Chun Wah Kam, that had this chicken in their steam table selection. The ladies that worked there were so generous, they'd stuff the takeout box completely full and apologize when they couldn't close the lid! That's hospitality. The best part was when my cousin Mary Jean got a job there while in college. Got the hookup big time—always extra ginger-scallion on the side.

As much as I loved eating it, making cold ginger chicken for the menu at Lineage taught me some valuable lessons: You have to almost go overboard in flavoring the poaching liquid, otherwise you end up with a bland bird. And though it takes a little patience, the most foolproof method for tender and moist chicken is to never let the bird sit in full-on boiling water, since it toughens the meat. Some people like ginger chicken at room temperature, some like it chilled. Me? I eat some at room temp first, then eat any leftovers straight from the fridge. You do you.

As any cold ginger chicken fanatic will tell you, the sauces are just as important as the poultry. I make two: an aromatic "pesto" of minced ginger and scallion blanched in hot oil—a classic condiment that improves all leftovers or plain rice—and a thick savory paste made from black beans and black truffles, which provides an earthy contrast to the bright ginger relish. (If you don't feel like blowing your grocery budget, use mushrooms instead of truffles. Still very delicious.)

Kosher salt
5 scallions, cut into 2-inch lengths
3-inch piece fresh ginger, sliced and crushed
4 cloves garlic, crushed and peeled
2 cinnamon sticks
2 star anise
3 wide strips orange zest (use a vegetable peeler)
1 whole chicken (4 to 5 pounds)
Black Bean Truffle Paste (recipe follows)
Ginger-Scallion Relish (recipe follows)

Fill a pot with just enough water to submerge the chicken. Add a few big pinches of salt, the scallions, ginger, garlic, cinnamon sticks, star anise, and orange zest (don't add the chicken yet!). Bring the water to a boil, then remove from the heat. Carefully place the chicken in the pot, cover, and let sit for 1 hour.

Return the pot to medium heat. When tiny bubbles start appearing, turn off the heat and let sit, covered, for another hour.

Carefully remove the chicken from the pot. Check the temperature by inserting a thermometer in the thigh; if the temperature is below 160°F, return the chicken to the broth and simmer, covered, in 5-minute increments as required, making sure the liquid never reaches a full boil.

(recipe continues)

When the internal temperature is reached, remove the chicken from the poaching liquid and let it air-dry on a wire rack for at least 1 hour. (If desired, save the poaching liquid to make stock.)

Carve the chicken using a sharp knife: Remove the legs by cutting through the thigh joints, then separate the thighs from the drumsticks. Carve the breast meat from the bone and slice each breast crosswise into 4 pieces. Arrange pieces on a platter (if desired, add the bones to the poaching liquid if making stock).

Smear a small amount of the black bean paste over the chicken slices and generously spoon the ginger-scallion relish over the top, with more served on the side as needed.

BLACK BEAN TRUFFLE PASTE

MAKES ¾ CUP

2 tablespoons fermented black beans, rinsed and soaked in hot water for 30 minutes
2 tablespoons toasted sesame oil
1 tablespoon minced garlic
1 tablespoon Shaoxing wine or dry sherry
¼ cup black truffle paste or ½ cup finely chopped mushrooms (any kind)
1 teaspoon sugar
1 teaspoon sambal oelek or Kudeesh Sauce (page 39)
Shoyu (soy sauce)

Drain the soaked black beans, mash with a fork, and set aside. In a small saucepan, heat the sesame oil over high heat until shimmering-hot. Add the garlic and cook until browned and slightly fragrant, about 1 minute. Reduce the heat to medium-low and stir in the Shaoxing wine, mashed black beans, and truffle paste and cook for 2 minutes or so until combined and fragrant (if using mushrooms, cook until they're softened and browned, about 5 minutes). Stir in the sugar and sambal and remove from the heat. Taste and season with shoyu, if needed.

GINGER-SCALLION RELISH

MAKES ABOUT 2 CUPS

½ cup roughly chopped peeled fresh ginger (about 2 ounces, or two 4-inch pieces)
2 cups thinly sliced scallions (about 1 large bunch)
½ teaspoon ground white pepper
1½ teaspoons Diamond Crystal (or 1 teaspoon Morton) kosher salt, plus more to taste
½ cup neutral oil

Place the ginger in the bowl of a food processor and process until the ginger is finely minced but not mushy. Scrape the ginger into a large heatproof bowl. Add the scallions to the food processor and process until finely minced but not mushy, then scrape them into the bowl as well. Stir in the white pepper and salt. Taste and add more salt if needed (don't be wary of saltiness here; the oil will mellow it out).

In a saucepan, heat the oil until shimmering-hot, about 4 minutes. Carefully pour the hot oil over the ginger-scallion mixture (it will bubble up a little) and stir lightly. Let cool to room temperature and serve. Keeps, covered and refrigerated, for up to 2 weeks.

PORTUGUESE BEAN SOUP

SERVES 8

On the Big Island, this "everything but the kitchen sink" soup is one of our favorite rainy day comfort foods (and in Hilo, it rains a lot). The foundation of the dish is smoked Portuguese sausage flavored with warm spices like cinnamon and cloves. Dad always kept a few links stashed in our freezer just in case the weather called for it.

The running joke in Hawai'i is that the Portuguese locals love to do two things: talk and eat. And the only way to keep them quiet is to make a hearty soup with *choke* (lots of) fillings: beans, potatoes, macaroni, cabbage, etc.

Perfect for a leisurely afternoon cook, this is one of those soups where you throw everything in the pot and simmer until *pau* (finished). Usually the strong seasoning of homemade sausage is enough to flavor the broth, but if you're using a milder store-bought variety like I often do, you can supplement the warm flavor with a little pumpkin pie spice.

2 pounds smoked ham hocks (2 to 3 hocks)
1 tablespoon neutral oil
¾ pound Portuguese sausage, store-bought or homemade (page 284), sliced or crumbled
1 large sweet onion, medium-diced
1 large carrot, sliced
3 stalks celery, medium-diced
3 cloves garlic, crushed and peeled
1 large baking potato, peeled and cut into 1-inch cubes
1 (15-ounce) can tomato sauce
1 (14.5-ounce) can diced tomatoes
1 (15.5-ounce) can kidney beans, undrained
¾ cup elbow macaroni

1 tablespoon sugar
1 teaspoon Diamond Crystal (or ½ teaspoon Morton) kosher salt, plus more to taste
1 teaspoon freshly ground black pepper, plus more to taste
1 teaspoon pumpkin pie spice
½ medium head green cabbage, cored and chopped, or 1 bunch kale, trimmed and chopped

FOR SERVING
Basic or Simeon-Style Chili Pepper Water (page 265) or Tabasco sauce
Portuguese Sweet Rolls (page 256)

In a large pot or Dutch oven, combine the ham hocks and 3 quarts water to cover the hocks. Bring to a boil, then reduce the heat and simmer gently, covered but with the lid askew, until the hocks start to fall apart when poked with a spoon, 2 to 3 hours.

Remove the hocks from the pot and pour the broth into a separate container (the broth should have now reduced to about 2 quarts; add water if necessary to get to this amount). Once the hocks have cooled enough to handle, pick all the meat from the bones and set aside.

Wipe out the pot you used to simmer the ham hocks. Add the oil and heat over medium-high heat until shimmering-hot. Add the sausage and brown on all sides, about 5 minutes. Reduce the heat to medium-low and stir in the onion, carrot, celery, and garlic. Continue cooking, stirring occasionally, until the onion is soft and translucent, about 12 minutes.

(recipe continues)

Add 2 quarts of the reserved broth, the potato, tomato sauce, diced tomatoes, kidney beans (with liquid), macaroni, sugar, salt, pepper, and pumpkin pie spice and stir. Increase the heat and bring to a boil, then reduce the heat and cook at a gentle simmer, covered, for 1 hour.

Stir in the cabbage and cook until crisp-tender, about 5 minutes. Remove from the heat and let the soup sit, covered, at room temperature for 2 to 3 hours before serving. Even better if you let it chill in the fridge overnight. Reheat until warmed through, and adjust the seasoning with more salt and black pepper as needed.

Serve with chili pepper water and Portuguese sweet rolls.

THE INFLUENCERS
THE PORTUGUESE COMMUNITY

Portuguese immigrants began to arrive in Hawai'i starting around 1878 and continuing until 1911. A majority of the sixteen thousand or so who came were from the offshore islands of the Azores and Madeira in the eastern Atlantic. Being European, they were often given higher-paying contracts at the plantations compared to Asian workers, and often served as supervisors for the sugarcane field crews. Their long passage also meant that many Portuguese brought their families with them and planned to stay after their work contracts finished. Most went on to open their own businesses, including restaurants or bakeries, or got into cattle ranching, becoming part of the islands' unique *paniolo* (cowboy) culture. With the Portuguese came a taste for pork, tomatoes, pepper, garlic, and vinegar, along with a signature style of sweet bread that would become associated with Hawai'i thanks to local bakers. Generously spiced dishes like Portuguese Bean Soup (page 144) and Portuguese Sausage (page 284) developed a reputation as hearty local comfort foods.

COOK REAL HAWAI'I

CHICKEN PAPAYA

SERVES 4 TO 6

In the Philippines, this ginger-scented chicken soup is called *tinola*, a name that I wasn't even aware of until probably five years ago. In Hilo we knew it as chicken papaya, a local translation that nods to the squash-like unripe papaya chunks simmered along with the chicken.

Because it was so easy to make, the comforts of chicken papaya weren't only enjoyed by Filipinos in Hawai'i. This is the type of soothing soup you might cook a big pot of and gift to a friend or family member who was sick—basically the Pinoy penicillin.

When we cooked it at home, we used leaner but more flavorful mature chickens that were better for stewing. There was a poultry farm near our house that, once a year, would sell all the old hens that didn't lay eggs anymore for $1. All my uncles and aunties would buy like thirty birds each and all the *hanai* (extended cousins) would spend the whole day plucking and butchering and then cook some chicken papaya.

Because they were readily available around Hilo, we always used green papaya and bitter melon or chili pepper leaves. If you can find those, do use them. But even in the Philippines, cooks use all kinds of vegetable options for this dish. I've written this recipe with two easy substitutes: mild-flavored chayote squash instead of unripe papaya and any spicy or peppery green—watercress or dandelion greens or arugula. As locals like to say, "Make do with what get."

2 tablespoons neutral oil

1 medium yellow onion, sliced

2-inch piece fresh ginger, peeled and thinly sliced

4 cloves garlic, sliced

2 pounds chicken wings or drumsticks

2 tablespoons fish sauce

6 cups low-sodium chicken stock or water

4 bay leaves

2 tablespoons shoyu (soy sauce)

3 large chayote squash or 1 medium green papaya (about 1½ pounds), peeled and cut into 1-inch cubes

2 cups packed watercress

Kosher salt and freshly ground black pepper

Cooked rice, for serving

In a large saucepan or pot, heat the oil over medium heat until shimmering-hot. Add the onion, ginger, and garlic and cook until the onion has softened, about 5 minutes.

Add the chicken pieces and fish sauce and cook, stirring, until the chicken is well coated and its fat begins to render, about 5 minutes. Add the chicken stock, bay leaves, and shoyu, increase the heat, and bring to a boil. Then reduce the heat, cover, and simmer until the chicken is nearly tender, about 20 minutes. Skim away any scum that floats to the surface, but leave the chicken fat, which supplies flavor.

Add the chayote and simmer until tender, 10 to 15 minutes. Stir in the watercress and simmer until wilted, less than a minute. Season to taste with salt and pepper. Serve immediately with cooked rice.

LOCAL-STYLE BEEF STEW

SERVES 8

Good old beef stew. We love it as much in Hawai'i as they do anywhere, perhaps even more so.

My dad was a big beef stew guy, but the catch was he never made it in sensible batches. It was always cooked in a stockpot that was big enough to crawl inside. His logic was that if you're going to do it, go for broke.

That meant for us, beef stew was a three-day event. We never had room in the fridge for all the leftovers, so the pot of stew sat covered on the stove with the flame on super low until we finished it off. On the second day, my favorite, the vegetables became like custard and the cooked-down beef frayed into strands. By the third day any discernible chunks had dissolved and it had just become a thick gravy that we spooned over rice. And yet I never got tired of it.

What distinguishes local beef stew, aside from additions like shoyu and ginger, is that it is often made with other starches besides potato, including *kalo* (taro) and *'ulu* (breadfruit). Here I use potatoes, but if you happen upon an 'ulu tree, go for it.

Though any kind of beef chuck or stew meat can be used, I like the combination of short rib and brisket best, two marbled cuts that offer beef flavor and hold up during the long cook.

Since beef stew is a common option at plate lunch restaurants, a lot of locals enjoy the combination of Mac Salad (page 223) and beef stew. At our house, however, we usually only made mac salad for parties, so instead we used the next best thing: mayo. Yes, mayonnaise. On beef stew. With Tabasco. So 'ono (delicious). We each had our own technique: My brother would smear it over the rice, my cousin would stir it into the stew, and I would dollop it right over the top. Don't knock it until you try it.

1 pound boneless short rib, cut into 1½-inch cubes

1 pound brisket, cut into 1½-inch cubes

1 teaspoon Diamond Crystal (or ½ teaspoon Morton) kosher salt

1 teaspoon freshly ground black pepper

2 tablespoons all-purpose flour

2 tablespoons neutral oil

½ medium yellow onion, finely chopped

½ cup celery leaves, finely chopped

4 cloves garlic, minced

2 tablespoons shoyu (soy sauce)

1 (6-ounce) can tomato paste

4 cups beef broth

2-inch piece fresh ginger, peeled and minced

2 bay leaves, halved

2 large carrots, cut into ¾-inch pieces

2 celery stalks, cut into ¾-inch pieces

1 large sweet onion, roughly chopped

1 large baking potato, peeled and cut into 1-inch cubes

FOR SERVING

Cooked rice

Tabasco sauce or Basic or Simeon-Style Chili Pepper Water (page 265)

Mayo

In a medium bowl, season the short rib and brisket with the salt and pepper, then toss in the flour to coat.

In a large pot or Dutch oven, heat the oil over medium-high heat until shimmering-hot. Add the beef and brown on all sides, about 8 minutes total. Stir in the yellow onion, celery leaves, and garlic. Reduce the heat to low and cook, stirring occasionally, until the onion is soft and translucent, about 10 minutes.

Stir in the shoyu and tomato paste to coat. Add the broth, ginger, bay leaves, carrots, celery, sweet onion, and potato. Increase the heat and bring to a boil, then reduce the heat, cover, and simmer until the beef is extremely tender, about 1½ hours. Check on it occasionally to make sure it hasn't come back up to a boil.

Remove from the heat and let it sit, covered, at room temperature for 2 to 3 hours before serving. Even better, let it chill in the fridge overnight. Reheat until warmed through.

Serve with rice, Tabasco or chili pepper water, and mayo.

SWEET SOUR SPARERIBS

SERVES 6 TO 8

Chinese in origin, these tangy braised and glazed ribs—tossed with pineapple chunks and stewed daikon—have evolved over generations to become a widespread local favorite, one that has transcended any particular ethnicity.

Though you'll see them at Cantonese Chinese restaurants here and there, sweet sour spareribs are mostly a nostalgic party dish in Hawai'i, often stealing the show at church fundraisers or first birthdays. In the Simeon household, cooking them warranted use of our *silyasi*, a wide metal wok-slash-cauldron that was about the size of a truck tire and heated by a propane burner. Fortunately, making spareribs in your home won't require that much firepower.

Browning the ribs first thing might seem like an extra step, but it's what helps the vinegary glaze really cling to the meat. After the ribs are crispy, they're braised until nearly falling apart, infusing their porky richness into the sauce. It might be tempting to toss in the carrot and daikon at the same time as the pineapple when simmering, but hold off until almost the end. The vegetables will turn tender with a slight crunch right when the liquid has reduced.

5 pounds pork spareribs, cut into bite-size riblets (see Note)

1½ cups packed dark brown sugar

1½ cups apple cider vinegar

½ cup rice vinegar

1 cup shoyu (soy sauce)

1 (6-ounce) can pineapple juice

1 (20-ounce) can juice-packed pineapple chunks, drained and juice reserved

6 star anise

3 bay leaves

3 tablespoons cornstarch

1 tablespoon Diamond Crystal (or 2 teaspoons Morton) kosher salt

1 tablespoon freshly ground black pepper

Neutral oil, for shallow-frying

4 cloves garlic, crushed and peeled

2 large (4-inch) pieces fresh ginger, peeled and thinly sliced

¼ cup oyster sauce

2 medium carrots, sliced on the diagonal

1 medium daikon radish, peeled and halved lengthwise, then sliced crosswise into half-moons

Cooked rice, for serving

Place the riblets in a large pot or wok with water to cover. Bring to a boil, then reduce the heat and simmer for 5 minutes. Drain the riblets well and set aside to cool slightly.

Meanwhile, in a medium bowl, whisk together the brown sugar, cider vinegar, rice vinegar, shoyu, pineapple juice (the 6-ounce can, plus the reserved juice from the chunks), star anise, and bay leaves. This is the sauce mixture.

In a large bowl, toss the riblets with the cornstarch, salt, and pepper until thoroughly coated.

Wipe out the large pot or wok that you used to simmer the ribs and fill it with about 1 inch of oil. Heat the oil over high heat until shimmering-hot, or until it sizzles when you flick in a drop of water. Working in batches, fry the riblets until browned on all sides, about 8 minutes per batch.

(recipe continues)

Transfer the browned spareribs to a sheet pan. Once all the riblets are browned, remove the pot from the heat and pour off almost all of the frying oil, leaving about 1 tablespoon in the pot.

Return the pot to medium-high heat. Once the oil is shimmering-hot, add the garlic and ginger and sauté until fragrant, 20 to 30 seconds. Add the riblets and the sauce mixture, tossing to coat. Add enough water to cover the ribs. Bring to a boil, then reduce to a simmer. Stir in the pineapple chunks, then cover and cook until the rib meat is tender, about 1 hour.

Remove the cover and increase the heat to high. Once at a boil, stir in the oyster sauce, carrots, and daikon. Continue cooking, stirring often, until the sauce has reduced by half and the vegetables are tender, about 15 minutes. Serve warm with cooked rice.

NOTE: *Ask your butcher to cut a rack of pork spareribs across the ribs into 1½-inch-wide strips, then to make cuts between the bones to create bite-size riblets (you can also do the last step yourself). This style is sometimes labeled "Chinese cut" at Asian markets. If you're not able to find a helpful butcher, you can substitute about 3¾ pounds boneless country-style pork ribs (which are actually shoulder cuts), cut into 1½-inch pieces.*

OKINAWA PIG'S FEET

SERVES 6 TO 8

As one of the largest ethnic groups that came to the islands, Japanese immigrants and their descendants have had a huge impact on the culture of Hawai'i. A significant portion of those immigrants arrived from Okinawa, the southernmost prefecture of Japan, comprising hundreds of islands. Proud and fiercely independent, Okinawans in Hawai'i often refer to themselves as Okinawans as opposed to Japanese and have a unique history all their own.

Here's one story I love in particular: After World War II ended, word got back to Hawai'i that war-torn Okinawa was badly in need of food. Hawai'i Okinawans rallied their community and raised enough money to buy 550 pigs, which a handful of locals then escorted to Japan via ship. With those gift pigs, the Okinawa pork supply was eventually replenished to a healthy level.

One of the most beloved Okinawan dishes in Hawai'i is *rafute*, also called shoyu pork. The first time I made it was during my early days at Aloha Mixed Plate, when for nightly specials I would cook dishes I was studying in culinary school. Rafute was a major highlight: fatty hunks of pork cooked down with brown sugar, mirin, and a special Okinawa rice liquor called awamori, the whole thing simmered until meltingly tender. (Since awamori can be tricky to come by, I use a combination of sake and whiskey here.)

Many cooks use pork shoulder or belly for rafute, but the best version I ever tasted was made with pig's feet. The sweet reduced shoyu mixes with the sticky gelatin in the hocks to create the richest, glossiest, most decadent sauce ever, one that would make any pork-loving homesick Okinawan weep with joy. Eat that over two scoops rice, *hoo*. I'm drooling on the keyboard as I write this.

3 pounds fresh (unsmoked, uncured) pig's feet, cleaned and cut into 3-inch rounds by the butcher

2 tablespoons Diamond Crystal (or 1½ tablespoons Morton) kosher salt

4 bay leaves

8 cloves garlic, crushed and peeled

4 ounces fresh ginger, peeled and julienned

¾ cup sake

¼ cup whiskey

1 cup shoyu (soy sauce)

½ cup packed light brown sugar

½ cup mirin

2 pounds daikon radish, peeled and cut into 1-inch cubes

FOR SERVING

Cooked white rice

Salt-Pickled Cabbage (page 266)

Chinese hot mustard (optional)

Place the pig's feet in a large pot and add the salt and water to cover. Bring to a boil and cook for 5 minutes. Discard the water and rinse the feet thoroughly.

In the same pot, combine the bay leaves, garlic, ginger, sake, whiskey, shoyu, brown sugar, and mirin. Return the pig's feet to the pot and add enough water to cover. Bring to a boil, then reduce the heat to a simmer, cover, and cook for 1½ hours. Stir occasionally and replenish the water as needed.

(recipe continues)

After 1½ hours, uncover and stir in the daikon and continue simmering, uncovered, until the daikon is tender and the feet are soft enough to insert a chopstick into them, another 30 to 45 minutes. Increase the heat to medium-high and cook, stirring occasionally, until reduced and a thick sauce forms. Remove from the heat.

Serve warm with rice and pickled cabbage. Dab hot mustard on the side, if desired.

NOTE: *I've written this recipe for a standard pot, but you could also speed up the braising process by using a pressure cooker (cook 20 minutes at high pressure, natural release).*

PORK BELLY ADOBO

SERVES 4 TO 6

Adobo is in my blood. From the moment I got my first tooth, I was eating spoonfuls of this iconic savory-sour stew, considered to be the national dish of the Philippines.

At the Simeon house, our adobo recipe went through countless tweaks and twists over the years, from what types of vinegar were used, what brand of shoyu, to how long we let the sauce thicken at the end. Pork shoulder was great, sure, but pork belly in big chunks was even better. We discussed and analyzed so much that we could all have had PhDs in Adobo Theory.

For me, the best adobo was not too soupy, ideally reduced until all the liquid is gone and a glaze forms. All the different seasonings—garlic, bay leaf, peppercorns—should meld together as one. At the end, the meat should start to fry in its own rendered fat, like a confit.

But a few years ago, while filming a show with chef Ed Kenney, I was able to travel to the Philippines for the first time and visit Ilocos Norte, the region where my grandparents were from. I cooked adobo with a local chef, and I noticed he did something different than us, which was to fry the pork before braising it in the sauce. At home, we did the opposite. So I went back to Hilo and cooked that adobo for my dad and told him the story. He looked at me and sort of scratched his head: *You know, this actually tastes more like what your grandma used to make.*

I realized that our family recipe had been changed or modified or misremembered, at some point, between three generations and thousands of miles. Having that chance to connect with my roots, however, snapped everything back into focus. We didn't have to debate over the right way to make adobo now because we knew by looking backward. From then on, we cooked adobo the new way, which was, in fact, the old way. One thing that never changes though: We always eat it with white rice and raw tomato, the perfect foil to the rich, tangy sauce.

¼ cup neutral oil

2 pounds pork belly, skin removed, cut into 2-inch cubes

3 tablespoons minced garlic (about 10 cloves)

¼ cup shoyu (soy sauce)

2 tablespoons oyster sauce

¼ cup cane vinegar

¼ cup apple cider vinegar

3 bay leaves

½ teaspoon freshly ground black pepper

3 cups halved cherry tomatoes (about 1 pound), for serving

Cooked rice, for serving

In a large, deep skillet, wok, or Dutch oven, heat the oil over high heat until shimmering-hot. Pat the pork dry with paper towels. Sear it in the hot oil, turning, until evenly browned on all sides, about 6 minutes. Add the garlic and sauté until fragrant, about 30 seconds.

Stir in the shoyu, oyster sauce, both vinegars, the bay leaves, and pepper and toss to coat the pork belly. Reduce the heat to low, cover, and simmer until the pork has started to soften and most of

(recipe continues)

the fat has rendered, 40 to 50 minutes. What you're going for is not a melt-in-your-mouth bite, but rendered fat and meat with some texture to it, like spareribs almost.

Once the pork is cooked, remove it with a slotted spoon and set aside. If desired, skim off some of the rendered fat and discard (I usually keep it). Increase the heat to medium and reduce the sauce, stirring constantly, until a sticky glaze starts to form. Return the pork belly to the sauce and toss to coat.

Serve with tomatoes and cooked rice.

NOTE: *Although pork belly adobo is my favorite, you can also try substituting other cuts of pork, dark meat chicken, turkey, beef, fish, seafood, or tofu. Adjust the simmering as needed, since some proteins will cook more quickly than others.*

THE INFLUENCERS
THE FILIPINO COMMUNITY

Though Filipinos were the last major immigrant group to come to Hawai'i, they arrived in full force. The first waves started in 1906, mostly made up of unmarried men who came from the rural provinces of Ilocos (where my grandpa was from) and Visaya. Eventually the *sakadas*, or Filipino migrant workers, would make up two-thirds of the sugar plantations' labor force, but they were also the lowest paid of all the immigrant groups and often assigned the most backbreaking work. By 1946, nearly 125,000 Filipinos had come to Hawai'i, with many sending for their families after working for a few years. Many sakadas found resourceful ways to make ends meet, planting their own gardens, fishing, and taking on extra jobs. Over the decades, immigration from other parts of the Philippines continued, and by 2010 Filipinos had surpassed Japanese as the largest ethnic group in Hawai'i. By the time the Filipino community became established in Hawai'i, many of the ingredients that made up the cuisine were already well stocked on the islands, with the exception of patís (fish sauce) and *bagoóng* (shrimp or fish paste). Japanese shoyu and Portuguese vinegar and spices could be used to season Pork Belly Adobo (page 155); Chinese noodles were available for Pancit (page 180); and vegetables like eggplant, bitter melon, and long beans were staples for Pinakbet (page 158). Rice flour desserts like cascaron (see page 71) and bibingka (see page 247) slotted in easily beside mochi and manjū.

PINAKBET

SERVES 8

Pinakbet, a hearty one-pot vegetable braise, was one of my mom's signature recipes. Made from whatever produce is in season, the most famous versions of this "farmer's stew" come from Ilocos Sur, the rural region in the Philippines that my mom and her family emigrated from in the 1970s. For Ilocanos, the go-to seasoning for pinakbet is *bagoóng isda*, a sharp and salty fermented sardine paste, which is distinct from the slightly sweeter *bagoóng alamang*, a fermented shrimp paste used in southern regions.

What is universal, however, is the way pinakbet is cooked: The vegetables are stacked in a wide pot according to their cooking time, a technique that allows them to steam and simmer in their own juices without needing to stir the pot. On the Big Island, where many families had little gardens in their yards, pinakbet was a righteous way to use what the tropical sunshine and volcanic soil had provided you. (And since Filipinos are gonna Filipino, most recipes sneak a little pork in there, too, for flavor.)

When I think back to my mom making pinakbet, I remember her knack at what Ilocanos called *tal tal*, or "toss toss," a move that involved vigorously shaking the pan back and forth so all the colorful layers—eggplant, bitter melon, okra, lima beans, tomatoes, squash—would fly up and mix together without being squished by a stirring utensil. It takes real skill, I've learned. When I try it at home with my Le Creuset I just end up with sore arms. My suggestion here would be to use a silicone spatula to fold together the vegetables once they're cooked to keep them as intact as possible.

Bagoóng isda, sometimes labeled as salted fish sauce or salted anchovies, can be found at Filipino or Asian markets, though a 50/50 mixture of patís (fish sauce) and shrimp paste will get you close. Also remember that the amount of bagoóng used is subjective: My mom's first-generation family went hard on the stuff, while my dad's side, second-generation "local" Filipino, tended to go lighter. Adjust the salt-to-bagoóng ratio as desired.

1 pound pork shoulder (pork butt), cut into
¾-inch cubes
2 tablespoons neutral oil
Kosher salt and freshly ground black pepper
2 slender Japanese eggplants (about 10 ounces
total), halved lengthwise and cut into
2-inch pieces
1 medium Chinese bitter melon (about
5 ounces), halved lengthwise, seeds and
inner pulp removed, and sliced crosswise
2 heaping cups 2-inch pieces Chinese long
beans or green beans (about 8 ounces)
3½ cups sliced okra (about 12 ounces)
1 small kabocha squash (about 1½ pounds),
peeled, seeded, and cut into 1-inch cubes

1 heaping cup snow peas or snap peas
(about 4 ounces)
1 cup frozen lima beans
2 large tomatoes, chopped
1 (14.5-ounce) can diced tomatoes
8 cloves garlic, crushed and peeled
2-inch piece fresh ginger, peeled and
thinly sliced
½ large yellow onion, chopped
¼ cup bagoóng isda (fermented fish paste), or
2 tablespoons fish sauce plus 2 tablespoons
shrimp paste
Cooked rice, for serving

Pat the pork dry with paper towels. In a large, heavy pot, heat the oil over medium-high heat until shimmering-hot. Add the pork and season with a big pinch each of salt and pepper. Sear the pork, turning every couple minutes, until browned on all sides, about 8 minutes. Remove the pork from the pot and set aside.

Without wiping out the pot, return to medium heat and layer in the vegetables, scattering each one over the last in this order: eggplants, bitter melon, long beans, okra, squash, snow peas, lima beans, chopped fresh tomatoes, canned tomatoes, garlic, ginger, and onion.

Place 2 cups warm water in a bowl. Stir in the bagoóng and 1 tablespoon Diamond Crystal (or 2 teaspoons Morton) kosher salt just to combine. Pour into the pot and bring to a boil. Then reduce the heat to medium-low, cover, and simmer, without stirring, until the vegetables are tender but not collapsing, 20 to 25 minutes.

Use a spatula to gently fold in the pork, mixing the layers of vegetables together in the process. Continue cooking until the pork is warmed through. Adjust the seasoning with salt and pepper to taste. Serve with cooked rice.

PORK AND PEAS

SERVES 4 TO 6

Also known as pork *guisantes*, this dish was the most requested main course in all of the Simeon repertoire. Anytime our family was invited to cook for a big party, someone would inevitably ask my dad, *Uncle Rei, you making pork and peas, no?*

Our streak of stardom for this comforting, creamy, tomato-based stew goes back before I was born. According to family legend, my dad's uncle started adding Campbell's cream of mushroom soup as his secret ingredient, which made the dish richer and creamier than its competitors (he also swapped in thicker tomato paste for the tomato sauce).

I've cooked so many huge batches of pork and peas in our family garage, portions that fed a few hundred people, that when I decided to put it on the menu at Lineage, adapting the family recipe for a restaurant kitchen proved a challenge. I'm embarrassed to admit that I even briefly considered serving a "deconstructed" version with pea puree and sous vide pork loin. Thankfully, good taste prevailed and I stuck with the classic style, presented here.

My favorite thing about making pork and peas is a specific moment at the end, right when you stir in the frozen peas (gotta be frozen). After the peas have cooked for a minute or two, they suddenly turn a bright shade of green, the brightest green ever against the creamy rust-colored sauce. If you turn off the heat right then, you can capture them in their vivid luster. Try not to overcook the peas, is what I'm saying.

2 pounds pork shoulder (pork butt),
    cut into 1½-inch chunks
1 teaspoon Diamond Crystal (or ½ teaspoon
    Morton) kosher salt, plus more to taste
1 teaspoon freshly ground black pepper, plus
    more to taste
3 bay leaves
¼ cup shoyu (soy sauce)
3 tablespoons apple cider vinegar

2 tablespoons neutral oil
½ large yellow onion, thinly sliced
4 cloves garlic, minced
3 tablespoons canned condensed cream of
    mushroom soup
3 tablespoons tomato paste
1½ cups frozen green peas, slightly thawed
½ teaspoon ground cinnamon
Cooked rice, for serving

Place the pork in a large bowl and toss it with the salt, pepper, bay leaves, shoyu, and vinegar until well coated. Cover and refrigerate for 1 hour, or up to overnight.

In a large pot or Dutch oven, heat the oil over high heat until shimmering-hot. Add the onion and garlic and sauté until translucent and fragrant, about 2 minutes. Add the pork with the marinade and sauté until cooked on the outside, about 4 minutes. Once boiling (the pork will have released a good amount of liquid at this point), reduce the heat to a gentle simmer, cover, and cook until the pork is cooked through and begins to soften (the meat should be tender, but not falling apart), 30 to 40 minutes.

Stir in the cream of mushroom and tomato paste and continue to cook for about 3 minutes, until everything is incorporated and warmed through. Stir in the green peas and cook for another 2 minutes, until the peas are tender and bright green. Remove from the heat and stir in the cinnamon. Season with more salt and pepper to taste. Serve over rice.

MAHI MAHI LUAU

SERVES 4

The reason we call a luau a luau is this classic Hawaiian dish. Made with stewed taro leaves and coconut milk, luau requires a long simmer to break down the tough leaves, which is how it became synonymous with special occasions where you would invest many hours in the cooking. Back in the olden times, that meant during traditional feasts called *pā'ina* (now called luau). These days, luau might show up at a first birthday, a wedding, or a graduation party.

In terms of technique, luau isn't too far from the long-braised greens you might find in the South, it just takes a lot longer. But since fresh taro leaves are tricky to find on the mainland (and I'm not a huge fan of the precooked frozen ones), I've built this recipe around quicker-cooking Swiss chard, a braising green that provides a similar sweet earthiness when simmered with baking soda, which removes some of the acid and breaks down the leaves. If you are using fresh taro leaves, remove the stems and roughly chop, then simmer as directed for an hour or so until tender before proceeding with the rest of the recipe.

Some locals think of traditional luau as sweet, but in my opinion it's more like balanced. Adding just a touch of sugar is common, though I've noticed Maui locals tend to prefer theirs sweeter than other islands. Me? I lean toward savory, but I was also the kid who finished everyone's canned spinach at the school cafeteria. Adjust as needed.

Commonly luau is topped with braised *he'e* (octopus), but honestly it goes great with most proteins, particularly seafood or pork or seared tofu. At Lineage, we would use whatever fresh catch came in that day from our fish guys, simply seared in the pan and laid over the luau, finished with sweet onions and sesame seeds—all together a real party in the mouth.

2 pounds Swiss chard
Kosher salt
1 tablespoon baking soda
2 small sweet onions, finely sliced
1 tablespoon roasted sesame seeds
2 teaspoons granulated sugar
4 tablespoons (½ stick) salted butter
1 (13.5-ounce) can full-fat coconut milk
2 tablespoons light brown sugar, or to taste
4 mahi mahi or other firm white fish fillets (6 to 8 ounces each)
Ground white pepper
1 cup all-purpose flour
2 tablespoons neutral oil
Cooked rice, for serving

Remove the leaves from the stems of the Swiss chard. Roughly chop the leaves, and finely chop the stems.

(recipe continues)

In a large pot, combine the Swiss chard, a big pinch of salt, and baking soda and cover with water. Bring to a boil, then reduce the heat and simmer for 20 to 30 minutes, until the leaves and stems are extremely tender. Drain, let cool a bit, and squeeze out the excess water.

Place half the onions in a bowl and cover with ice water. Let soak for 20 to 30 minutes, then drain and pat dry. Set aside.

Heat a small nonstick skillet over medium heat. Add the sesame seeds, granulated sugar, and a pinch of salt. Cook, stirring constantly, until the sugar has melted and caramelized around the sesame seeds, 2 to 3 minutes. Scrape onto a plate to cool, then crush it up and set aside.

In a large saucepan, melt 2 tablespoons of the butter over high heat. Add the unsoaked onions and cook until they are translucent, about 5 minutes. Add the coconut milk and bring to a boil, then reduce to a simmer. Stir in the chard and brown sugar and continue to simmer for 30 to 40 minutes, stirring occasionally, while you prepare the fish (when the chard begins to break down and dissolve into the coconut milk, it's done).

Pat the fillets dry and season generously with salt and white pepper on both sides. Place the flour on a shallow plate and dredge the fish, pressing down firmly but shaking off any excess flour.

In a large skillet, heat the oil over high heat until shimmering-hot. Add the remaining 2 tablespoons butter. Once melted, sear all 4 fish fillets until golden brown and crispy, 2 to 3 minutes per side.

To plate, spoon the chard into bowls and top with the pan-fried fish. Garnish with the soaked onions and candied sesame seeds. Serve with cooked rice.

DELUXE LAULAU

SERVES 12 TO 24

The best laulau I ever made was for Anthony Bourdain. It was during the filming of the Hawai'i episode of *Parts Unknown*, an unreal experience. I got to eat Spam with the guy, go hunting, and spend the whole day roasting a pig in an *imu* (earthen oven) that we dug ourselves.

But to step back: Let's talk about laulau. It's a traditional Hawaiian food that has many elements of the cuisine bound up in one package, literally. Chunks of pork and cured fish are seasoned with Hawaiian salt and wrapped in taro leaves (which you eat), then wrapped again in ti leaves (which you don't eat), then cooked in the hot coals of a fire. For the original Hawaiians, it was the ultimate combo meal, made from what the *'aina* (land) provided.

Today it's more common to steam the laulau in the oven, but the general concept remains the same. When my 'ohana made laulau it was always a communal effort, where everyone chipped in a few pieces of meat or fish and there was a big wrapping party. Making it that time for Bourdain, at my friend Shep Gordon's house on Maui, I went all out with the best ingredients: short rib, Kurobuta pork belly, chicken wings, local cod that I salted myself, taro and sweet potato, all of it wrapped in fresh taro leaves. I layered the packages into a hotel pan and put them inside the imu where they cooked for hours, the drippings filling the pan and basically confit-ing them as they steamed. They were so delicious I was speechless. Even the Hawaiian families at the party, who had eaten plenny legit laulau, were blown away.

This recipe is a tribute to that renowned day of laulau, though obviously it's fine to cook them in the oven (like I do at home) rather than digging a pit in the sand. If you use all the fillings, which you don't have to (pork and fish are the most traditional), remember these will end up mean-size buggahs, not unlike the ones at Hilo's Kuhio Grille: *Home of the One-Pound Laulau!*

1 pound butterfish (sablefish), black cod, or
    salmon fillets, cut into 1-inch strips
12 chicken wing flats or drumettes
2 pounds pork shoulder (pork butt),
    with fat cap, or country-style pork ribs,
    cut into 1½-inch chunks
Hawaiian sea salt or kosher salt
1 pound boneless short rib, cut into 1½-inch
    chunks
1 tablespoon shoyu (soy sauce)
2 medium sweet potatoes (about 1 pound),
    cut into 1½-inch chunks (optional)

24 ti leaves, thick midribs removed (or 3 to
    4 banana leaves, cut into 6 × 12-inch strips)
36 taro leaves, large Swiss chard leaves, or
    other braising green (about 3 pounds),
    washed and stems removed

FOR SERVING
Cooked rice or poi
Lomi Salmon (page 220)
Basic or Simeon-Style Chili Pepper Water
    (page 265)

In a large bowl, combine the fish, chicken, and pork and sprinkle on a few big pinches of salt. Toss thoroughly to coat, then cover and let sit overnight in the fridge.

In another bowl, toss the short rib meat with the shoyu, then cover and let marinate overnight in the fridge.

(recipe continues)

When you're ready to assemble, remove the meat from the fridge. Place the sweet potato (if using) in a bowl and sprinkle with a few pinches of salt, tossing to coat.

To assemble the laulau, place a 1½-foot length of foil on a clean, dry work surface. On top of that, arrange 2 ti leaves or banana leaf strips to form a cross. On top of that, stack 3 taro leaves smooth-side up in a crisscross fashion, with the largest leaf at the bottom and the other leaves both crossing it and overlapping one another. Into the center of the leaves, place one chicken wing and pieces of fish, pork, short rib, and sweet potato. Fold in the sides of the taro leaves, then fold the top and bottom to form a squarish bundle. Flip the bundle over so it is facing seam-side down, then wrap the bundle with the ti or banana leaves in the same fashion. Flip that bundle over so it is facing seam-side down, then wrap in the same fashion with the foil. Set the finished bundle aside. Repeat the process until you've used up all the meat and leaves (you should have 12 bundles).

Preheat the oven to 325°F.

Fill a large roasting pan with ½ inch or so of water. Place a metal rack inside the roasting pan, making sure the water line sits just below the rack (you can also create an impromptu rack using folded foil). Arrange the bundles evenly on the rack so they sit over the water without touching it. Cover the pan tightly using a lid or foil so steam does not escape. Roast for 5 hours, then remove the laulau and let cool slightly. Unwrap just before serving, removing and discarding the foil and the ti or banana leaf layers.

Serve warm with rice or poi, lomi salmon, and chili pepper water.

RICE AND NOODLES

Rice is great when you're hungry and want two thousand of something.
    –Mitch Hedberg

Rice or noodles? It's one of those hypothetical questions that local kids debate to stave off boredom or kill time on a long flight. If you could only eat one for the rest of your life, which would it be? The noodle crowd tends to pick noodles because they're more interesting on their own, and rice lovers pick rice because what else would you eat with all the foods that taste delicious over rice.

Thankfully, rice or noodles is never a choice we'll actually have to make, at least in Hawai'i. The demand for rice on the islands started as soon as the first Chinese workers arrived; it turned out that the swampy fields where taro patches grew also made for good rice paddies. As waves of Japanese, Koreans, and Filipinos later arrived, the local appetite for the staple grain only grew larger and eventually had to be supplemented, so much so that almost all rice these days eaten in Hawai'i is imported from elsewhere. Rice isn't grown much on the islands now, but back when it was, during my grandparents' generation, it was often cooked in these huge pots over wood fires for luaus and big events. Couldn't have a party without plenny rice. The process was tricky—scorch the bottom of the pot and the entire batch is ruined—but absolutely fundamental. Locals elevated rice cooking to an art form. Still, makes me grateful for the automatic functions on my rice cooker!

No matter what kind of household you grew up in, making rice was the one daily chore you learned at a young age. Come home from school, cook rice. Woe be unto the kid who forgot to hit the start button on the rice cooker and had to explain to his parents why no rice. There's even a local saying, "go home, cook rice," which is a more polite way of telling someone to f*** off when they can't do anything right. Rice also made sure you stretched every last bite of a dish into a meal. I remember when my dad would come home from work with leftover tea in his Thermos; he'd tell us to pour it over leftover rice and season it with furikake—eat rice soup. Nothing wasted.

But there was always plenty room for noodles in our diet, too. The instant kind was a constant snack, one that I loved even more when I graduated from making soup to learning to fry the noodles in the pan and sprinkle them with the seasoning packet.

Before I opened my first restaurant, Star Noodle, I spent months studying and eating and dreaming about every type of noodle you could imagine, experimenting with different flours and cooking techniques. We even found a vintage saimin noodle machine in Wailuku that had a lot of *mana* (good energy) in it; the owner decided to retire after decades of making tofu and fresh noodles and sold us his recipes as well as his equipment. We locals say eating noodles brings good luck and in my experience that tends to be true.

In this chapter you'll find many local dishes that are classic comfort foods—saimin, fried rice, loco moco. In general, rice and noodles usually play a supporting role, but here they get the spotlight they deserve. May your rice cooker never run empty and your noodles never be cut short.

OTHER GRINDS   MUM

SPICY CHICKEN SANDWICH 7   → BIBIN
                                            BC
DRY MEIN 8
                                      → PONO
GARLIC   NOODLES 7   LIL

SAIMIN BOWL 10   CH
                                      UA
FAT CHOW FUNN 7   MA
                                      BA
KALE SALAD 6

BEET BOX 5

CHICKEN HEKKA
SERVES 4 TO 6

Hekka is an old-fashioned dish you'll often see at church potlucks and social events. I even know an uncle or two who don't consider a gathering *official* unless someone brings hekka.

Most food scholars described hekka as a local take on Japanese sukiyaki, but being local, there's probably some Chinese influence in there as well. Somewhere between a braise and a stir-fry, hekka is an ideal "clean out the fridge" meal because you can use whatever vegetables and greens are on hand and add them to the pot. The constant part of hekka is what we call long rice, dried cellophane noodles that are soaked in water first, then finished in the pot, absorbing the flavors of shoyu, mirin, ginger, garlic, and chicken broth.

Even though there are already noodles in the dish, many people like to eat hekka with rice, which is a testament to how much Hawai'i loves rice and how little we worry about carbs. While rice is nice, it's not strictly necessary here—hekka makes for a balanced and flavorful one-pot meal all by itself.

¾ cup packed light brown sugar

¾ cup shoyu (soy sauce)

¾ cup mirin

6 dried shiitake mushrooms

6 ounces dried cellophane or glass noodles, or rice vermicelli

2½ tablespoons toasted sesame oil

2 pounds boneless, skin-on chicken thighs, sliced into 1-inch-wide strips

2 tablespoons grated fresh ginger (from a 2-inch piece)

2 tablespoons minced garlic (about 6 cloves)

1 cup diagonal-cut carrot slices

1 medium yellow onion, thinly sliced

1 (14-ounce) can baby corn, halved lengthwise on the diagonal

1 cup canned sliced bamboo shoots

4 cups chicken broth

2 cups fresh watercress, cut into 3-inch pieces

2 small baby bok choy, trimmed and cut into 2-inch pieces

4 ounces abura age (deep-fried tofu), sliced into ½-inch-wide strips, or 8 ounces extra-firm tofu, cubed

6 scallions, cut into 2-inch pieces

Cooked rice, for serving (optional)

In a small bowl, whisk together the brown sugar, shoyu, and mirin and set aside. Place the dried shiitakes in a bowl and cover with warm water to soften. Place the noodles in a bowl and cover with warm water to soften.

In a large wok or Dutch oven, heat the sesame oil over medium-high heat. Add the chicken, increase the heat to high, and sauté until the meat is mostly cooked, 3 to 4 minutes. Add the ginger and garlic and sauté until fragrant. Add the carrots, onion, baby corn, bamboo shoots, shoyu mixture, and chicken broth. Reserving the soaking liquid, drain the mushrooms, cut off and discard any stems, and slice the caps. Add them and the soaking liquid to the pan. Bring all of this to a boil, then reduce the heat and simmer for 10 minutes.

Drain the cellophane noodles (they should be softened at this point) and cut into 3-inch lengths. Add them to the pan along with the watercress, baby bok choy, abura age, and scallions and simmer until the greens are blanched but firm, 2 to 3 minutes longer. Serve with cooked rice, if desired.

HOUSE CAKE NOODLE WITH OYSTER SAUCE GRAVY

SERVES 4 TO 6

As far as I know, "cake noodle"—a local delicacy of noodles pressed into cakes and pan-fried—can only be found at old-school Cantonese Chinese restaurants in Hawai'i. Ask for them at any Chinese restaurant on the mainland, or even in China, and you'll probably get a confused look.

Made from compacted chow mein noodles cut into squares, the perfect cake noodle is crunchy and golden on the outside and soft and chewy on the inside, a textural one-two punch. Depending on where you go, cake noodles can be served on their own as a starch, or smothered with a gravy-rich stir-fry like beef broccoli. Some places will throw Crispy Gau Gee (page 42) on top, which is one of the most awesome combinations to ever grace a lazy Susan.

Though they might seem intimidating to prepare, cake noodles are fairly easy to crisp up at home, like making a giant pancake out of al dente noodles. My favorite way to eat them is in a classic Cantonese stir-fry loaded with a "house special" coalition of vegetables and meats (use as many or as few as you like). Oyster sauce provides the bulk of the flavoring in the gravy, so make sure you find a brand labeled "premium oyster sauce," which boasts a deeper, more complex umami than the low-budget kind.

CHICKEN
8 ounces boneless, skinless chicken thighs,
    cut into 1-inch chunks
1 teaspoon cornstarch
1 teaspoon toasted sesame oil
1 teaspoon shoyu (soy sauce)
1 teaspoon Shaoxing wine or dry sherry
Pinch of ground white pepper

CAKE NOODLES
Kosher salt
20 ounces fresh chow mein noodles

STIR-FRY GRAVY
1 tablespoon neutral oil
3 cloves garlic, minced
2 teaspoons minced fresh ginger
2 teaspoons sugar
¼ medium yellow onion, sliced

1 stalk celery, sliced
¼ cup canned sliced mushrooms, drained
1 (8-ounce) can sliced water chestnuts, drained
½ medium carrot, thinly sliced
½ cup snow peas
½ cup fresh or frozen broccoli florets
6 ounces baby bok choy, ends trimmed, sliced
4 ounces peeled and deveined large shrimp
    or sliced char siu (optional)
2 tablespoons oyster sauce
1 tablespoon shoyu (soy sauce)
1 tablespoon Shaoxing wine or dry sherry
1 cup chicken stock
1 tablespoon cornstarch

TO FINISH
Neutral oil, for the cake noodles
1 teaspoon toasted sesame oil

For the chicken: In a medium bowl, toss the chicken with the cornstarch, sesame oil, shoyu, Shaoxing, and white pepper. Set aside to marinate for 20 minutes or until you're ready to use.

(recipe continues)

To start the cake noodles:
Bring a large pot of salted water to a boil and blanch the fresh noodles according to the package directions (or cook until they're pliable but firm, not more than a minute or two). Drain well and set aside while you make the stir-fry gravy.

For the stir-fry gravy: In a large skillet or wok, heat the neutral oil over high heat until shimmering-hot. Add the garlic and ginger and stir-fry until fragrant and lightly browned, about 1 minute. Add the marinated chicken and sugar and stir-fry until the chicken

is cooked on the outside, 1 to 2 minutes. Add the onion, celery, mushrooms, water chestnuts, carrot, snow peas, broccoli, bok choy, and shrimp (if using) and stir-fry until the carrot is tender but crisp, 2 to 3 minutes. Add the oyster sauce, shoyu, Shaoxing, and chicken stock, tossing to coat.

In a small bowl, stir together the cornstarch and 1 tablespoon water to form a slurry, then stir it into the sauce. Bring it to a boil to thicken, then remove from the heat while you cook the cake noodles.

To finish the cake noodles: Coat the bottom of a large skillet with a generous layer of neutral oil and set over high heat. In a bowl, toss the noodles evenly with the sesame oil. When the oil in the pan is shimmering-hot, add the noodles to the pan and evenly distribute them so that they cover the entire surface. Fry the noodles until golden-brown and crispy, 5 to 7 minutes on each side (carefully flip the whole thing like a pancake), watching it closely, making sure it doesn't burn. Transfer to a cutting board and let cool slightly before cutting into 2-inch squares.

Arrange the crispy noodles on a plate and top with the stir-fry gravy, reheating briefly if needed. Serve immediately.

HOPPIN' JUAN

SERVES 4 TO 6

One of the coolest parts of being on *Top Chef: Charleston* (my second season on the show) was being exposed to all manner of Southern cuisine while I stayed there. What surprised me most was how much I felt connected to it, from the Filipino cooking I grew up with: lots of pork, homegrown vegetables, deep flavors, and the tradition of taking one salty or fatty piece of meat and building it into a complete meal using broth, beans, or rice.

Hoppin' John, a Carolina Lowcountry dish of brothy stewed black-eyed peas and rice, checked all those boxes, and in particular reminded me of an Ilocano dish from my mom's side of the family. When I put my version on the menu at Lineage, enriched with luscious braised oxtails, I called it Hoppin' Juan, since a lot of Filipinos are named Juan (I know, explaining a joke makes it funnier, haha). My suggestion is to serve the beans over the rice and have people mix it up as they like with a side of tangy pickled jalapeños. If you can't get ahold of oxtails, a similar amount of ham hock makes for a good substitute (since ham hocks come already brined, omit the salt used in the first step).

2 tablespoons neutral oil
1½ pounds oxtails
1½ tablespoons Diamond Crystal
  (or 3 teaspoons Morton) kosher salt
2 teaspoons freshly ground black pepper
6 cups chicken stock
2 cups dried black-eyed peas, soaked overnight
  or quick-soaked (see Note)
2 cups diced yellow onions (about 2 medium)
2 cups diced carrots (about 4 medium)

2 cups diced celery with leaves (about 4 stalks)
4 cloves garlic, thinly sliced
5 fresh thyme sprigs
3 bay leaves

FOR SERVING
Cooked rice
½ cup chopped scallions
Quick-Pickled Jalapeños (recipe follows)

In a large pot or Dutch oven, heat the oil over high heat until shimmering-hot. Pat the oxtails dry and season evenly with 1½ teaspoons of the Diamond Crystal (or 1 teaspoon Morton) kosher salt and 1 teaspoon of the black pepper and place in the pot. Cook until browned on all sides, about 4 minutes per side.

Remove the oxtails and drain off any drippings from the pot, leaving behind any browned bits. Add the stock and bring to a boil, using a wooden spoon to scrape the bottom. Return the oxtails to the pot and reduce the heat to medium-low. Cover and simmer until tender, 1½ to 2 hours.

Using a slotted spoon, transfer the oxtails to a plate and set aside to cool slightly. Add the black-eyed peas, onions, carrots, celery, garlic, thyme sprigs, and bay leaves to the oxtail stock. Season with the remaining 1 teaspoon pepper and 1 tablespoon Diamond Crystal (or 2 teaspoons Morton) kosher salt. Bring to a boil, then reduce to a simmer, partially cover, and cook until the peas are soft, about 1 hour.

(recipe continues)

While the peas cook, pick the oxtail meat from the bones. Once the peas are cooked, stir in the oxtail and cook for a few minutes until the meat is heated through.

To serve, ladle the stew over bowls of rice and garnish with scallions and pickled jalapeños. Mix it all up together before eating.

NOTE: *Quick-soak your beans by adding them to a pot of boiling water and boiling for 2 minutes. Remove from the heat and let stand for 1 hour. Discard the soaking water and use them as directed.*

QUICK-PICKLED JALAPEÑOS

MAKES 1 CUP

1 cup apple cider vinegar
2 tablespoons sugar
1 tablespoon Diamond Crystal (or 2 teaspoons Morton) kosher salt
1 cup thinly sliced jalapeños (about 8 peppers)

In a saucepan, combine the vinegar, sugar, salt, and ½ cup water. Bring to a boil. Add the jalapeño slices, stir, and remove from the heat. Let cool completely before using. Place any leftovers in a jar and cover with the brine. They will keep for several months in the fridge.

PANCIT

SERVES 4

At the Filipino gatherings of my youth, you could always count on ample amounts of pancit, a noodle stir-fry seasoned with oyster sauce and fish sauce. On my mom's side of the family we usually ate *pancit bihon* (made with thin, dried rice noodles) and on my dad's side it was usually *pancit Canton* (thick, Chinese-style egg noodles). Chewy and substantial, the latter style was the one that called me back for second (and third, and fourth) helpings.

Pancit recipes vary, but they tend to take shape based on whatever you toss in the wok: bean sprouts, tomato, sliced cabbage, or carrots. Unlike some stir-fries, the goal is not to get a crazy hot sear, but simply to get everything warmed through and cooked, which makes this an easy dish to scale up for a crowd. For us, pancit was also a great "peasant" food—you could always stretch a small amount of meat or vegetables with a huge quantity of noodles. If done right, pancit would be the dish piled high on *balon* plates, an Ilocano term for the foil-covered plates filled with leftovers that always get brought home after parties.

At Migrant, the riff on pancit we had on the menu was designed to flip the traditional script: All the superb local vegetables and meats we used in the kitchen became the stars while the noodles took on a supporting role. This recipe splits the difference, with lots of noodles and lots of fillers both, everything tossed in a salty-savory sauce that ties the dish together.

Salt

1 pound fresh chow mein noodles (pancit Canton) or other fresh thin egg noodle

1 tablespoon plus 3 tablespoons neutral oil

⅔ cup chicken stock

¼ cup oyster sauce

1 tablespoon plus 1 teaspoon fish sauce

2 teaspoons instant dashi powder (such as HonDashi)

1 teaspoon ground annatto

2 tablespoons minced garlic

6 ounces boneless, skinless chicken thighs, cut into 1-inch pieces

6 ounces ground pork

10 peeled and deveined large shrimp, roughly chopped

4 ounces mushrooms (any kind), stems discarded and caps thinly sliced

1 medium carrot, thinly sliced

4 ounces napa cabbage, leaves halved lengthwise and cut into 2-inch pieces

½ medium red onion, thinly sliced

1 medium tomato, cored, seeded, and cut into strips

3 scallions, dark green tops only, cut into 2-inch pieces

¼ cup Fried Garlic (page 283)

Calamansi or lemon wedges, for serving

Tabasco or your favorite hot sauce, for serving

Bring a large pot of salted water to a boil and blanch the fresh noodles according to the package directions (or cook until they're pliable but firm, not more than a minute or two). Drain well and toss with 1 tablespoon of the neutral oil.

In a small bowl, whisk together the stock, oyster sauce, fish sauce, dashi powder, and annatto.

In a wok or very large skillet, heat 3 tablespoons of the oil over high heat until shimmering-hot. Add the garlic, chicken, and pork and stir-fry until the meat is mostly cooked, about 2 minutes.

Add the shrimp and stir-fry until the shrimp are pink, another 2 minutes. Add the mushrooms and carrot and stir-fry until the mushrooms are softened, about 3 minutes.

Add the noodles, cabbage, onion, tomato, and the oyster sauce mixture and stir-fry until the noodles are heated through and the sauce is absorbed, about 3 minutes. Remove from the heat and toss in the scallion greens.

Transfer to a serving plate. Garnish with fried garlic and serve with citrus wedges and hot sauce.

MIKI NOODLES

SERVES 4

When I think about my late mom—Juanita Janet "Joanne" Moreno Simeon—the dish that comes to mind is her miki noodles. A hearty chicken noodle soup colored with red annatto seed, miki was a homey staple from Ilocos that she usually cooked for my brother and me when we were under the weather. Even though it had noodles in it already, we'd eat it with bowls of rice, just to soak up every last drop. I still refer to miki as my ultimate "death row meal."

Since Filipinos are big on mixing pork with seafood, I've enriched this deluxe version with smoked ham hocks and a little bit of fresh shrimp. The hocks add a porky oomph of flavor to the soup, and you can use the shredded meat to garnish the noodles.

About those noodles: What sets miki apart for me is that the noodles are always cooked *in* the broth until they're soft and supple, which makes them give off their starch and thicken the luscious broth. What you end up with is a lot like chicken and dumplings. For this purpose, fresh noodles can't be beat. I know making your own noodles at home sounds intimidating, but for these very simple flour noodles it's incredibly straightforward: just three ingredients and a rolling pin. Don't worry about making your noodles look picture-perfect—rustic strands that vary are part of the charm.

4 dried shiitake mushrooms

2 large smoked ham hocks (about 2 pounds total)

8 cups chicken broth

4 cloves garlic, crushed and peeled, plus 6 garlic cloves, thinly sliced

1 medium yellow onion, halved

2 bay leaves

1 teaspoon black peppercorns

2 tablespoons neutral oil

8 ounces boneless, skin-on chicken thighs, cut into 1-inch pieces

4 peeled and deveined large shrimp, roughly chopped

2 tablespoons fish sauce, plus more to taste

1 teaspoon ground annatto (or ½ teaspoon paprika plus ½ teaspoon turmeric)

1¼ pounds Easy Handmade Noodles (recipe follows)

FOR SERVING

1 bunch scallions, thinly sliced

Fried Garlic (page 283)

Soft-boiled eggs, peeled and halved

Lemon Olive Oil (page 278)

Place the dried shiitakes in a bowl, cover with ½ cup hot water, and set aside to soften.

In a pressure cooker or Instant Pot (see Note), combine the ham hocks, broth, crushed garlic, onion, bay leaves, and peppercorns. Cook on high pressure for 25 minutes. Quick-release the pressure. Strain the broth, reserving the ham hocks and broth. When cool enough to handle, pick the meat from the hocks (discard the bones). Set the broth and meat aside.

Drain the soaked shiitakes, reserving the soaking liquid. Cut off and discard any stems, and thinly slice the caps.

(recipe continues)

In a large skillet, heat the oil over medium heat until shimmering-hot. Pat the chicken dry and cook it until golden-brown all over, about 6 minutes. Add the shrimp, sliced garlic, and shiitakes and cook until the shrimp are opaque and the garlic is fragrant, about 1 minute. Stir in the fish sauce and annatto, then add the reserved shiitake soaking liquid and 6 cups of the reserved broth. Bring to a simmer and add the noodles. Cook, stirring occasionally, until the noodles are very tender and the broth has thickened slightly, about 15 minutes. Remove from the heat. Season with more fish sauce to taste.

Divide the noodles and broth among bowls. Top with the reserved ham hock meat, scallions, fried garlic, and eggs. Drizzle with lemon olive oil and serve immediately.

NOTE: *If you don't have a pressure cooker, place those ingredients in a large pot and bring to a boil. Reduce the heat to maintain a simmer, cover, and cook until the meat falls from the bone, 2 to 3 hours, replenishing with water as needed.*

EASY HANDMADE NOODLES

MAKES 1¼ POUNDS

2¾ cups all-purpose flour, plus more for
    kneading
1¼ cups room temperature water
½ teaspoon Diamond Crystal (or a pinch
    of Morton) kosher salt

In a large bowl, add the flour, then slowly pour in the water a little at a time while mixing into the flour. Keep adding water until there is no more dry flour left, being careful not to add too much water (the dough should be soft and sticky but not runny). The amount of water needed might shift slightly depending on your flour.

Sprinkle a clean, dry work surface generously with flour. Knead the dough until the surface turns smooth and the dough develops a springy, elastic texture, about 10 minutes. Dust your hands or the work surface with more flour as needed to keep the dough from sticking.

Shape the dough into a ball and place back in the bowl. Cover with a damp cloth and let rest for around 1 hour.

Place the dough ball back on a floured work surface and cut into 4 equal pieces. Knead each piece of dough a few times and shape it into a ball.

Working with one dough ball at a time, use your palms to flatten it onto the work surface. Use a rolling pin to roll the dough into a thin sheet, about ⅛-inch thick (or as close as you can get to that). The dough will keep pulling into itself, so make sure to roll the dough evenly and continuously, dusting with more flour as needed.

Sprinkle both sides of the rolled-out dough with flour. Starting with the side closest to you, roll the edge of the dough toward the middle, stopping halfway, then roll the opposite side to the middle as well (you should end up with something that looks like a long, flat scroll). Repeat with the remaining dough balls.

Cut the dough scrolls crosswise into ¾-inch-wide noodles (or whatever width you prefer). Gently unfurl each noodle and arrange them into 4 bundles, gently shaking off any excess flour.

SOMEN SALAD SUPREME

SERVES 4 TO 6

About once a year, usually on a hot day, I get a mean craving for somen salad. Refreshing and chewy, the star of this dish is chilled somen, Japanese-style wheat noodles, tossed with a colorful "who's who" of julienned meats and vegetables (usually whatever is in the fridge) and a mellow sweet dressing made with mirin and sesame oil.

It's a great potluck dish, but it's also sold premade in plastic containers at superettes, local shops that are half grocery store, half mini-mart. At the public school cafeteria, I remember veggie somen salad being the lone meatless option on the menu. In other words, somen salad is totally customizable, easily becoming as fancy or as basic as you need it to be.

Once you've cooked the noodles and diced the toppings, putting the salad together is a snap. A good idea is to prepare it ahead of time and pack it away for the beach; just toss in the dressing when ready to eat. As for toppings, crunchy vegetables are a must for texture, and usually I add at least one protein such as cooked egg, canned meat, char siu, kamaboko, or tofu.

DRESSING

¼ cup sugar

1 teaspoon instant dashi powder (such as HonDashi)

¼ cup shoyu (soy sauce)

¼ cup mirin

2 tablespoons toasted sesame oil

2 tablespoons rice vinegar

1 tablespoon roasted sesame seeds

SALAD

6 dried shiitake mushrooms

2 large eggs

Garlic salt

Ground white pepper

Neutral oil

1 (9-ounce) package somen noodles, cooked, rinsed with cold water, and drained

1 cup shredded napa cabbage or iceberg lettuce

1 cup bean sprouts

1 large carrot, julienned

1 small Japanese cucumber or ½ English cucumber, julienned

4 ounces snow peas (about 1 cup), julienned

4 leaves baby bok choy or 1 handful watercress, trimmed and thinly sliced

8 ounces Easy Char Siu (page 286) or smoked ham, julienned

4 scallions, dark green tops only, thinly sliced

¼ cup roughly chopped cilantro leaves

4 ounces kamaboko (fish cake), julienned

¼ cup beni shōga

¼ cup shredded dried nori

For the dressing: In a small saucepan, stir together ¾ cup water, the sugar, dashi powder, shoyu, mirin, sesame oil, and rice vinegar and bring to a boil. Reduce the heat and simmer for 5 minutes, then remove from the heat and stir in the sesame seeds. Store in the refrigerator until ready to use, up to 2 weeks.

For the salad: Place the dried shiitakes in a bowl and cover with hot water to soften while you prepare the other ingredients, 15 to 20 minutes. Drain the mushrooms, cut off and discard any stems, and thinly slice the caps.

In a small bowl, beat the eggs and season with a pinch each of garlic salt and white pepper.

In a skillet, add enough oil to lightly coat the pan and heat over medium-high heat until shimmering-hot. Add the eggs and cook until the edges start to set, about 30 seconds. Use a spatula to push the cooked edges toward the center while tilting the pan so the uncooked eggs spread out. Continue cooking for another minute until most of the egg has set, then carefully flip or roll the omelet to the other side (it doesn't have to be perfect). Cook for another minute, then remove the omelet from the pan and let cool. Cut into ½-inch-wide strips.

To assemble the salad, arrange the somen on a large platter and garnish with the shiitakes, omelet strips, and all the remaining ingredients except the shredded nori. When ready to serve, add the dressing and sprinkle the nori over the top and toss.

SAIMIN

SERVES 4

Saimin, saimin
Anytime is saimin time
Be it breakfast, lunch or dinner
Or a snack after dinner
It's a proven winner
—Franz Shiro "Mistah Saimin" Matsuo

How can I explain what saimin means to Hawai'i? It's comfort food. It's nostalgia. It's a simple soul-warming bowl of noodles that you crave again and again.

As a kid I didn't know what cereal was because my breakfast was always saimin, pronounced sigh-min, made from a packet of instant noodles (I could never figure out why we called it saimin when the package read T-O-P R-A-M-E-N; for a while I thought I was illiterate). In later years, it was my favorite late-night snack and what I filled up on before and after work. Like everyone else, I eat saimin at snack bars, luncheonettes, coffee shops, and fast-food chains (even McDonald's has it on the menu).

Completely unique to the islands, saimin is noodle soup at its most elemental. The noodles are thin, white, chewy, and a little curly. The dashi-based broth is light and clear, usually made with some combination of pork, chicken, shrimp, mushrooms, ginger, and dried *kombu* (kelp). The quintessential toppings are chopped scallions, egg (scrambled or boiled), char siu or Spam, and a slice of pink-and-white *kamaboko* (fish cake). It's a satisfying, affordable, everyday meal that doesn't require much dressing up to spark joy. As my friend and all-around wise braddah chef Mark Noguchi is fond of saying: "Ramen is trendy, saimin is life."

The name saimin comes from a combination of two Chinese words, *sai* meaning thin and *min* meaning noodle. Nobody quite knows who invented it in Hawai'i—the half-joke in the islands is that the Chinese think it's a Japanese dish and the Japanese think it's a Chinese dish—but most people agree that it emerged during the plantation era in the late 1800s, eventually spreading beyond the various ethnic work camps and becoming a staple at casual food stands.

Now you'll often encounter versions bulked up with add-ins like wontons, cabbage, bok choy, or bean sprouts; my favorite old-school saimin shop, a place on Oahu called Shiro's Saimin Haven, sells over sixty-four kinds of saimin, topped with anything from pork adobo to mochiko chicken to Vienna sausage. And, of course, you gotta have a few barbecue Teri Beef Sticks (page 85) on the side.

As someone who has eaten my fair share of instant noodles, my saimin recipe is laid-back. I tend to focus my energy on making the broth, which in this case is chicken broth infused with a bunch of umami-rich additions. As for noodles, there are tiers of preference. At the top is fresh or frozen saimin, which can be found at some Asian markets. Just below that is any kind of fresh noodle similar to ramen (one of the biggest ramen suppliers in the United States, Sun Noodle, started in Honolulu making saimin). Chow mein, yakisoba, or even udon will work, too. If all else fails, use instant dried noodles or "faux-min" (pasta cooked in alkaline water; see page 292), which I have used several times when cooking on the mainland. Whatever you're using, try to cook the noodles more on the al dente side—proper saimin has some chew to it.

The best way to eat saimin is with chopsticks and a deep soupspoon, alternating between mouthfuls of broth and noodles, dipping them in shoyu and hot mustard as needed (see Dry Mein, page 192). Slurp, too—there is no quiet way to eat saimin.

SAIMIN BROTH

8 cups chicken broth

1 pound pork spareribs

2 strips dried kombu (about 4 grams), optional

1 cup dried shrimp

6 dried shiitake mushrooms

6 cloves garlic, crushed and peeled

1 leek, including dark green tops, sliced

1 medium carrot, sliced

1-inch piece fresh ginger, sliced and crushed

TO FINISH

Salt

1 pound fresh saimin, ramen, or chow mein noodles (or "faux-min" noodles; see page 292)

4 tablespoons shoyu (soy sauce)

4 teaspoons instant dashi powder (such as HonDashi)

½ teaspoon ground white pepper

¼ cup thinly sliced scallions

4 ounces kamaboko (fish cake), sliced

½ pound Easy Char Siu (page 286), sliced

Soft-boiled eggs, peeled and halved

In a large pot (see Note), combine the chicken broth, spareribs, kombu (if using), dried shrimp, shiitakes, garlic, leek, carrot, and ginger and bring to a boil. Reduce the heat to a simmer and cook for 2 hours. Skim off any foam that rises to the top. Strain the broth, reserving the spareribs for another use if desired, and keep warm in the pot over low heat.

To finish: Bring a large pot of salted water to a boil. Loosen the noodles and add to the boiling water. When the water returns to a boil, the noodles should be nearly done (2 to 3 minutes; or follow the package directions). Check the noodles by taste or touch. They should be tender but springy. Drain.

Place 1 tablespoon shoyu, 1 teaspoon dashi powder, and a pinch of white pepper in the bottom of each of four soup bowls. Add about 1½ cups of hot broth to each bowl. Place a serving of noodles in each bowl and stir with chopsticks or tongs. Garnish with scallions, kamaboko, char siu, and egg just before serving.

NOTE: *You can speed up the broth in a pressure cooker or Instant Pot. Add the ingredients to the cooker and cook at low pressure for 45 minutes. Allow the pressure to release naturally. Strain as directed and return the broth to the pot.*

DRY MEIN

SERVES 4

Dry mein is a close cousin of saimin, originally made famous at Sam Sato's, a popular Japanese-owned saimin shop in Happy Valley Village on Maui. The quickest explanation is that dry mein is simply saimin without broth, but there are also some significant differences.

I find dry mein tends to emphasize the toppings and garnishes more and uses a stronger seasoning to coat the noodles; a cup of broth usually comes on the side for dipping, sipping, or splashing, but you can also omit it altogether. My favorite way to eat dry mein is to use a chopstick to mix together hot mustard with shoyu until the heat is mellowed slightly, then dip the noodles in the resulting brownish-yellow sauce before each bite. The strong sharp-salty flavor goes beautifully with the starchy chew of the noodles (you can use this same dip for regular saimin, too).

Salt

1 (12-ounce) can Spam, julienned

6 tablespoons neutral oil

4 large eggs

Garlic salt

Ground white pepper

4 ounces (about 1½ cups) bean sprouts

1 pound fresh saimin, ramen, or chow mein noodles (or "faux-min" noodles; see page 292)

¼ cup shoyu (soy sauce), plus more for serving

1 tablespoon oyster sauce

2 teaspoons instant dashi powder (such as HonDashi)

4 ounces kamaboko (fish cake), sliced

¼ cup thinly sliced scallions

Chinese hot mustard, for serving

Instant Saimin Broth (optional; recipe follows), for serving

Bring a large pot of salted water to a boil over high heat.

In a large skillet over medium-high heat, arrange the Spam in a single layer and cook until crispy and browned on all sides, about 6 minutes. Remove the Spam from the pan and set aside. Add 3 tablespoons of the oil to the pan. Crack in the eggs and fry, undisturbed, until the yolks are cooked and the edges are crispy, seasoning with garlic salt and white pepper to taste. Remove the eggs to a cutting board. Once the eggs are cooled, slice into ½-inch-wide strips.

Place the bean sprouts in a colander and set the colander in the sink. Loosen the noodles and add to the boiling water. When the water returns to a boil, the noodles should be nearly done (2 to 3 minutes; or follow the package directions). Check the noodles by taste or touch. They should be tender but springy. Drain the noodles over the bean sprouts in the colander. Let both drain thoroughly.

While the noodles are still warm, in a large bowl, whisk together the remaining 3 tablespoons oil, the shoyu, oyster sauce, dashi powder, and a pinch of white pepper. Add the noodles and bean sprouts and toss to coat with the sauce.

Transfer the noodle/sprout mixture to a serving bowl or individual bowls and garnish with the Spam, sliced eggs, kamaboko, and scallions. Serve with a small dish of hot mustard, drizzled to taste with shoyu. If desired, serve with a cup of saimin broth.

INSTANT SAIMIN BROTH

MAKES 4 CUPS

2 teaspoons instant dashi powder (such as
    HonDashi)
2 teaspoons chicken bouillon powder
4 teaspoons garlic oil (reserved from Fried
    Garlic, page 283)

In a small bowl, combine the dashi powder
and bouillon. Place 1 teaspoon of the mixture
into each of four cups or small bowls. Bring
4 cups water to a boil and pour 1 cup into
each bowl, stirring to dissolve the powder.
Top each with 1 teaspoon garlic oil and serve
immediately.

BREAKFAST FRIED RICE

SERVES 2 TO 4

Fried rice wears many hats in Hawai'i: quick lunch, clear-the-fridge dinner, hearty breakfast of champions. Most cooks don't have a formal recipe—*just throw rice in the pan and fry 'um*, says Uncle—but that doesn't mean locals are short on strong opinions on the best way to make it.

One thing nearly everyone agrees on is using day-old refrigerated rice, which dries out a bit and provides a tender-chewy texture when fried. Some people even freeze their rice if they're in a hurry. Beyond that, fried rice is a storehouse of possibilities, as simple and complex as you prefer, and a great vehicle for improvisation.

I enjoy the process of making fried rice—the flow of it, which can be quite meditative—as much as I do eating it. The best thing to do is get up early and fry last-night's rice with assorted breakfast meats—no better way to wake up the house than with Spam and bacon sizzling.

My formula is fairly standard: rice, eggs, shoyu, two kinds of onion. One twist taught to me by my Thai friend Sunday, who cooked at Star Noodle, was to mix a raw egg into the rice before it's fried: The egg coats each grain and keeps them fluffy and separated. I'm also of the opinion that too often fried rice is underseasoned (rice can hold a lot of flavor), so in addition to shoyu I use oyster sauce, garlic salt, and a few pinches of sugar to dial up the taste.

Although it's sometimes enjoyed as a quick meal, fried rice in Hawai'i is also often eaten as a side. Think of it as an upgrade over plain starch and try eating it with main dishes that would normally be accompanied by rice (except raw dishes, like poke).

2 tablespoons neutral oil

3 large eggs

3 cups cooked rice, refrigerated overnight

6 slices bacon, chopped fine

½ cup diced or crumbled Portuguese Sausage (page 284)

½ cup diced Spam

½ medium yellow onion, diced

2 cloves garlic, minced

½ teaspoon garlic salt

2 tablespoons shoyu (soy sauce)

1 tablespoon oyster sauce

1 teaspoon sugar

1 teaspoon toasted sesame oil

½ cup thinly sliced scallions (about 5 scallions)

In a large skillet or wok, heat 1 tablespoon of the oil over medium heat. In a small bowl, lightly beat 2 of the eggs. Add to the pan and cook, stirring, until scrambled. Transfer the eggs to a cutting board and chop into small pieces.

Beat the remaining egg in the same egg bowl. In a large bowl, combine the rice and the beaten egg. Using your hands to combine, make sure every rice grain is coated and there are no clumps.

Wipe the pan clean. Set over medium-high heat and heat the remaining 1 tablespoon oil until shimmering-hot. Add the bacon and fry until lightly browned. Add the sausage and Spam. When lightly browned, add the onion and garlic and cook until lightly browned, about 2 minutes. Stir in the rice/egg mixture. Add the garlic salt, shoyu, and oyster sauce. Stir and toss until combined. Increase the heat to high and continue to fry until the rice is hot. Reduce the heat to medium and stir in the chopped eggs, sugar, and sesame oil. Stir and toss to combine. Remove from the heat and stir in the scallions. Serve immediately.

FRIED GARLIC NOODLES

SERVES 4

Simple and flavorful, fried noodles seasoned with shoyu is one of those more-than-a-snack, not-quite-a-meal foods you find all over Hawai'i. On the Big Island they sell it at okazuya, on Oahu it's sold from the famed "manapua man" trucks, on Maui you can find it at swap meets and farmers' markets.

The version I serve at my restaurants takes that salty fried base and adds three dimensions of garlicky flavor: fresh garlic, fried garlic, and garlic-infused oil, boosted with a sprinkle of umami-rich dashi powder. Extremely customizable, these noodles can be eaten several ways: on their own, as a seasoned base for dishes like Chop Steak (page 111), fried cutlets, or Tin Roof Pork Belly (page 108), or combined with whatever stir-fry-friendly chopped meats (char siu, Spam, kamaboko, chicken) or vegetables (cabbage, carrots, onions, celery, bean sprouts) are on hand to make a fast weeknight meal.

1 pound fresh saimin, ramen, or chow mein noodles
  (or "faux-min" noodles; see page 292)
3 tablespoons Microwave Fried Garlic (recipe follows),
  with reserved oil
2 tablespoons minced garlic (about 8 cloves)
3 tablespoons shoyu (soy sauce)
1 tablespoon oyster sauce
2 teaspoons instant dashi powder (such as HonDashi)
¼ cup chopped scallions
Sambal oelek or Kudeesh Sauce (page 39), for serving (optional)

Bring a large pot of water to a boil over high heat. Loosen the noodles and add to the pot. When the water returns to a boil, the noodles should be nearly done (2 to 3 minutes; or follow the package directions). Check the noodles by taste or touch. They should be tender but springy. Drain thoroughly.

In a wok or skillet, heat 3 tablespoons of the garlic oil over high heat until shimmering-hot. Add the raw garlic, stir-frying until fragrant but not browned, a few seconds. Add the noodles and toss to coat. Add the shoyu, oyster sauce, and dashi powder and continue to stir-fry for another minute or two until the sauce is absorbed.

Remove the pan from the heat and transfer the noodles to a serving plate or individual bowls. Reheat the fried garlic in the microwave until crispy, 10 to 15 seconds, keeping an eye (and a nose) on it so it doesn't burn.

Garnish the noodles with scallions and fried garlic before serving. Top with sambal or kudeesh sauce if desired.

MICROWAVE FRIED GARLIC

MAKES ABOUT 3 TABLESPOONS

¼ cup minced garlic
   (about 12 cloves)
Neutral oil
Kosher salt
Sugar

Place the garlic in a microwave-safe
bowl and add enough oil to cover (at
least 3 tablespoons). Microwave for
1 minute, then stir. Repeat, stirring
and microwaving in 30-second
increments until the garlic begins
to brown. Then repeat, stirring
and microwaving in 15-second
increments, until the garlic is a deep
gold. (This could take between 2 and
4 minutes total, depending on your
microwave.) In a sieve set over a bowl,
drain the garlic, reserving the oil.
Transfer the garlic to a plate lined
with paper towels and season with a
pinch each of salt and sugar. Set aside
to cool.

LOCO MOCO GRAVY RICE

SERVES 4

Perspective is a funny thing. During my time on *Top Chef,* and later when I was fortunate enough to travel around the country, I found myself having to explain foods I'd been eating my whole life—saimin, smoke meat, manapua, etc.—to mainlanders who had no idea what I was talking about.

Of course, as a born-and-bred local boy, this was a two-way street. For me, ceviche was poke with lime juice. Everything bagels were covered in haole furikake. And the first time I ate risotto, part of me thought, *Ho, brah, this gravy rice.*

Gravy rice, which is what it sounds like, plays a crucial role in loco moco, the famous hamburger-topped dish that was proudly invented in Hilo. If you were a restaurant in Hilo that didn't have loco moco on the menu, people were suspicious. It's everywhere. Most people assume the hamburger patty is the most important part of loco moco, but just like a flavorful broth is key to a proper risotto, a good rich brown gravy is what makes the dish sing.

As if to prove this specific point, I made this dish, with all the oniony beefy flavor of classic loco moco but presented like risotto, at a pop-up I did with my friend chef John Tesar in Dallas. And I didn't have to explain a thing because if there're folks who deeply understand beef and gravy, it's Texans. Maybe I should have taken it one step further and called it "Hilo Boy Risotto."

3 tablespoons unsalted butter or neutral oil

1 medium yellow onion, sliced into half-moons

Kosher salt

1 pound ground beef (80/20)

4 cloves garlic, minced

¼ cup all-purpose flour or 2 tablespoons cornstarch

1½ cups beef broth

2 teaspoons Worcestershire sauce

2 teaspoons shoyu (soy sauce), plus more to taste

4 cups cooked white rice, hot

Freshly ground black pepper

4 soft-poached eggs (see Note), for serving

Tabasco sauce, for serving

In a skillet or wide pan, heat the butter or oil over medium heat until sizzling (butter) or shimmering (oil). Add the onion and season with a generous pinch of salt. Cook, stirring, until the onion is softened and slightly translucent but not browned, 4 to 5 minutes. Remove the onion from the pan and set aside.

Add the ground beef and the garlic and cook over medium heat, stirring occasionally, until browned, 4 to 5 minutes. Break up the meat as much or as little as you like. Sprinkle the flour over the top and stir to combine (if using cornstarch, mix it with 2 tablespoons of water to form a slurry, then stir it in after the beef broth has come to a simmer). Once the flour is fully absorbed, add the beef broth, Worcestershire sauce, and shoyu. Continue cooking until the broth thickens

(recipe continues)

and a gravy-like sauce forms. Remove from the heat and stir in the rice. Season with black pepper to taste and add more shoyu, if needed.

To serve, portion the gravy rice into individual bowls and top each with sautéed onions, a poached egg, and a few dashes of Tabasco.

NOTE: *The easiest way to poach eggs is to crack a very fresh egg into a fine-mesh sieve and wipe away any runny, stringy bits that come out the bottom. Add the drained egg to a pot of boiling water at least 4 inches deep and cook for 2 to 3 minutes, or to taste. The egg should stay intact and you don't have to deal with any wispy egg strands polluting the water.*

LOCO MOCO FAMILY

LOCO MOCO▪	4.35
DOUBLE LOCO▪	8.45
SUPER LOCO▪	8.95
KILAUEA LOCO▪	8.45
SPAM LOCO▪ 4.55 BACON LOCO▪	4.55
PORTUGUESE SAUSAGE LOCO▪	4.55
SMOKIE SAUSAGE LOCO▪	4.55
TERIBURGER LOCO▪	5.30
TERIBEEF LOCO▪	5.30
HOT DOG LOCO▪ 4.30 CHORIZO LOCO▪	5.30
AHI LOCO▪	5.45
OYAKO OR GRILLED CHICKEN LOCO▪	5.30
CHILI LOCO▪	5.30
GARDENBURGER LOCO▪	5.30
HEKKA OR VEGETABLE LOCO▪	5.30
STEW LOCO▪	5.30

LAHAINA FRIED SOUP (FAT CHOW FUN)

SERVES 4

When I was planning out the menu for Star Noodle, one of the first things I did was write down all the nostalgic noodle dishes in Hawai'i, from any culture, as sort of a brainstorming exercise. Eventually that led to poring through vintage community cookbooks, looking through old newspapers at the library, and prying recipes from every auntie and uncle I knew to call.

One recipe in particular that sent me down a rabbit hole was a little-known noodle dish from Lahaina that was called "Fry Soup" or "Fried Soup." When I first moved to Maui, I tried it at a first birthday luau, but nobody knew much about where it came from, even the family cooking it. The name was a misnomer because there wasn't actually any soup— it was these chewy thick-cut chow fun noodles, more like pinkie-size rice cakes really, that were wok-fried with ground pork and bean sprouts and topped with scallions and sesame seeds.

Later I learned that back in the '50s or '60s there was a popular place called Liberty Restaurant on Front Street in Lahaina, owned by the Yamafuji family, that sold the homemade "fried soup" noodles in little pink cones made out of butcher paper for 50 cents. Since then the dish had mostly faded into obscurity, except among a few deep-rooted families on Maui.

One of my philosophies as a chef is that it's better to revive a dish from the past than invent something new. I knew that I wanted "Lahaina Fried Soup" on the Star Noodle menu, not only because it was delicious, but because it represented a special part of Maui's history. We just had to figure out how to make it.

Following in the footsteps of the Yamafuji 'ohana, we made the "fat chow funn" (the two n's is a local spelling) noodles by steaming batter in hotel pans and cutting them into French-fry lengths; we swapped in wheat flour (thin chow fun are usually made with rice flour) since we found it held up better against the rigors of a hot wok. Pan-fried in a little pork fat, the chunky noodles took on a toothsome mochi-like texture on the inside and a crispy shell on the outside, almost like a fried gnocchi. Seasoning them with shoyu, oyster sauce, and a sprinkle of powdered dashi made them extremely habit-forming. They ended up being such a hit at Star Noodle that when I opened Tin Roof, customers began asking for the noodles by name, so now I serve them there as well.

The last revelation came while working on this book, when I realized that instead of cooking the noodles in a steamer, it could also be done in the microwave at home. Absolute game changer. Grab a pan and go forth to spread the Lahaina Fried Soup gospel.

3 tablespoons neutral oil

4 ounces Spam or Easy Char Siu (page 286), roughly diced

½ pound ground pork

2 cloves garlic, minced

1 tablespoon minced fresh ginger

1 pound Fat Chow Fun (recipe follows)

1 tablespoon oyster sauce

1 tablespoon shoyu (soy sauce)

1 tablespoon instant dashi powder (such as HonDashi)

1 tablespoon toasted sesame oil

6 ounces bean sprouts

6 scallions, cut into 1-inch sections

Ground white pepper

1 teaspoon roasted sesame seeds

(recipe continues)

In a large skillet or wok, heat 1 tablespoon of the oil over high heat until shimmering-hot. Add the Spam and sear on all sides, about 3 minutes. Add the ground pork, garlic, and ginger and stir-fry until the pork is cooked through, 3 to 4 minutes. Remove the pork mixture from the pan and set aside.

Add the remaining 2 tablespoons oil to the skillet. Heat over high heat until the oil begins to smoke. Add the noodles and cook, stirring occasionally, until seared at the edges, about 2 minutes.

Add the oyster sauce, shoyu, dashi powder, and sesame oil, tossing to coat. Once the noodles are coated, add the bean sprouts and scallions, tossing for about 30 seconds, until the bean sprouts have softened. Return the pork mixture to the pan and toss once more to mix. Season with a pinch of white pepper to taste and remove from the heat. Garnish with sesame seeds and serve immediately.

FAT CHOW FUN

MAKES ABOUT 1 POUND

1½ cups all-purpose flour
¼ cup plus 2 tablespoons tapioca starch or cornstarch
1 egg white
1 teaspoon neutral oil, plus more for brushing
¼ teaspoon Diamond Crystal (or a pinch of Morton) kosher salt

Sift together the flour and starch into a bowl. In a large bowl, whisk together the egg white, 1 teaspoon oil, salt, and 1¾ cups warm water. Gradually stir in the flour mixture until a smooth batter forms (strain through a fine-mesh sieve to make sure there are no lumps). Cover the bowl and refrigerate for 1 hour.

Lightly brush oil over the bottom and sides of a square or rectangular microwave-safe pan or dish (whatever size will fit your microwave is fine). Pour in enough batter to come ¼ inch up the sides (set the remaining batter aside). Cover the pan with plastic wrap or a damp paper towel and microwave on high until the noodle sheet is firm and springy but not dry, about 2 minutes. Depending on the wattage of the microwave and the size of the pan, more time may be required (if so, continue microwaving in 20-second increments). Let cool and carefully remove the noodle sheet from the dish with a spatula and set aside. Repeat the process with the remaining batter, making sure to brush the pan with oil each time.

Brush the noodle sheets lightly with oil so they don't stick together and place in a stack. Cut into strips ½ inch wide and 2½ inches long (they all don't have to be exactly the same size). Carefully separate the noodles, brushing with more oil if needed, and cover with plastic wrap or parchment paper. Refrigerate until ready to stir-fry.

CHICKEN (OR TURKEY) ARROZ CALDO

SERVES 4 TO 6

It's a common local tradition to make rice porridge with leftover turkey the day after Thanksgiving, but what you called it depended on your roots. For Chinese and Korean families it was *jook;* Japanese families, *okayu* or *zosui;* and for Filipino families, *arroz caldo,* a dish that translates to "rice broth" in Spanish.

There's no agreed upon recipe for arroz caldo, per se; it's more of a simple equation of rice, salt, and water doctored up with whatever seasonings are handy. Some people like their arroz caldo soupy, others prefer it cooked longer so the rice breaks down and it becomes thick and starchy. Since most of the year you won't have a turkey carcass to pick from, this version uses chicken thighs (though the leftover turkey option is also included). And since half the appeal of arroz caldo is in the toppings, I use a grip of them here: fresh scallions, fried garlic, pork rinds, boiled eggs, citrus, and a spicy umami-bomb condiment we make at Lineage called Hilo X.O.

2 pounds bone-in, skin-on chicken thighs
   (or 3 cups shredded cooked turkey meat)
1½ teaspoons garlic salt
½ teaspoon ground white pepper
2 tablespoons neutral oil
1 medium yellow onion, diced
6 cloves garlic, minced
1 tablespoon minced fresh ginger
1 cup uncooked rice

6 cups chicken or turkey broth
1 tablespoon fish sauce, plus more to taste

FOR SERVING (ALL OPTIONAL)
Calamansi or lime wedges
Fried Garlic (page 283) or crushed pork rinds
1 bunch scallions, thinly sliced
Hilo X.O. (page 273)
Soft-boiled eggs, peeled and halved

Place the chicken in a large bowl and sprinkle with the garlic salt and pepper. Toss to coat, then set aside. (If using turkey, you will season it with garlic salt and white pepper and add it later.)

In a large pot, heat the oil over medium-high heat until shimmering-hot. Add the onion, minced garlic, and ginger and cook, stirring occasionally, until softened and fragrant, about 5 minutes. Add the chicken and cook, stirring occasionally, until the skin begins to brown and the fat renders, about 5 minutes.

Stir in the rice so that it's coated in chicken fat and cook for another 5 minutes, until the rice smells toasted and nutty. (At this point, if you're using cooked turkey, season the shredded meat with garlic salt and white pepper to taste and add to the pan.) Pour in the broth.

Increase the heat and bring to a boil. Reduce it to a low simmer and cook, stirring occasionally, until the chicken is nearly falling off the bone and the rice grains have broken down significantly, 45 minutes to 1 hour. Remove the chicken from the pot and let cool. (If you're using turkey, just leave it in there.) Adjust the consistency with water as desired.

When the chicken is cool enough to handle, remove the meat from the bones and roughly chop, then stir it back into the arroz caldo. Season with the fish sauce, then divide among bowls. If desired, squeeze a calamansi or lime wedge over the top (serve extra wedges on the side) and garnish with fried garlic, scallions, X.O. sauce, and a soft-boiled egg.

MEAN GREENS

One of the perks of living in paradise is the produce. Where else in America can you find potato-like *'ulu* (breadfruit) falling from neighborhood trees, squash vines climbing chain-link fences, and pink-hued guavas so sweet that birds (literally) get drunk off their nectar?

When I opened Lineage, one of the goals I had was to celebrate the products of Hawai'i in ways that I hadn't seen before, or at least seen in ambitious restaurants. That I was even able to consider doing this owed a lot to the generation of Hawai'i chefs who came before me. They helped bring attention to local farmers who used their skills to grow strawberries, tomatoes, spinach, and other fruits and vegetables that blew away anything you could find on the mainland.

What I wanted to capture in my food was the way that immigrants to Hawai'i—including my family—used flavors they knew from home to shape the foods they found around them. Chef Ed Kenney, a good friend, likes to talk about how in the ancient days of Hawai'i, the original voyagers would bring *limu* (seaweed), *pa'akai* (sea salt), and *'inamona* (roasted candlenuts)—staple seasonings of traditional Hawaiian cuisine—with them wherever they traveled, using those base flavors to heighten the taste of whatever they found.

When you look at it a certain way, that helps explain my cooking, too. I've been fortunate to see parts of the world outside of Hawai'i and be introduced to ingredients I might not have otherwise known. But no matter what you hand me, I'm going to use the flavors I know by heart to turn it into something delicious.

Which brings me to this chapter. Most people don't associate local food with fresh vegetables, and for an understandable reason: Our most famous salad is macaroni and mayo. Part of me loves that, but I also want to show how wide our roots go. The heart of cooking is respecting what you're given, and for this chapter that means taking produce that is around you, wherever you may be, and bringing out its best side. Bust out your kale, your beets, your sweet potatoes. Here's what we would do with them in Hawai'i.

POHOLE SALAD

SERVES 4 TO 6

Pohole, or what the mainland knows as fiddlehead ferns, goes by many names. Maui calls it *pohole*, the Big Island and Oahu call it *hō'i'o*. It's also known as *pako* in the Philippines, *warabi* in Japan, and *kosade* in Korea.

Pohole is fresh, crunchy, earthy-sweet, and extremely green-tasting, almost like a mix between baby asparagus and okra. It's one of the fastest-growing plants on earth and since all it needs is water and sunlight, it tends to shoot up through the forests and gulches all over the islands. This is especially true around Hilo, where frequent rain showers mean that wild pohole patches pop up year-round. Before any big party at the Simeon house, the kids would be sent down to Papaikou or Hakalau Gulch to compete to see who could pick the most. The old-timers always knew where the best patches were and passed the info along to other families, since there was always more than enough to go around. The key was to find ferns that were young and tender, which often grew in the shade or near rivers and springs. Sometimes you could chop down the large ferns with a machete and then come back in a day or two when fresh shoots appeared in their place.

But it wasn't all fun and games! Fiddleheads can be finicky to prepare. Flecks of soil tend to get caught in the curled tips of the fern, so you have to make sure they're washed thoroughly. They need to be blanched, but leave the ferns in hot water too long and they'll turn black, so you need ice water to halt the cooking process. But I promise the effort is worth it.

Pohole salad involves the ferns and a few other ingredients tossed in a salty-umami dressing. Our family recipe is nice and straightforward, made with tomato, sweet onion, and sliced *kamaboko* (fish cake). Rather than a dressing, the saltiness and umami in our version comes from dried shrimp and *shio kombu* (Japanese salt-dusted shredded seaweed), which absorb the moisture from the pohole and became tantalizingly dressing-esque.

If you're on the mainland and don't have a pohole patch near you, the good news is that fiddlehead ferns will keep in the fridge for about 1 week. During summertime you can find them through specialty produce vendors. Mainland fiddlehead ferns are thicker and tougher (and earthier in flavor) than their supple Hawaiian cousins, so they might take longer to become tender when blanched. Otherwise, pencil-thin baby asparagus or long beans are the best substitute.

1 pound fresh pohole (fiddlehead ferns) or baby asparagus
Kosher salt
½ medium sweet onion, thinly sliced
2 medium plum tomatoes, cored and diced, or 6 ounces cherry tomatoes, halved
4 ounces kamaboko (fish cake), julienned
3 tablespoons dried shrimp
3 tablespoons shio kombu
2 tablespoons toasted sesame oil

Before using, wash and rinse the ferns thoroughly until the water runs clear, making sure to clean out any trapped dirt in the curled fern heads. Trim off the woody stems. Half-fill a large bowl with ice and enough cold water to cover the ice.

(recipe continues)

Bring a large pot of well-salted water to a boil. Cut the ferns into 2-inch pieces (the ones in Hawai'i are usually 8 to 12 inches long; if yours are shorter than 2 inches, trim the bottom stems and leave them whole). Blanch them for about a minute, until bright green, working in batches if necessary. The blanching time will vary based on the size and maturity of your ferns; keep a close eye on them as they change color. Drain and immediately place them in the ice bath, stirring the ferns until cooled. Drain thoroughly and return the ferns to the large bowl.

Add the onion, tomatoes, kamaboko, dried shrimp, and shio kombu and gently toss with your hands until everything is evenly distributed. Transfer to the fridge and chill for at least 15 minutes. Just before serving, drizzle with the sesame oil and season with a pinch of salt, if needed. Any leftovers will keep in the fridge for a day.

MAUI KALE SALAD
WITH SWEET ONION DRESSING

SERVES 4 TO 6

Here's how this salad came together. A few days before we opened Tin Roof, we had the menu 90 percent set. Mochiko chicken, pork belly, chop steak—the essentials all locked in. Then somebody in the kitchen pointed out that we had no salad (other than mac salad) on the menu. Maybe we needed something with actual greens in it?

Cue the *Top Chef* quickfire music. Within 30 minutes we had pulled together a salad based on what was in our pantry and what I picked up from the Costco down the street. The dressing was a crowd-pleasing sweet onion recipe that we'd used at Old Lahaina Luau. We took roasted peanuts and coated them with sweet-spicy kochujang and garlic salt. We added crushed potato chips for crunch and more salt, dried cranberries for chew and sweetness. We used kale and cabbage because we figured they would taste better after sitting around in the dressing for a while; eventually we figured out that if you *lomi* (massage) the leaves with a little salt it makes them even more tender. It turned out to be a very good salad: easy but interesting enough to hold your attention, robust but balanced.

2 large bunches kale, rinsed and roughly chopped
   (remove any midribs and stems if they're too tough)
½ medium head green cabbage, cored and thinly sliced
½ cup sweetened dried cranberries
½ cup Sweet Onion Dressing (recipe follows)
1 cup crushed potato chips (Maui onion flavor preferred)
¾ cup roughly chopped Kim Chee Peanuts (recipe follows)
Kosher salt

In a large bowl, combine the kale, cabbage, cranberries, and sweet onion dressing. Toss to coat and mix thoroughly, using your hands if desired. Transfer to the fridge and let chill for at least 15 minutes.

When ready to serve, add the potato chips and peanuts and toss to combine. Season with a pinch of salt, if needed.

(recipe continues)

SWEET ONION DRESSING

MAKES ABOUT 2 CUPS

¼ cup apple cider vinegar
½ cup sugar
1 medium sweet onion, quartered
2 teaspoons celery salt
2 tablespoons Dijon mustard
¼ teaspoon freshly ground black pepper
1 cup neutral oil

In a blender, combine the vinegar, sugar, onion, celery salt, mustard, and black pepper and process until smooth. With the blender on its lowest speed, gradually add the oil in a steady stream until the dressing is thickened. Transfer to a jar or sealable container and store in the refrigerator for up to 2 weeks.

KIM CHEE PEANUTS

MAKES ABOUT 2 CUPS

2 tablespoons sugar
1 tablespoon neutral oil
1 tablespoon kochujang (Korean chili paste)
½ teaspoon kochugaru (Korean chili flakes)
1 teaspoon garlic salt
2 cups raw peanuts

Preheat the oven to 325°F. Line a baking pan with parchment paper.

In a large saucepan, stir together the sugar, oil, and 1 teaspoon water over medium heat. Once the sugar is dissolved, remove it from the heat and stir in the kochujang, kochugaru, and garlic salt. Add the nuts, stirring to coat evenly.

Spread the nuts out in the baking pan. Bake until the nuts are toasted and glossy, 15 to 20 minutes, stirring once. Break the mixture apart. Cover and store at room temperature for up to 2 weeks.

"BOTTOM OF THE PLATE LUNCH" SALAD

SERVES 4 TO 6

After my shifts at Aloha Mixed Plate, I'd always take home a huge plate of kalbi with rice, mac salad, and extra shaved cabbage. Once the ribs were polished off, there were a couple final bites at the bottom that held my attention: the sweet-salty drippings from the meat mingled with the starchy mayo from the mac salad to form a kind of creamy dressing that coated the cabbage. Some people regard that roughage as filler, but it was my favorite part. So I thought, *What if I made shaved cabbage the hero instead of an afterthought?* Thus was born one of my signature dishes.

The dressing for this shaved cabbage salad combines two sauces, one being a mac salad puree—make sure to cook the macaroni until very soft—and the other, a quick shoyu-sugar dressing made with the drippings from Local-Style Kalbi (page 82). If you aren't making kalbi to go with the salad, use bacon fat or regular oil in the dressing and garnish the salad with some thinly sliced teriyaki beef jerky.

1 medium green cabbage

MAC SALAD PUREE
1 cup well-cooked macaroni noodles (very soft, not al dente)
1 hard-boiled egg, peeled and roughly chopped
1 cup mayonnaise
1 tablespoon apple cider vinegar
½ teaspoon garlic salt
½ teaspoon freshly ground black pepper

KALBI DRESSING
3 tablespoons beef drippings or bacon fat
½ cup shoyu (soy sauce)
½ cup sugar
1 tablespoon toasted sesame oil
1 teaspoon sambal oelek or Kudeesh Sauce (page 39)
1 teaspoon minced fresh ginger
2 cloves garlic, minced

FOR SERVING
2 scallions, finely chopped
1 tablespoon roasted sesame seeds
2 tablespoons thinly sliced teriyaki beef jerky or Pipikaula (page 38), optional

Shave the cabbage as thinly as possible (a mandoline works great for this) and set aside.

For the mac salad puree: In a blender, combine the macaroni, egg, mayo, vinegar, garlic salt, and pepper and blend until smooth. The puree should be thick, but you can also add a few teaspoons of water if necessary. Transfer to a squeeze bottle (or a zip-top plastic bag with a corner cut off to serve as a piping bag).

For the kalbi dressing: In a small saucepan, combine the beef drippings, shoyu, sugar, sesame oil, sambal, ginger, and garlic and bring to a simmer over medium-high heat, stirring until the sugar is dissolved. Remove from the heat.

To serve, place a pile of cabbage on a serving platter and drizzle on the mac salad puree to taste. Spoon the kalbi dressing on the top just before serving and garnish with the scallions, sesame seeds, and beef jerky (if using).

TOFU WATERCRESS

SERVES 4 TO 6

In Hawai'i, tofu watercress is a salad your oldest auntie might bring to the family potluck. It's not flashy, but it's fresh, healthy, tasty, and can be tossed together during a commercial break of *The Young and the Restless*.

The anchors of this nostalgic dish are firm, high-quality tofu and fresh watercress, a peppery crisp green that is commonly farmed here. Seafood often serves as a seasoning. I love using *taegu*, a Hawai'i Korean side dish of dried shredded fish (usually cod, pollack, or cuttlefish) tossed in sweet-spicy chili paste (taegu makes a great snack with rice, too). If fish jerky isn't your jam, you can also substitute canned salmon, a pantry essential that all my aunties stocked up on when it went on sale at Longs Drugs.

Then there's the dressing. There's an old-school brand here called Tropics that makes a soy/sesame/ginger "Oriental Dressing" that has dominated the salad scene for decades. It's an iconic name in some circles. The actual recipe is a trade secret, of course, so I've done my best to replicate it below (I'm about 90 percent sure on the steak sauce that's in it, so just trust me on that).

1 (14-ounce) block extra-firm tofu, drained and cut into ¾-inch cubes
1 tablespoon grated fresh ginger
5 tablespoons Tropics Oriental dressing, store-bought
    or homemade (recipe follows)
½ medium sweet onion, thinly sliced
1 cup packed Spicy Taegu (recipe follows)
1 large tomato, diced
1 bunch watercress, trimmed and roughly chopped
2 tablespoons finely chopped dried shrimp
1 teaspoon roasted sesame seeds
Freshly ground black pepper

In a small bowl, toss the tofu cubes with the ginger and 2 tablespoons of the dressing and let marinate for 20 minutes at room temperature.

Place the onion in a bowl with a handful of ice and rinse under cold water until the ice melts, then drain and dry on a paper towel.

Transfer the marinated tofu to a serving platter and evenly top with the spicy taegu. In the same bowl you used to marinate the tofu, toss the tomatoes with 1 tablespoon of the dressing. Layer the tomatoes over the taegu, followed by the onion and watercress. Top with dried shrimp, sesame seeds, and black pepper to taste. Spoon on the remaining dressing just before serving.

(recipe continues)

SPICY TAEGU

MAKES ABOUT 1 CUP

1 tablespoon kochujang (Korean chili paste)
1 teaspoon kochugaru (Korean chili flakes)
2 teaspoons honey
2 teaspoons toasted sesame oil
1 teaspoon garlic salt
1 cup packed shredded dried cuttlefish
    (about 2 ounces) or 1 (5-ounce) can salmon,
    drained and patted dry
Neutral oil, as needed
Kosher salt

In a bowl, combine the kochujang, kochugaru, honey, sesame oil, garlic salt, and dried cuttlefish and mix thoroughly. If the mixture is too sticky, add a few drops of neutral oil. Season with salt to taste.

TROPICS ORIENTAL DRESSING

MAKES ABOUT 1½ CUPS

½ cup rice vinegar
3 tablespoons sugar
2 tablespoons plus 1 teaspoon shoyu (soy sauce)
2 tablespoons toasted sesame oil
2 teaspoons A.1. steak sauce
2 teaspoons roasted sesame seeds
1 teaspoon minced fresh ginger
1 teaspoon garlic powder
¼ teaspoon ground black pepper
¾ cup neutral oil

In a blender, combine the vinegar, sugar, shoyu, sesame oil, A.1., sesame seeds, ginger, garlic powder, and pepper. With the blender on its lowest speed, slowly pour in the neutral oil. (Alternatively, combine everything but the oil in a bowl, then briskly whisk in the oil until emulsified.) Store in the refrigerator until ready to use, up to 1 month.

FILIPINO OKRA SALAD

SERVES 4 TO 6

Nutrient-rich okra gets a lot of love in Filipino cooking. I noticed during *Top Chef: Charleston*, however, that the okra dishes I ate in the South tended to involve longer cooking times, yielding soft (and what some people might call slimy) okra instead of the crisp, snappy style I knew growing up.

Both ways can be delicious, of course, but that's part of why I created this simple salad: to spotlight a fresher, crunchier side of okra that's just as enticing. Tomato, celery leaves, and boiled eggs are sidekicks for the blanched okra here, sluiced with a sweet-tangy fish sauce dressing. Shrimp chips or pork rinds, two puffed snacks found in most pantries here, are fantastic crushed over the top. Add them just before serving so they stay crunchy.

Kosher salt
12 ounces okra pods, stems removed, halved lengthwise on the diagonal
½ cup cane vinegar
1 tablespoon plus 1 teaspoon fish sauce
1 teaspoon grated fresh ginger
1 teaspoon minced garlic
1 tablespoon neutral oil
Freshly ground black pepper
1 cup loosely packed celery leaves, rinsed and roughly chopped
1 large tomato, diced
2 medium-boiled eggs, peeled and quartered
Lemon Olive Oil (page 278)
¼ cup crushed shrimp chips or pork rinds, for garnish

Bring a large pot of well-salted water to a boil. Meanwhile, half-fill a large bowl with ice and enough cold water to cover the ice.

Blanch the okra for about a minute, until bright green. Drain and immediately place in the ice bath. Drain thoroughly and leave the okra in the bowl.

In a small bowl, combine the vinegar, fish sauce, ginger, and garlic and whisk in the oil until emulsified. Season with pepper to taste.

Add the celery leaves and tomato to the large bowl with the okra. Add the dressing to taste and toss to coat. Gently fold in the eggs and transfer the salad to a serving plate. Drizzle with lemon olive oil to taste and garnish with shrimp chips just before serving.

LOMI SALMON

SERVES 4 TO 6

If you've ever been to a luau you've probably seen the little cups of lomi salmon and poi that are served alongside kālua pig (imu-roasted pork). Made with salt-cured salmon, tomatoes, and sweet onions, lomi salmon has roots in the whaling industry days: Whalers would bring salted salmon with them from Alaska and the Pacific Northwest and trade it with the Hawaiians.

The word *lomi* means "to massage," which is a nod to how the salad is mixed together. Some people will tell you to let the salmon sit, preserving, in salt for a day, but I let it cure for just a couple hours instead, so you can still taste the freshness of the fish. You're probably not preparing for a month-long sailing voyage, I bet.

When I helped cook at the Old Lahaina Luau, one of my occasional tasks was to mix together forty pounds of lomi salmon for the dinner crowds. Picture me up to my elbows in a giant mixing bowl (lomi salmon is always better when tossed by hand), soaked in tomato juice. One thing I learned: Don't use fancy peak-season tomatoes here. They'll turn mushy. You want something that's firmer and slightly acidic. Plum tomatoes are nice.

Lomi salmon is traditionally eaten with poi (see page 24) and Hawaiian dishes like Deluxe Laulau (page 165), but it can also be served with rice or alongside roasted or grilled main dishes.

1 pound skinless salmon fillet, cut into ¾-inch cubes
Kosher salt
6 medium plum tomatoes, seeded and diced
2 small sweet onions, small-diced
4 scallions, thinly sliced
Tabasco sauce or Basic or Simeon-Style Chili Pepper Water (page 265)

In a small bowl, combine the cubed salmon and enough salt to coat thoroughly. Use your hands to massage the salt into the salmon for a few minutes, then cover and let sit for 2 hours at room temperature or 4 hours in the fridge.

While the salmon is curing, in a medium bowl, combine the tomatoes, onions, scallions, and a few generous pinches of salt and gently toss with your hands. Cover the bowl and refrigerate.

When the salmon is finished curing, rinse it well under cold water and drain well, patting away any excess water with a paper towel. Remove the tomato-onion mixture from the fridge and pour off the liquid. Stir in the salmon and gently mix with your hands. Season with a few dashes of Tabasco, adding more salt, if needed. Serve chilled.

MAC SALAD

SERVES 4 TO 6

Second only to two scoops rice, mayo-rich mac salad is a cornerstone of local cuisine. No proper plate lunch is without it: a creamy and comforting side at diners, potlucks, lunch wagons, drive-ins, and picnics. What makes a dish that is so elemental—it's literally 90 percent mayo and starch—so craveable? Allow me to dive deep for a minute.

Some believe the origins of mac salad in Hawai'i came from European potato salad, which classically trained chefs cooked for the wealthy haole families who ran the plantations. Local workers then added cheaper dried macaroni to the potatoes. Much like a mouthful of rice, the soothing blandness of mac salad helps break up a meal, contrasting with a saucy main dish like adobo or beef stew. I guess if you're not from here, you either love it or hate it, depending on how you feel about mayo. But I've also seen supposed mayo haters converted, too, so who really knows.

There are many recipes for mac salad out there, but I believe this one, which I serve at Tin Roof, is the peak of the form. Some people like to add peas, ham, tuna, celery, imitation crab, things like that, but I don't mess—simplicity is king. I do add potatoes and boiled eggs, because I feel they complement the macaroni without being too distracting. Grated carrots are for a touch of color.

What I can't stress enough is that you *must* overcook the macaroni until the noodles are fat and soft, definitely not al dente. It seems crazy when you do it, but it's what helps the pasta soak up the mayo and become super flavorful. For mayonnaise, it's got to be Best Foods (sold as Hellmann's east of the Rockies). No dispute on that. The first time you make mac salad, the almost 2-to-1 ratio of mayo to starch also seems crazy, but just like when you make chicken or egg salad, the two ingredients become one homogenous thing as they sit in the fridge. Done right, mac salad should be so creamy and lush that you have to take a drink of water after a few bites!

As a cherry on top, I like to serve chilled mac salad over a bed of shredded iceberg, which is often done at local diners. To me it adds a touch of class—and some welcome crunchy freshness.

Kosher salt

8 ounces macaroni

1 pound russet potatoes, peeled and cut into ½-inch cubes

4 hard-boiled eggs, peeled and chopped

3 cups mayonnaise

1 tablespoon garlic salt

1 teaspoon freshly ground black pepper, plus more for serving

1 medium carrot, grated

Shredded iceberg lettuce, for serving

Bring a pot of well-salted water to a boil over high heat. Cook the macaroni a minute or two longer than the package directions, until very tender. Drain and rinse under cold water. Place in the refrigerator to cool and further drain for a minimum of 2 hours.

In the same pot, combine the potatoes and fresh water to cover by 1 inch. Salt it well and bring to a boil. Reduce the heat to a simmer and cook until tender, about 10 minutes. Drain well.

In a large bowl, stir together the eggs, mayonnaise, garlic salt, pepper, and carrot. Fold in the potatoes and chilled macaroni. Refrigerate until ready to eat.

Serve on a bed of shredded lettuce with a sprinkling of black pepper.

GRILLED DINENGDENG

SERVES 6 TO 8

Filipinos are famous for their green thumbs. Most of our 'ohana on Hilo had gardens in their front yards or backyards, growing all kinds of vegetables and greens. At gatherings, we'd cook dishes that made use of this big medley of produce, like Pinakbet (page 158) or *dinengdeng*, a gingery fish soup that my grandpa loved to prepare for large crowds.

The twist of this recipe is that it takes the salty-sour broth of dinengdeng and condenses it down to a gingery fish sauce vinaigrette, used to flavor vegetables that have been cooked on the grill until they're smoky and slightly charred.

The veggies below are more of a loose guideline than a firm list, so feel free to substitute with anything in season, or whatever you scrounge up from the garden. Squash, zucchini, peppers, eggplant, broccoli, bok choy, or even Brussels sprouts would be great here.

Kosher salt

20 okra pods

½ pound green beans or long beans, trimmed

3 pounds kabocha squash, peeled, seeded, and cut into wedges

2 tablespoons fish sauce

2 tablespoons apple cider vinegar

1½ tablespoons sugar

1 tablespoon grated peeled fresh ginger (from a 1-inch piece)

1 tablespoon minced garlic

3 tablespoons neutral oil, plus more for the grill

3 large tomatoes

1 cup squash tendrils or pea tendrils (or any fresh microgreen)

2 tablespoons olive oil

Freshly ground black pepper

Bring a large pot of well-salted water to a boil. Meanwhile, half-fill a large bowl with ice and enough cold water to cover the ice.

Blanch the okra for about a minute until bright green, then transfer immediately to the ice bath. Repeat with the green beans. Add the squash to the boiling water and cook until a fork can easily pierce the flesh, about 6 minutes. Drain and set the pieces aside to cool on a baking sheet, removing the skin from the cooked squash if desired.

In a small bowl, whisk together the fish sauce, vinegar, sugar, ginger, and garlic. Slowly drizzle in the neutral oil while continuing to whisk.

Preheat a grill or grill pan to high heat. Using tongs, oil the grates of the grill with an oiled rag or paper towels. Place the tomatoes on the grill and cook, turning often, until charred all over, about 10 minutes. Grill the okra, beans, and squash, turning often, until charred on all sides, 3 to 4 minutes. Cut the okra in half on the diagonal, cut the beans into 4-inch pieces (if needed), and cut the tomatoes into wedges.

In a large bowl, toss all the grilled vegetables, except the tomatoes, with the dressing. Gently fold in the tomatoes and transfer to a serving platter. Garnish with the squash tendrils. Drizzle with the olive oil and season with a pinch of pepper before serving.

SWEET-AND-SOUR ROASTED BEET MUI

SERVES 4 TO 6

When I think about beets, a popular vegetable for trendy chefs these days, I think about my dad eating canned beets topped with shoyu mayo and a splash of vinegar. Always canned! I thought it was a strange combination as a kid, but nowadays I would crush that—the richness of the mayo and earthy tang of the beets go together like yin and yang.

At Tin Roof, we have a dish on the menu called the Beet Box, which plays on that same dynamic, layering roasted beets with garlic aioli and a handful of furikake and crushed chips for crunch. This version ups the ante further, adding in quick-pickled beet greens (use every part of the vegetable!) and tossing the beets in a sweet-sour vinaigrette made with li hing mui powder (see page 291), which brings the root vegetable's natural sweetness into focus.

2 pounds large beets, with tops
Olive oil
Garlic salt
¼ cup rice vinegar
2 teaspoons sugar
½ teaspoon Diamond Crystal (or ¼ teaspoon Morton) kosher salt

⅓ cup Li Hing Mui Vinaigrette (recipe follows), or more to taste
⅓ cup Garlic Aioli (recipe follows)
2 tablespoons Furikake (page 262)
2 tablespoons crushed Funyuns or corn chips

Preheat the oven to 350°F.

Cut the tops off the beets, leaving about ¼ inch of stems, and set the greens aside. Peel the beets and cut into 1-inch chunks. In a bowl, toss the beets with olive oil to coat and season with ½ teaspoon garlic salt.

Spread the beets out on a sheet pan and roast until they are tender, about 45 minutes, tossing occasionally.

While the beets are in the oven, wash the greens in at least 2 changes of water to remove any grit. Separate the stems from the leaves. Slice the stems into ¼-inch pieces and transfer to a small heatproof bowl. Cut the leaves into 1-inch pieces.

In a small saucepan, heat a small splash of olive oil over high heat. Add the beet leaves and cook until wilted, about 3 minutes. Season with garlic salt to taste and remove to a bowl. Add the vinegar, sugar, and kosher salt to the pan. Bring to a boil and then pour it over the beet stems to make a quick pickle. Let stand for at least 30 minutes before using.

Remove the beets from the oven and let cool. Toss with the vinaigrette, tasting and adding more if needed.

On a serving plate, spread the aioli and arrange the beets on top. Garnish with sautéed greens and pickled beet stems. Sprinkle with the furikake and Funyuns just before serving.

(recipe continues)

LI HING MUI VINAIGRETTE

MAKES ABOUT ½ CUP

This vinaigrette is made with powdered li hing mui (see page 291), a salted dried sour plum.

¼ cup balsamic vinegar
2 teaspoons li hing mui powder, or to taste
½ teaspoon sugar
½ teaspoon garlic salt
2 tablespoons Lemon Olive Oil (page 278)
2 tablespoons neutral oil
½ medium shallot, grated

In a small bowl, whisk together all the ingredients. Keeps for about a week in the fridge.

GARLIC AIOLI

MAKES ABOUT 1 CUP

1 head garlic
1 tablespoon olive oil
Kosher salt
¾ cup mayonnaise

Preheat the oven to 425°F.

Cut the tops off the head of garlic to expose the cloves. Place the head on a large piece of aluminum foil, drizzle with the olive oil, and sprinkle with salt. Wrap the foil into a tight pouch and bake for 35 to 45 minutes, then remove from the oven and let cool. In a small bowl, squeeze out the roasted cloves from their skins and mash them with a fork. Add the mayo and stir until combined. Season to taste with more salt. This keeps for about a week in the fridge.

CHARRED CARROTS WITH MAC NUT DUKKAH AND LIMU VERDE

SERVES 4 TO 6

When you think about Maui, you probably don't think about carrots. But maybe you should. Some of the sweetest and most flavorful carrots I've ever tasted are grown here. At Lineage, I get mine from a guy we called Braddah Ross, the farmer responsible for managing a farm on Maui owned by a certain famous resident who prefers to keep a low profile. Let's just say her name rhymes with *schmoprah*.

Whichever talk-show icon you source your carrots from is not so important. What matters is how you season them. My idea for this dish was to take two very classic carrot toppers—Italian salsa verde and toasted nuts—and connect with them what we had on the islands. In the Limu Verde, herbs and lemon are mixed with fresh seaweed, adding salinity and a snap that crunches in a nice way between your teeth. The mac nut dukkah, a seasoned nut and spice mixture, is based off a riff my friend chef Mark Noguchi came up with when he was trying to approximate roasted Hawaiian 'inamona while cooking at The Greenbrier resort in West Virginia. I use crushed graham crackers in my version because they're a convincing sub for nutty kiawe flour, an ingredient made from the dried and ground beans of the kiawe (mesquite) tree. Between the brightness of the limu verde and the nuttiness of the dukkah, you get two contrasting garnishes that make the carrots pop with complexity. Here I cook the carrots in a skillet, but you could just as easily grill them for extra smokiness or roast them whole in a 425°F oven.

2 tablespoons neutral oil
1½ pounds carrots (preferably young and tender), cleaned,
    with a bit of the tops remaining and halved lengthwise
Kosher salt and freshly ground black pepper
4 tablespoons (½ stick) unsalted butter, at room temperature
2 tablespoons shiro (white) miso
1 teaspoon honey
⅓ cup Limu Verde (recipe follows)
⅓ cup Mac Nut Dukkah (recipe follows)

In a large skillet, heat the oil over high heat until shimmering-hot. Working in batches if necessary, add the carrots and season with salt and pepper. Cook, mostly undisturbed, for 7 to 8 minutes, until the carrots are slightly charred and tender, but with a slight snap in the middle.

Remove the carrots from the skillet and reduce the heat to low. Add the butter. When the butter starts to brown and smell nutty, remove the pan from the heat and use a whisk to stir in the miso, honey, and 1 tablespoon water. Continue whisking until a creamy and lump-free sauce forms, then return the carrots to the pan, tossing to coat.

Transfer to a plate and top with the limu verde and mac nut dukkah just before serving.

(recipe continues)

LIMU VERDE

MAKES ABOUT 1 CUP

¼ cup roughly chopped ogo seaweed
¼ cup roughly chopped chives or scallion tops
¼ cup coarsely chopped flat-leaf parsley
2 tablespoons minced Roof Lemons (page 275)
    or preserved lemon
Grated zest of 1 lemon
2 teaspoons shichimi tōgarashi
½ cup Lemon Olive Oil (page 278)
Kosher salt
Neutral or olive oil, as needed

In a bowl, combine the ogo, chives, parsley, roof lemon, lemon zest, tōgarashi, and lemon olive oil in a bowl until well incorporated and season with salt to taste. Store in an airtight container and cover with a thin layer of oil if necessary to keep it all covered in oil. This will keep in the fridge for up to 2 weeks.

MAC NUT DUKKAH

MAKES ABOUT 2 CUPS

1 cup finely chopped roasted macadamia nuts
1 cup crushed graham crackers
3 tablespoons butter, at room temperature
1½ teaspoons Diamond Crystal (or 1 teaspoon
    Morton) kosher salt
1 teaspoon fennel seeds
½ teaspoon smoked paprika
¼ teaspoon cayenne pepper
¼ teaspoon ground white pepper

Preheat the oven to 325°F.

In a bowl, stir together all the ingredients until well incorporated. Spread the mixture evenly onto a sheet pan and bake until golden brown, about 10 minutes. Cool and store in an airtight container for up to 2 weeks.

SALT LEMON BROCCOLINI
WITH FRIED GARLIC

SERVES 4 TO 6

I've always had a soft spot for broccoli, even as a kid. What I cared about was not so much the broccoli itself, but the ability of the tiny florets to soak up sauce like little green sponges. If you can picture a very saucy dish of beef broccoli at a Chinese buffet you'll understand what I'm talking about.

Broccolini, which is basically broccoli that went to prep school, might be even better at mopping up sauce thanks to its extra frilly fronds. At Lineage, my favorite broccolini topper involved roasting preserved lemons (see Roof Lemons, page 275) and blitzing them into a salty-sour dressing. As a side dish, it tastes a dozen levels more sophisticated than it actually is to cook. There's fried garlic on top, too, because in my experience you will never regret sprinkling fried garlic over roasted vegetables.

1 pound broccolini or sprouting broccoli, trimmed
1 Roof Lemon (page 275) or preserved lemon, rinsed, seeded, and thinly sliced
    crosswise (or ¼ cup diced Quick-Salted Lemon Peel, page 277, with pulp)
2 tablespoons plus ¼ cup Lemon Olive Oil (page 278)
Kosher salt and freshly ground black pepper
½ cup Fried Garlic (page 283)
1 tablespoon sugar
¼ cup rice vinegar

Preheat the oven to 425°F.

On a sheet pan, toss the broccolini and preserved lemon with 2 tablespoons of the lemon olive oil until evenly coated (if the pan is too crowded, arrange the broccolini on top of the lemon). Season to taste with salt and black pepper. Roast until the broccolini is bright green and starting to char in spots, 10 to 15 minutes.

Remove the lemon from the pan and set aside. Sprinkle the fried garlic over the broccolini and return to the oven until the garlic is fragrant and warmed through, another 2 to 3 minutes.

In a food processor or blender, combine the still-warm lemon, the sugar, vinegar, and 1 tablespoon water and blend until smooth, adding a little more water if necessary. Season to taste with salt and pepper.

Remove the broccolini from the oven (if you haven't already) and transfer to a plate. Spoon the lemon dressing over the top and serve.

HAWAIIAN SWEET POTATOES WITH COCONUT CREAM AND DRY AKU

SERVES 4 TO 6

Sweet potato with coconut is a classic pairing here in Hawai'i. Roasted sweet potatoes with coconut cream and toasted coconut is a staple at luaus, and one of Roy Yamaguchi's most famous dishes over the years was mashed sweet potatoes flavored with coconut and ginger.

Despite what you might think, plain coconut milk contains very little sugar, which is why I like seasoning it with salt and pushing it in a savory direction, providing a contrast to the tuber's natural sweetness. Adding umami to the salt creates depth, which here comes from dry *aku*, a local variety of dried fish made from skipjack tuna. If you can't find dry aku, you can substitute any type of fish jerky (including Sakura Boshi, page 41) or use a favorite Japanese ingredient of mine, *katsuobushi* (dried bonito shavings).

In this case I'm using Hawaiian purple sweet potatoes, which are sometimes called Okinawan sweet potatoes. You can find them at many Asian markets. Compared to regular sweet potatoes, they're dense and a little drier (hence cooking them in foil to seal in moisture) and more delicate in flavor, but otherwise similar. Orange or purple, you're good either way.

2 pounds purple sweet potatoes (about 4 medium)
1 (13.5-ounce) can full-fat coconut milk, unshaken and refrigerated overnight
Kosher salt
½ cup thinly sliced dry aku, or fish jerky, or firmly packed katsuobushi shavings
2 scallions, thinly sliced

Preheat the oven to 425°F.

Wash and dry the sweet potatoes well and pierce them a few times with a fork. Wrap tightly in foil and bake on a sheet pan until fork-tender, about 1 hour.

While the potatoes are baking, remove the coconut milk from the fridge, being careful not to shake it. Use a can opener to partially open the can from the bottom while holding it over a small container so the separated coconut milk drains into it (set the milk aside for now). Open the can fully and scoop the remaining cream into a small bowl and let it come to room temperature. Stir in a pinch or two of salt, adjusting to taste. Spread the coconut cream onto a large platter (if the cream seems too thick to spread easily, add back a bit of the coconut milk to thin it to a yogurt-like consistency). Reserve the coconut milk for another use.

Remove the potatoes from the oven and let them cool slightly before unwrapping. Cut them into 2-inch chunks and transfer them to the platter with the coconut cream. Garnish with the dry aku, scallions, and a pinch more salt, and serve.

HURRICANE ELOTE

SERVES 8

Even though it didn't really fit with the rest of the menu, one of the most popular dishes we had at Migrant was a version of Mexican "street corn," or *elotes*. We sold a truly insane amount. I assume this was because a) everyone loves grilled corn and b) the flavors of chili, lime, cheese, and cream/mayo/butter were instantly recognizable to those diners who were visiting from the mainland. For a while, I even served the corn "deconstructed" style with pieces of cob jutting up from the plate and these ridiculous artsy swirls of sour cream and chili powder. Yikes.

The funny thing is, I grill corn at home a lot—especially during the summer, when corn is extra sweet. Over time the elotes from Migrant evolved into this recipe, which boasts the same creamy-cheesiness but borrows from sweet-salty Hurricane Popcorn (page 40). All the original elote flavors are there, just remixed in a local way.

I would recommend making the Cotija mixture beforehand, since it keeps well in the fridge for a couple days. And if you don't feel like dealing with corn cobs or grills, you can apply this recipe to cooked kernels or, taken one step further, a baked sweet potato or yam.

Oil, for the grill
4 ounces Cotija cheese, crumbled (about ½ cup)
⅓ cup sour cream
¼ cup mayonnaise
2 tablespoons fresh calamansi juice (or 4 teaspoons Key lime juice
    plus 2 teaspoons orange juice)
2 teaspoons minced cilantro stems
1 teaspoon kochugaru (Korean chili flakes)
2 cloves garlic, minced (about 1 teaspoon)
1 teaspoon garlic salt
8 ears corn, shucked
¼ cup shredded or finely chopped dried nori
¼ cup crushed arare (rice crackers)
¼ cup cilantro leaves, chopped
2 teaspoons grated calamansi or Key lime zest

Preheat a grill or grill pan to high heat. Using tongs, oil the grates of the grill with an oiled rag or paper towels.

Place the Cotija in a food processor and pulse 5 times. Add the sour cream, mayonnaise, calamansi juice, cilantro stems, kochugaru, garlic, and garlic salt and pulse until the mixture just comes together but still has some texture. Transfer to a large bowl.

When the grill is hot, cook the corn, covered, until lightly charred on all sides, about 8 minutes. Transfer the corn, one at a time, to the bowl with the cheese mixture; turn to coat. Transfer to a serving platter; sprinkle with nori, rice crackers, cilantro leaves, and citrus zest.

SWEETS
AND DRINKS

When I picture the perfect dessert in Hawai'i, I think about all my aunties coming to a potluck clutching pans wrapped tightly with foil. As kids we would try and peek under to see what was inside. Guava cake. Mac nut bars. Banana lumpia. Chocolate haupia cream pie. If you were really lucky somebody might bring a box of goodies from the bakery: coco puffs with Chantilly, long johns with lemon custard, glazed stick doughnuts, or warm malasadas.

For me, there's something about local sweets that tugs on my heartstrings and transports me back to small kid time, even being the dedicated "savory" person that I certainly am. Part of that has to do with our history. Since the earliest plantation days, the legacy of cane sugar in Hawai'i has been strong. Both my grandpa and dad worked at the sugar mills; I remember raw crystals being scooped from a big bucket in our kitchen that was never empty. Sweet was always around to balance the salty. Sometimes it was as basic as the colorful cans of fruit-flavored "juice" that we sipped with our after-school musubi as kids.

Each culture that came to Hawai'i shaped this surplus of sugar to fit their own traditions. There were mochi and manjū from the Japanese, almond cookies and steamed niangao from the Chinese. There were Portuguese egg tarts and sweet bread, and Filipino bibingka and cascaron. Haoles brought cream puffs and chiffon cake. Dessert being one thing everyone agreed on, all those mouthwatering items mixed together over time, giving rise to the smorgasbord of tastes and textures you find today.

This chapter is hardly a complete survey of the favorite desserts (or drinks) of Hawai'i. That is worth its own dedicated cookbook! But a common thread in these treats is nostalgia. Not just the recipes I remember, but *how* I remember them, rethought and reimagined in ways that capture their essence. That might mean a dusting of Ovaltine on cheesecake, li hing mui thrown into a tequila cocktail, or a layer of rainbow sprinkles over chocolate butter mochi—a few twists for the sweet tooth.

HAUPIA WITH PASSION FRUIT CURD

SERVES 8 TO 16

A thick, extra-rich, sliceable coconut pudding, haupia is an iconic luau dessert that shows up at parties and festivities. In the olden days, haupia was made from freshly milled coconut thickened with ground arrowroot, which was then wrapped in ti leaves and baked in the *imu* (underground oven), almost like a flan. These days, most home cooks use instant haupia mix sold at the grocery store, but a superior version can be made in nearly the same amount of time using canned coconut milk, sugar, and arrowroot or cornstarch.

Creamy and not too sweet, with a texture halfway between Jell-O and custard, haupia has broad appeal. Many people prefer haupia on its own, but I think it also goes well with this silky *liliko'i* (passion fruit) curd, which lends a tart twang that contrasts with the butteriness of the coconut. Fresh passion fruit, frozen passion fruit puree, or 100% passion fruit juice—any of them can be used in this case.

Oil or butter, for greasing
5 tablespoons arrowroot powder or ⅓ cup cornstarch
1 (13.5-ounce) can full-fat coconut milk
⅓ cup sugar
1 teaspoon vanilla extract
1½ cups Passion Fruit Curd (recipe follows)
¼ cup coconut flakes, toasted, for garnish (optional)
Kosher salt, for garnish

Lightly grease an 8 × 8-inch pan. In a small bowl, whisk together the arrowroot powder and ¾ cup water until smooth.

In a medium saucepan, combine the coconut milk, sugar, and vanilla. Bring to a boil over medium-high heat. Stir the arrowroot mixture in its bowl to recombine, then add it to the saucepan in a slow and steady stream, while whisking constantly. After all of it has been added, reduce the heat to medium-low and simmer, whisking constantly, until the mixture is thick and looks slightly pearlescent, 6 to 8 minutes.

Pour the haupia into the prepared pan and let cool to room temperature before refrigerating to chill and firm up, at least 2 hours.

When ready to serve, slice into 2-inch squares and top with a few spoonfuls of passion fruit curd. Garnish with toasted coconut (if using) and a sprinkle of salt.

PASSION FRUIT CURD

MAKES ABOUT 1½ CUPS

1 cup passion fruit juice or
    puree
¼ cup sugar, or more to taste
4 large egg yolks
Kosher salt
6 tablespoons (¾ stick) cold
    unsalted butter, cut into
    pieces

Create a double boiler: Fill a
medium pot with a few inches
of water and bring to a simmer
over medium heat. Set a glass or
metal (nonaluminum) bowl big
enough to cover the mouth of
the pot. Add the passion fruit,
sugar, egg yolks, and a pinch
of salt, whisking constantly
until the sugar is dissolved.
Add the butter a piece at a time,
whisking until each is melted.
Continue whisking until the
curd reaches 160°F on an instant-
read thermometer and thickens
enough to coat the back of a
spoon (the whisk will begin to
leave lines in the curd that take a
moment to fill back in). This takes
about 12 minutes. Don't overcook
it, or the eggs will curdle. Remove
the bowl from the heat and cover
with plastic wrap, pressing it
against the curd to prevent a
skin from forming. Refrigerate
until chilled and fully set, at least
1 hour, before using.

CONDENSED MILK CHEESECAKE WITH OVALTINE CRUST

SERVES 8 TO 12

When we were coming up with the dessert menu at Migrant, the idea was to take things you'd find at resort restaurants and remake them local style. For classic cheesecake, we incorporated three ingredients that our *tutus* (grandmas) would always have in the cupboard: condensed milk, Nilla wafers, and rich chocolate Ovaltine.

Despite the decadence of condensed milk, this no-fuss cheesecake comes out very light and fluffy, a miracle of baking science I will likely never fully understand. Dusting the finished product with extra Ovaltine makes it resemble an upscale tiramisu—no one will guess the powder is actually the stuff they drank as kids to get their vitamins.

Butter, for greasing
1¼ cups finely crushed vanilla wafers or any cookie crumbs
½ cup Ovaltine powder, plus 2 tablespoons for garnish
8 tablespoons (1 stick) unsalted butter, melted
Kosher salt
3 tablespoons sugar
16 ounces cream cheese, at room temperature
½ cup sour cream
1 (13.5-ounce) can sweetened condensed milk
3 large eggs
2 tablespoons fresh lemon juice

Preheat the oven to 325°F. Grease a 9-inch pie plate or springform pan with butter.

In a large bowl, stir together the cookie crumbs, ½ cup of the Ovaltine, the melted butter, and a pinch of salt until moist crumbs form. Transfer to the greased pan and press evenly into the bottom and up the sides. Bake the crust until lightly browned, about 10 minutes. Remove and let cool. Leave the oven on.

While the crust is baking, in a bowl, with an electric mixer, mix together the cream cheese and sour cream until fluffy and smooth. Gradually fold in the condensed milk, stirring until incorporated, followed by the eggs and lemon juice. Pour the mixture into the prepared crust.

Return to the oven and bake until the center is set, 50 to 55 minutes. Test by poking it with a toothpick or a paring knife; if it comes out clean, it's done. Remove the cake from the oven and let cool for 1 hour, or longer in the refrigerator if preferred.

Dust with the remaining 2 tablespoons Ovaltine before slicing and serving.

FILIPINO CEREAL

SERVES 6

I used to joke that since I grew up eating Saimin (page 190) for breakfast, I didn't know what milk and cereal was until I moved out of my parents' house. At Lineage, that joke slowly turned into a question: What would a bowl of cereal look like in a Filipino household? The answer came to me when I thought about the sliced avocados we used to eat with milk and sugar, and the hardtack crackers my dad and uncles would eat with their black coffee, a real working man's breakfast.

The result was a not-too-sweet dessert with a lot of layers to it, so to speak: creamy cracker-flavored panna cotta topped with candied crackers, vanilla milk, and diced avocado. At the restaurant we served each bowl with a giant spoon, which made eating it feel like childhood and helped you get all the different textures in one bite.

A note on the crackers: I use two kinds from local brand Diamond Bakery. There's the slightly sweet Royal Creem crackers, which can be replaced by any vanilla cookie, and Saloon Pilot crackers (a style of hardtack biscuit introduced to the islands by nineteenth-century sailors), which can be replaced by low-sodium saltines.

PANNA COTTA

1 (¼-ounce) envelope unflavored gelatin
⅓ cup whole milk
2½ cups heavy cream
½ cup granulated sugar
8 Diamond Bakery Royal Creem Crackers, or vanilla sandwich cookies (filling removed), crushed

PILOT CRACKER CRUMBLE

3 tablespoons light brown sugar
2 sticks (8 ounces) salted butter, at room temperature

10 Saloon Pilot crackers, or 40 low-sodium saltines, crushed into cornflake-size pieces (about 3 cups)

SWEET MILK

2 cups whole milk
1½ tablespoons granulated sugar
1 teaspoon vanilla extract

FOR ASSEMBLY

2 medium avocados, diced
Turbinado sugar
Flaky sea salt

For the panna cotta: In a small bowl, sprinkle the gelatin evenly over 2 tablespoons water. Set aside. In a small saucepan, combine the milk, heavy cream, and granulated sugar and bring to a boil. Stir in the bloomed gelatin and continue boiling for about 30 seconds, stirring constantly. Stir in the crushed crackers and remove from the heat. Let steep for 10 to 15 minutes while the panna cotta mixture cools. Pour the mixture into a sieve set over a bowl, using a spoon to press out as much liquid as possible. Divide the liquid among 6 bowls or cups (between ⅔ and ¾ cup of mixture per bowl), being sure to leave room for the garnishes at the end. Transfer the bowls to the fridge and refrigerate for at least 4 hours, or overnight, until firm.

For the pilot cracker crumble: Preheat the oven to 350°F. Line a sheet pan with parchment paper.

In a small microwave-safe bowl, combine the brown sugar and butter and microwave for 30 to 45 seconds, stirring until the butter has melted into the sugar. In a medium bowl, toss the crushed crackers with the butter/brown sugar mixture until coated evenly.

Spread the cracker mixture onto the lined sheet pan. Bake until the crackers are golden brown and the sugar has caramelized, 10 to 12 minutes, stirring once. Remove from the oven and let cool.

For the sweet milk: In a bowl, whisk together the milk, granulated sugar, and vanilla until the sugar is dissolved.

To assemble: Top each panna cotta with an equal amount of avocado, then about ½ cup of the cracker crumble. Sprinkle a pinch of turbinado sugar and flaky sea salt over each. When ready to serve, pour about ⅓ cup of sweet milk over the top and eat with a big spoon.

CHOCOLATE BIRTHDAY CAKE BUTTER MOCHI

SERVES 12

Butter mochi is the best. The perfect mixture of chewy, squishy, dense, and sticky, these coconut and rice flour cake bars (a cousin of Filipino bibingka) are one of the most beloved island desserts out there.

Plain old butter mochi is great, but the kind we do at Tin Roof—developed after many hours of "research"—is on another level. Stoner food to the max. We start with chocolate butter mochi, which has the texture of soft-baked brownies, then spread it with a dead simple frosting made from creamy peanut butter, raw sugar, and Pop Rocks. And finally we shower the top with rainbow sprinkles because it's like throwing yourself a mini birthday party. What more could you want?

BUTTER MOCHI

12 tablespoons (1½ sticks) salted butter, cut into chunks, plus more for greasing

1 cup semisweet chocolate chips

2 cups granulated sugar

3 large eggs

2 teaspoons vanilla extract

1 (12-ounce) can evaporated milk

1 (13.5-ounce) can full-fat coconut milk

3 cups mochiko (sweet rice flour)

1 tablespoon baking powder

¼ cup unsweetened cocoa powder

FROSTING AND TOPPING

1 cup creamy peanut butter

1 cup demerara or turbinado sugar

¼ cup Pop Rocks candy (optional)

Rainbow sprinkles

For the butter mochi: Preheat the oven to 350°F. Grease a 9 × 13-inch baking pan.

In a microwave-safe medium bowl, melt the butter and chocolate chips by microwaving in 30-second increments, stirring and repeating as needed, until just melted.

Add the granulated sugar to the melted chocolate and stir until combined. Add the eggs, one at a time, mixing well after each addition. Stir in the vanilla, evaporated milk, and coconut milk.

In a large bowl, stir together the mochiko, baking powder, and cocoa powder until evenly distributed. Fold the chocolate mixture into the dry ingredients, stirring until thoroughly mixed. When the batter is totally smooth, pour it into the prepared pan.

Bake until a toothpick inserted in the center comes out clean, about 1 hour. Let cool slightly.

Meanwhile, for the frosting: In a bowl, with an electric mixer, vigorously whip together the peanut butter and demerara sugar until it has the texture of frosting.

When the butter mochi is still slightly warm, spread the frosting evenly over the top. Sprinkle with Pop Rocks (if using) and shower sprinkles over the top. Let cool to room temperature, then cut into 2-inch-ish squares and serve.

GURI GURI

SERVES 8 TO 12

Given our tropical climate, it's no surprise Hawai'i has an affinity for icy desserts. The most famous one is shave ice, a fluffy style of snow cone descended from Japanese *kakigōri*. But there's also the humbler ice cake, a no-frills treat made with syrup and evaporated milk frozen in a paper cup. A slightly more luxurious version of ice cake is called *guri guri*, a creamy sherbet made famous by the legendary shop Tasaka Guri-Guri in Kahului. The Tasaka 'ohana recipe is a closely guarded secret, but I feel I've done a serviceable job with my own version, which combines bubbly fruit soda with fruit nectar and two kinds of canned milk. Garnish with a handful of puffed rice for crunch, if you like.

1 (13.5-ounce) can sweetened condensed milk
⅔ cup evaporated milk
1 (12-ounce) can strawberry-guava nectar, or your favorite fruit nectar
1 (12-ounce) can strawberry or orange soda
1 (12-ounce) can lemon-lime soda
Puffed rice cereal, for garnish

In a large bowl, stir together the condensed milk, evaporated milk, and fruit nectar until combined. Gradually pour in the soda one can at a time, gently stirring, preserving as much carbonation as possible. Transfer the mixture to a shallow freezer-proof container or individual paper cups. Cover and freeze until firm, 3 to 4 hours total, removing the guri-guri from the freezer every hour to stir and break up the ice crystals. Garnish with puffed rice before serving.

POG

MAKES 2 QUARTS

Maybe you've heard of POG, also known as passion orange guava juice? A simple blend of three fruit juices—originally sold by Maui's Haleakala Dairy in 1971—POG is a tasty orange-pinkish beverage that is pretty ubiquitous here in Hawai'i. They even serve it on Hawaiian Airlines flights.

Though you can find POG in cartons at the grocery store, the kind I drank back in small kid time was either Aloha Maid or Hawaiian Sun, two canned "juice" brands that you'll find sold in just about every local market and lunch shop. I put juice in quotes because, well, POG is usually around 10 percent fruit juice, making it more like a soft drink. That said, it is delicious and tropically refreshing! As a kid, a day at the beach wouldn't be the same without an ice-cold can from the cooler.

There's a fair chance you can find POG at your local supermarket, but if not, I invite you to make a batch yourself, since all it requires is three ingredients in the proper ratio. Also, it's amazing with rum. POG is meant to be fruity, tangy, and sugary, but I've toned down the sweetness slightly for this recipe. Feel free to add more or less water to suit your taste.

3¼ cups guava nectar
2¾ cups passion fruit (liliko'i) juice or nectar
1½ cups fresh orange juice (no pulp)

In a large pitcher or bowl, combine the guava nectar, passion fruit juice, orange juice, and ½ cup cold water and stir to combine. Serve extremely chilled.

NOTE: *If you can't find passion fruit juice or nectar, substitute with equal parts limeade and pineapple juice.*

TROPICAL FRUIT BREAD

MAKES 1 LOAF

Mango season. Guava season. The mention of these words can strike terror into people who have these trees in their backyards, At first it's great—free fruit!—but soon you're overwhelmed with so much ripeness you can barely keep up.

That's where this succulent, extra-moist fruit bread comes in, the best use for mushy, overripe mangoes, guavas, and bananas (a lot of bananas grow here, too).

Fruit breads are a popular gift on the islands, often swapped between families or sold at roadside stands. Here everyone has their own hand-me-down recipe, maybe scribbled on an old index card or clipped from the local newspaper. This one is of my own design—engineered for maximum tenderness (the secret is cornstarch) and topped with a sweet coconut crumble. You don't have to use all three fruits, just make sure that whatever combination you use adds up to the total amount.

CRUMB TOPPING

3 tablespoons light brown sugar
2 tablespoons all-purpose flour
2 tablespoons unsweetened grated coconut
2 tablespoons unsalted butter, chilled

TROPICAL FRUIT BREAD

Butter and flour, for the pan
2 cups all-purpose flour
¼ cup cornstarch
1 teaspoon baking powder
1 teaspoon baking soda
1 teaspoon ground cinnamon
½ teaspoon Diamond Crystal (or ¼ teaspoon Morton) kosher salt
8 tablespoons (1 stick) unsalted butter, at room temperature
¾ cup granulated sugar
2 large eggs
1 teaspoon vanilla extract
1 cup mashed ripe banana (2 to 3 bananas)
1 cup mashed ripe mango (about 1 mango)
½ cup guava pulp or puree (see Note)

For the crumb topping: In a small bowl, use a fork to combine the brown sugar, flour, and coconut. Add the butter in chunks and mix with the back of a fork or fingertips until coarse crumbs are formed.

For the fruit bread: Adjust an oven rack to the middle of the oven and preheat to 350°F. Butter and flour a 9 × 5-inch loaf pan, tapping out the excess flour.

In a medium bowl, sift together the flour, cornstarch, baking powder, baking soda, cinnamon, and salt.

In a large bowl, with an electric mixer, cream together the butter and granulated sugar until light and fluffy. Beat in the eggs and vanilla. Once combined, add the banana, mango, and guava, one at a time, mixing after each addition. Using a spatula or wooden spoon, fold in the flour mixture until just incorporated. The batter should be thick but smooth. Don't overstir.

Transfer the batter to the prepared loaf pan and sprinkle with the crumb topping. Place the pan on a rack toward the rear of the oven and bake for 30 minutes, then rotate the pan 180 degrees. Continue baking for another 30 to 35 minutes, or until a toothpick inserted in the center comes out clean and the edges of the loaf pull away from the pan.

Let the bread cool in the pan on a wire rack for at least 30 minutes. Invert the bread onto the wire rack to cool completely. To store, wrap tightly in plastic wrap.

NOTE: *If using fresh guavas, peel and blend the fruit to make a puree, then strain out the seeds. Otherwise, look for store-bought guava puree, which can be found in the frozen section and is sometimes labeled guava pulp.*

PRUNE MUI

MAKES 6 CUPS

How to describe prune mui? The four S's: sweet, sour, salty, and sticky. Even though locals refer to it as "prune" mui (*mui* means preserved fruit in Chinese), it's actually made with a medley of dried fruits soaked in a mixture of lemon juice, sugar, spices, spirits, rock salt, and li hing mui powder (see page 291).

Prune mui is like the Hawaiian equivalent of fruit cake, only people actually enjoy eating it. During the holiday season, jars of prune mui are everywhere, passed around as gifts and shared with friends. Every tutu and auntie has her own recipe. There was always a batch in our family fridge, though I was never quite sure where it came from; it seemed like whenever the jar got low it was refilled by magic. These days I eat prune mui as a post-dinner snack, maybe paired with a nice glass of whiskey on ice.

Prunes and apricots are the most commonly used dried fruits, but you can also use cherries, cranberries, raisins, etc. Just remember the fruit needs to soak for at least 3 days before it reaches the right consistency, so plan ahead.

3 ounces fresh lemon juice
1 cup firmly packed dark brown sugar
3 whole cloves
1 teaspoon Chinese five-spice powder
2 teaspoons whiskey
1 tablespoon Hawaiian salt or Diamond Crystal kosher salt
21 ounces pitted prunes
12 ounces dried apricots
1½ ounces sweet red li hing mui (see page 291), or li hing mui powder, to taste
½ cup roughly diced Roof Lemons (page 275) or Quick-Salted Lemon Peel
   (page 277), rinsed

In a large bowl, whisk together the lemon juice, brown sugar, cloves, five-spice powder, whiskey, and Hawaiian salt. Don't worry about getting everything dissolved.

Roughly dice one-third of the prunes and leave the others whole. Add the prunes, apricots, li hing mui, and preserved lemons to the bowl with the lemon juice mixture and mix well. Transfer to jars or zip-top plastic bags and let cure at room temperature for a minimum of 3 or 4 days, shaking them once or twice per day. Once the liquid turns from opaque to clear, it means the fruit has absorbed the spices. But the flavor only improves the longer it sits.

LI HING MUI PALOMAS

SERVES 4

One tip for any aspiring restaurant owners out there: Always get to know your liquor distributor. It was my buddy Keli'i, a professional booze supplier that I've worked with for years, who turned me on to the Paloma, a tangy grapefruit and tequila cocktail that has become my favorite mixed drink.

I realize that if you live on the mainland, Palomas aren't exactly groundbreaking, but here in Hawai'i we like to add li hing mui (salted sour plums) that are a spot-on match for the tart and sweet flavor of the cocktail. Made with a nice bottle of tequila (mahalos, Keli'i), the flavor combination creates a thirst-quenching beverage that is dangerously easy to drink. Or to put it another way: First sip, you fall in love. Last sip, you fall down.

1 cup tequila reposado
16 sweet red li hing mui (see page 291)
Hawaiian salt, for garnish
2 (12-ounce) cans grapefruit soda
2 small limes, halved

In a jar, combine the tequila and li hing mui and let soak for at least 1 hour in the fridge (overnight is best).

Wet the rims of 4 Collins glasses and dip them in Hawaiian salt. Fill the glasses with ice and divide the tequila and the li hing mui among them. Top each drink with grapefruit soda (about half a can) and squeeze half a lime over the top. Stir, drink, repeat.

NOTE: *The best way to make this drink is to infuse the tequila overnight, but if you're pressed for time you can place the li hing mui and tequila in a jar and shake vigorously for a few minutes, or until the dried plums look slightly hydrated.*

PORTUGUESE SWEET ROLLS

MAKES 16 ROLLS

Thanks to the popularity of King's Hawaiian Bakery (founded in Hilo back in 1950), most people on the mainland tend to associate Hawai'i with this style of slightly sweet, fluffy bread—based on Portuguese *pão doce*.

Though a majority of locals buy their sweet rolls from a grocery store or bakery these days, there is still a proud tradition of Portuguese grandmas baking their weekly loaf from scratch. Soft as clouds and fluffy as spun cotton, this bread is amazing eaten hot from the oven, spread with butter and guava jelly, or served with a bowl of Portuguese Bean Soup (page 144). Mini sandwiches made with sliced Spam, mustard, and mayo aren't a bad idea either.

½ cup milk

4½ teaspoons active dry yeast (2 packages)

½ cup sugar

1 cup evaporated milk or half-and-half

5 tablespoons salted butter, at room temperature, plus more for greasing and for serving

4 large eggs

1 teaspoon grated lemon zest

Pinch of nutmeg

3½ cups bread flour, plus more for the work surface

¼ cup instant mashed potato flakes

1 teaspoon Diamond Crystal (or ½ teaspoon Morton) kosher salt

In a small saucepan or in the microwave, gently warm the milk until it's 100° to 110°F. (If you overwarm it, let it cool to this range.)

In a large bowl, whisk together the warmed milk, yeast, and 1 teaspoon of the sugar. Let the mixture sit until the yeast has bloomed and tiny bubbles form, about 10 minutes.

Add the evaporated milk, the rest of the sugar, the butter, 3 of the eggs, the lemon zest, and nutmeg. Separate the remaining egg and add the yolk to the bowl. Set the white aside. Stir the milk and egg mixture until thoroughly combined.

In a medium bowl, combine the flour, potato flakes, and salt and pour this into the liquid ingredients. Mix with a spatula until a cohesive dough forms. It'll be soft and sticky at first.

Dust a work surface with flour and turn the dough onto it. Knead until smooth and elastic, 6 to 8 minutes. Grease a bowl and place the dough in it, turning once to coat the top. Cover and let rise in a warm place until doubled, about 1½ hours.

Butter a 9 × 13-inch baking pan. Gently punch down to deflate the dough and tip it onto a work surface. Divide the dough into 16 equal pieces, rolling each piece into a ball and placing it in the prepared pan. Cover the pan lightly with plastic wrap and set aside to double again, about 1 hour, until the rolls are nearly peeking out of the baking pan.

Near the end of the rising time, preheat the oven to 350°F. Mix the reserved egg white with 1 tablespoon cold water and brush some onto the surface of the rolls; this will give them a glossy sheen.

Bake the rolls until puffy and golden, 20 to 25 minutes. Remove the rolls from the oven and let cool slightly, then turn them out onto a wire rack.

Brush the tops with salted butter and serve warm. Leftovers can be stored in a sealable container at room temperature for several days, or frozen for longer storage.

MALASADAS
MAKES 16 DOUGHNUTS

Every island has its own famous spot for *malasadas*, puffy, pillowy Portuguese doughnuts rolled in sugar and more often than not filled with pastry cream, custard, or jam. There's Komoda Store on Maui, Tex Drive-In on the Big Island, and the legendary Leonard's Bakery on Oahu.

Though not as easy as strolling to the closest bakery, frying your own malasadas at home is worth it, especially because you can eat them as soon as they emerge from the hot oil, when they are at their absolute summit of deliciousness. For simplicity's sake, I've based this recipe on the dough used for Portuguese sweet rolls, since both pastries draw from the same background.

1 batch dough from Portuguese Sweet Rolls (page 256)
Butter or oil, for greasing
Neutral oil, for deep-frying
Sugar, for dusting
Optional filling: 2 cups jam, jelly, or instant pudding (your favorite flavors)

Prepare the Portuguese sweet roll dough through the first rise. Punch down the dough, divide into 16 equal portions, and flatten each into a round about ¾ inch thick. Place them on a greased sheet pan and cover with plastic wrap or a clean towel. Let rise in a warm place until doubled in size, about 1 hour. The dough should look puffy and spring back quickly when pressed.

Set a wire rack in a sheet pan. Fill a large, heavy-bottomed pot or Dutch oven with at least 2 inches of oil, making sure to leave a few inches of clearance from the top of the pot. Heat over medium-high heat until the oil reaches 350°F (use a thermometer), adjusting the heat as needed to maintain temperature.

Dip your fingers in softened butter or oil to keep the raw dough from sticking, or grease the business end of a pair of tongs. Working in batches, fry the malasadas for about 3 minutes on each side, flipping once, until golden brown. Transfer to the wire rack and let cool slightly.

Meanwhile, pour the sugar in a shallow bowl.

Once the malasadas are cool enough to handle, toss in the sugar. If filling the doughnuts, spoon the filling into a pastry bag with a medium tip or a zip-top plastic bag with one corner cut off. Use a paring knife to cut a slit into the middle of each malasada. Pipe about 2 tablespoons of filling into each, refilling the bag as necessary.

Serve the malasadas immediately; eating them warm is essential.

ODDS AND ENDS

Preservation plays an important, if undersung, role in the kitchens of Hawai'i. The home cooks I looked up to were the ones who always had a stash of empty jars and bottles in their pantry or garage, ready to preserve whatever edible windfall came their way . Empty mayo jars were our mason jars. If someone's auntie was making a batch of prune mui or pickled onions, you might say to them, *Eh, save me one mayo jar*. But those important condiments were often the ones taken for granted until the family member who made them passed on—Grandpa's chili pepper water, Mama's kim chee, Uncle's takuan. What was that recipe again?

In this chapter, you'll find different kinds of pickles, seasonings, oils, and sauces, all of which can be made well ahead of time, then mixed and matched with proteins, vegetables, or rice to round out a meal or transform a humdrum dish into something special. Each immigrant culture in Hawai'i has at least a few in their repertoire. Flavor boosters like crunchy furikake or fried garlic can be used as savory toppings. Lemon oil adds vibrancy and silkiness when drizzled over finished dishes. I've even included instructions for char siu and Portuguese sausage, two cherished meats that can be made ahead of time, refrigerated or frozen, then used to bulk up fried rice or noodles on the fly. Master these recipes, and you'll never be without the necessary tools to cobble together a delicious meal.

FURIKAKE

MAKES ABOUT ¼ CUP

My theory is that everyone who grew up in Hawai'i had a phase when they *really* got into putting furikake on everything. Salty, sweet, crunchy, loaded with umami—add this flavorful Japanese dry seasoning to almost anything and it will taste good (I've thoroughly tested this theory). Rice, vegetables, and fish are the most obvious candidates, but salty snacks like popcorn (see Hurricane Popcorn, page 40) and crackers, or even desserts like ice cream and cookies, are delicious topped with a sprinkle.

There are many variations of furikake out there, but in its most basic state it's this: shredded dried seaweed, sesame seeds, salt, and sugar. Dried shaved fish (*katsuobushi*) is often added to the mix as well.

At Tin Roof, putting furikake on our rice bowls was a given. But over time our restless spirits started to get creative by mixing new ingredients into the classic formula, like dehydrated vegetables, crushed chips, fried garlic, cheese powder, chili flakes, etc. Everything was fair game. We sold packets of this daily seasoning in tiny zip-top plastic bags. Thus, the dime bag was born—the ultimate seasoning for ultimate grinds.

Below is a basic recipe in case you can't find furikake in stores. However, the easiest route is to buy a container of furikake in the Asian food section of the grocery store and then spice it up with whatever mix-ins capture your imagination (suggestions at right). I prefer the kinds labeled Nori Fumi, Nori Komi, or Aji Nori Furikake (any brand), which are simple seaweed-and-sesame varieties that lend themselves well to modifications.

⅔ cup sesame seeds

3 sheets unseasoned nori (dried seaweed), about ¼ ounce

2 tablespoons dried bonito flakes

2 teaspoons sugar

2 teaspoons Diamond Crystal (or 1½ teaspoons Morton) kosher salt

In a dry pan or skillet, toast the sesame seeds over medium heat until lightly toasted, about 2 minutes, stirring often. (If your seeds are sold roasted, skip this step.) Transfer to a small bowl and let cool completely.

If the nori sheets are not crisp enough to crumble easily, carefully toast them by waving them over a gas flame or placing under a broiler for a few seconds.

In a food processor, combine the sesame seeds, nori, bonito flakes, sugar, and salt. Pulse 8 to 10 times or until mixture is well blended. Store in a sealable container in a cool, dry place for up to 1 month.

O.G. DIME BAG

MAKES 4 BAGS

¼ cup Furikake (recipe at left)

2 tablespoons plus 2 teaspoons crushed arare (rice crackers) or Funyuns

1 tablespoon plus 1 teaspoon Fried Garlic (page 283)

In a bowl, mix everything together until combined. Portion out 2 tablespoons into small plastic baggies or bundles of wax paper tied with string. Distribute as necessary.

FURIKAKE MIX-INS (ADD TO TASTE)

Togarashi spice

Wasabi powder

Kochugaru (Korean chili flakes)

Crushed arare (rice crackers)

Crushed potato chips

Crushed corn chips

Crushed corn nuts

Dehydrated kale

Dried onion flakes

Citric acid

Dried shrimp (ebi) powder

Mac and cheese powder

Li hing mui powder

CHILI PEPPER WATER

One of the signature table condiments for local cuisine, chili pepper water is a tangy, thinned-out hot sauce that gets splashed on everything except dessert. Most fridges in Hawai'i have at least one bottle hanging out in the back, and down-home restaurants all have their own special recipe.

The most basic style of chili pepper water—which is how native Hawaiians originally prepared it when the chili pepper was first introduced to the islands in the early 1800s—is a blend of water, salt, and the fiery so-called Hawaiian chili pepper, also known as 'nioi. It's small and skinny (about 2 inches or so in length) and bright red when ripe. Mixing it with salt water works as a seasoning and a preservative, so the flavor of the chilies develops over time as they slowly ferment. But there isn't one monolithic recipe, per se. As immigrant groups arrived, they brought seasonings with them and made chili pepper water their own. Portuguese and Filipinos contributed garlic, vinegar, bay leaves, and fish sauce. Japanese and Chinese brought shoyu and ginger. All of those influences mixed together and you ended up with what you have today, with each household developing their own blend.

I like to describe chili pepper water as somewhere between a condiment and a pickleback. It can be splashed onto foods at the table or sipped between bites of hearty dishes like beef stew or laulau. Either way, the sharp, spicy flavor slices through richness like a machete. In the Simeon household, my dad and uncles would pass around homemade chili pepper water in mismatched old whiskey bottles, pouring themselves glugs in little cups and taking shots throughout the meal.

The recipes that follow reflect two different styles of this versatile condiment-slash-chaser. One uses just a handful of ingredients—white vinegar, chilies, salt, and garlic—to deliver sharp flavor and spice. The other, which is more like my family's recipe, uses sweeter and tangier apple cider vinegar along with shoyu and fish sauce.

You can swap Hawaiian chili peppers for any hot red chili, but pequín and Thai bird's eye chilies bring a fair bit of heat. For a milder flavor, use finely chopped red jalapeños or red serrano peppers. Fun fact: The closest relative of the Hawaiian chili pepper is the Tabasco pepper, which might explain why locals also really love putting Tabasco sauce on their food.

BASIC CHILI PEPPER WATER

MAKES ABOUT 2½ CUPS

¼ cup distilled white vinegar
4 cloves garlic, crushed and peeled
8 Hawaiian or 4 bird's eye chilies, thinly sliced
2 teaspoons coarse Hawaiian sea salt or Diamond Crystal kosher salt

In a clean heatproof jar or sealable container, combine the vinegar, garlic, and chilies. In a small saucepan, bring the salt and 2 cups water to a boil over high heat. Pour over the ingredients and let the jar cool to room temperature. Taste and adjust the salt if needed. Chill in the fridge for at least a day before serving. Keeps in the fridge indefinitely.

SIMEON-STYLE CHILI PEPPER WATER

MAKES ABOUT 3 CUPS

¼ cup apple cider vinegar
2 teaspoons shoyu (soy sauce)
1 teaspoon fish sauce
2 bay leaves
4 cloves garlic, crushed and peeled
8 Hawaiian chili peppers or 4 bird's eye chilies, thinly sliced
2 teaspoons coarse Hawaiian sea salt or Diamond Crystal kosher salt

In a clean heatproof jar or sealable container, combine the vinegar, shoyu, fish sauce, bay leaves, garlic, and chilies. In a small saucepan, bring the salt and 2½ cups water to a boil over high heat. Pour this over the ingredients and let the jar cool to room temperature. Taste and adjust the salt if needed. Chill in the fridge for at least a day before serving. Keeps in the fridge indefinitely.

SALT-PICKLED CABBAGE (KOKO)

MAKES ABOUT 3 CUPS

This simple cabbage dish, which many locals lovingly know by the nickname *koko*, is one of the most basic varieties of *tsukemono* (Japanese pickles). It doesn't involve fermentation and requires only a small amount of seasoning and an hour or so to prepare.

After being tossed with salt, the cabbage is pressed down under a weight, which helps (along with the salt) in drawing out tasteless water. Once "pickled" this way, the vegetable develops a refreshing taste and a squeaky crunch.

We serve a side of koko with most rice bowls at Tin Roof, since its salty snap is a nice minimalist contrast to the big and bold flavors found in dishes like Chop Steak (page 111), Garlic Shrimp (page 106), and Mochiko Fried Chicken (page 112).

You can scale this recipe up or down, depending on your needs. If you have a kitchen scale and a calculator, a general rule of thumb is to use 3% of the cabbage's weight in salt. And since koko is so easy to prepare, you can start making it before you start cooking; that way it will be ready to eat when the main event is finished.

1 pound green or napa cabbage

1 tablespoon Diamond Crystal (or 2 teaspoons Morton) kosher salt, plus more as needed

¼ teaspoon instant dashi powder (such as HonDashi), optional

Core the cabbage and cut into 2-inch squares, breaking the layers apart. Place the cabbage in a large bowl and sprinkle with the salt, using a spatula or your hands to distribute the salt evenly and massage it into the leaves.

Use an inverted plate to cover and press the cabbage and place a heavy object on top, like a tin can or large stone. Let sit at room temperature for 1 hour. Remove the weight and toss the cabbage. If there are parts of cabbage that haven't turned slightly translucent, sprinkle them with a little more salt and toss again. Replace the weight and let sit for another 30 minutes.

Remove the cabbage from the bowl and place in a colander over the sink. Use your hands to squeeze out as much moisture as possible. Don't rinse it! Once the cabbage has been squeezed, sprinkle on the dashi powder (if using) and toss to coat. Chill until ready to serve. Keeps for about 1 week in the fridge.

PORTUGUESE PICKLED ONIONS

MAKES ABOUT 4 CUPS

Technically called *sabula de vinha,* this recipe is known by most locals simply as Portuguese pickled onions, a reference to the brine flavored with classic "Pocho" spices like cloves, peppercorns, and bay leaves. Vinegary with a touch of sweetness and heat, this is a great all-purpose pickle that is often eaten as a drinking snack.

3 medium sweet onions (about 1½ pounds), peeled and each cut into 8 wedges
1 medium green bell pepper, cut into strips
½ teaspoon black peppercorns
½ teaspoon whole cloves
2 bay leaves
4 cloves garlic, crushed and peeled
3 Hawaiian chili peppers, thinly sliced, or a large pinch of red chili flakes
½ cup distilled white vinegar
½ cup apple cider vinegar
½ cup sugar
1 tablespoon Diamond Crystal (or 2 teaspoons Morton) kosher salt

Wash and sterilize a 2-quart canning jar or nonreactive heatproof container big enough to fit all the onions and bell pepper. Add the peppercorns, cloves, bay leaves, garlic, and chilies to the jar, then alternate with layers of onion and bell pepper.

In a small saucepan, combine both vinegars, the sugar, salt, and 1 cup water and bring to a boil, stirring until the sugar and salt are dissolved. Remove from the heat and pour over the onions. Cover the jar tightly. Let sit at room temperature for 24 hours, then store in the refrigerator. Keeps in the fridge for up to 1 month.

TAKUAN

MAKES ABOUT 1 QUART

One of the more popular tsukemono on Hawai'i, *takuan* is a crunchy pickled daikon identifiable by its highlighter-yellow color. Slices of takuan are often tucked into bento boxes, or served with savory dishes like nori chicken or teriyaki beef. Raw daikon has a sharp, spicy flavor that mellows with vinegar and sugar, producing a sweet-salty pickle that is very balanced. Here I use turmeric for earthiness and color, but if you want the dramatic bright yellow hue found in store-bought brands, you can add a drop or two of yellow food coloring.

1 large or 2 small daikon radishes (about 2 pounds total), peeled
¼ cup Diamond Crystal (or 3 tablespoons Morton) kosher salt
1 cup sugar
¾ cup rice vinegar
¼ teaspoon ground turmeric
2 Hawaiian chili peppers, thinly sliced (optional)

Halve the daikon lengthwise, then cut crosswise into ½-inch-thick slices. Place the daikon in a colander and toss with the salt. Let sit for 2 hours at room temperature to draw out excess moisture.

Meanwhile, in a saucepan, combine the sugar, vinegar, ¼ cup water, turmeric, and chilies (if using) and bring to a boil. Remove from the heat and let cool to room temperature.

Rinse the salt-cured daikon with water and squeeze dry, then pack into a 1-quart jar. Pour the cooled liquid over the top and store in the fridge for at least 2 days before eating. The flavor will continue to develop as the daikon sits. It will keep, refrigerated, for about 1 month.

BRASSICA KIM CHEE

MAKES ABOUT 2 QUARTS

Facts: You can kim chee just about anything. Hawai'i takes that lesson to heart, as the kim chees we eat here go far beyond the standard cabbage/daikon/cucumber triad. At Lineage, we often made kim chee out of whatever local produce came through our door, from pineapple to shiso leaves. A clear winner of the bunch was this kim chee made with cauliflower and Brussels sprouts, two vegetables that absorb the flavor of the marinade nicely while maintaining a crisp bite. Use as you would any other kim chee, eaten as a side dish or chopped up and added to fried rice.

1 pound Brussels sprouts, trimmed and quartered
1 pound cauliflower (about 1 medium head), cut into bite-size florets
¼ cup Diamond Crystal (or 2½ tablespoons Morton) kosher salt
¼ cup kochugaru (Korean chili flakes)
¼ cup mochiko (sweet rice flour) or all-purpose flour
3 tablespoons fish sauce
3-inch piece fresh ginger, peeled and thinly sliced
8 cloves garlic, crushed and peeled
4 scallions, roughly chopped
1 small Fuji apple, sliced into wedges

In a large bowl, toss the sprouts and cauliflower with the salt. Let sit at room temperature for 1 hour, tossing frequently.

Meanwhile, to make the kim chee paste, in a food processor or blender, combine the kochugaru, mochiko, fish sauce, ginger, garlic, scallions, and apple and puree until a smooth paste forms, adding a few teaspoons of water if needed.

Once the sprouts and cauliflower have finished curing, drain the vegetables in a colander (rinse out the bowl). Rinse the vegetables thoroughly and gently press out any remaining water.

Add the kim chee paste to the drained sprouts and cauliflower and toss until well coated. Transfer to a large jar (or split among several jars), seal, and let sit at room temperature overnight. Refrigerate for 1 to 2 days before serving (the longer it sits, the riper and funkier the kim chee will become). Keeps in the fridge for up to 1 month.

SESAME BEAN SPROUTS

SERVES 4

Referred to as *namul* in Hawai'i, this Korean-style bean sprout salad is a good way to turn a main dish with rice into a well-rounded meal. We blanch the bean sprouts so they retain their crunch, then briefly marinate them in a salty sauce enhanced with nutty sesame oil, pungent garlic, and a hint of vinegar. Though this recipe makes a decent-size batch, you might be surprised how quickly namul disappears at the table. Can always double it!

Kosher salt
1 (12-ounce) package bean sprouts, rinsed
1 tablespoon toasted sesame oil
2 teaspoons shoyu (soy sauce)
1 tablespoon roasted sesame seeds
2 cloves garlic, grated
1 scallion, thinly sliced
2 Hawaiian chili peppers, thinly sliced, or a pinch of kochugaru
  (Korean chili flakes)
1 tablespoon rice vinegar

Bring a pot of well-salted water to a boil. Blanch the bean sprouts for 1 to 2 minutes until slightly wilted, then rinse under cold water. Drain well and squeeze out excess water.

In a medium bowl, whisk together the sesame oil, shoyu, sesame seeds, garlic, scallion, chilies, and vinegar. Add the bean sprouts and toss. Season to taste with kosher salt. Chill before serving; keeps for up to 2 days in the fridge.

CUCUMBER NAMASU

MAKES ABOUT 3 CUPS

Namasu, a simple side dish that involves gently pickling vegetables in sugar and vinegar, is a standard on Japanese tables in Hawai'i. It's sort of like a salad but is generally served condiment-style alongside other dishes and rice. While namasu made with cucumber is the most familiar, you'll also see it made with carrots, radishes, onions, bitter melon, lotus root, and seaweed. Some recipes add shellfish or fish cake as well. The end result is sweet and sour, crunchy and chewy, mouthwatering and refreshing. There's always room for namasu at the potluck.

Similar to koko (page 266) and takuan (page 268), the trick here is to briefly cure the cucumbers and carrots in salt before tossing them in the tangy dressing; this drives out water and turns the veggies snappy and crisp while also seasoning them. Chill down your namasu for at least a couple hours. Mo' bettah cold!

¼ ounce dried wakame (optional; see Note)
2 Japanese cucumbers or 1 large English cucumber or 3 Persian cucumbers
1 medium carrot, peeled, halved lengthwise, and thinly sliced
1½ teaspoons Diamond Crystal (or 1 teaspoon Morton) kosher salt, plus more to taste
⅓ cup rice vinegar
¼ cup sugar
1 teaspoon grated fresh ginger
½ teaspoon instant dashi powder (such as HonDashi) or 1 teaspoon shoyu (soy sauce)
1 Hawaiian chili pepper, thinly sliced (optional)
Roasted sesame seeds, for serving

Place the dried wakame in a bowl and cover with cool water. Let sit for 5 to 10 minutes, until the seaweed is tender, then drain well and roughly chop.

Peel a few strips of skin from the cucumbers, then slice them in half lengthwise. Using a spoon, gently scrape out the seeds, then slice them diagonally, about ⅛ inch thick. Place the cucumbers and sliced carrot in a bowl and toss with the salt. Let sit at room temperature for 15 minutes (don't let them sit too long or they'll lose their crunch).

In a small bowl, whisk together the vinegar, sugar, ginger, dashi powder, and chili pepper until the sugar has dissolved.

Drain the salted vegetables and place them in a piece of cheesecloth or paper towels, squeezing to remove the excess liquid (try not to squish the cucumbers too much).

In a medium bowl, combine the vegetables, seaweed, and dressing. Season with salt, if needed; the tanginess-sweetness-saltiness should taste balanced. Chill in the fridge for at least 2 hours before serving. Sprinkle with sesame seeds when ready to eat. Keeps in the fridge for up to 1 week.

NOTE: *Wakame, a mild-flavored, leaf-shaped seaweed often used in Japanese salads and miso soup, can be found at most Asian markets in the dried seaweed section.*

HILO X.O.

MAKES ABOUT 2 CUPS

At Lineage, we made our own X.O.-style sauce—a spicy flavor-bomb condiment traditionally flavored with Chinese smoked ham and dried seafood. Rather than a standardized recipe, our cooks often used whatever bits and pieces were around that day, and it always included some blend of sweet, smoky, salty going on—a balanced approach reflected in the recipe below.

Considering its profound wallop of flavor, a couple spoonfuls go a long way. Use it to season cooked rice or noodles, top roasted vegetables and grilled meats, or dab onto steamed fish or seafood.

3 ounces dried shrimp

3 ounces dried cuttlefish or squid jerky, roughly chopped

2 jalapeños, seeded and roughly chopped

4 cloves garlic, minced

½ medium sweet onion, roughly chopped

2 tablespoons finely chopped fresh lemongrass (cut from the tender center of 1 stalk)

2 small links lap cheong (Chinese sausage; about 3 ounces total), sliced

½ cup neutral oil

¼ cup sambal oelek or Kudeesh Sauce (page 39)

2 tablespoons oyster sauce

1 tablespoon plus 2 teaspoons light brown sugar

2 teaspoons fish sauce

2 tablespoons Cognac or other brandy

½ teaspoon Chinese five-spice powder

1 tablespoon toasted sesame oil

Place the dried shrimp and cuttlefish in a microwave-safe bowl and cover with water. Microwave for 4 minutes, or until the cuttlefish is tender and shreds apart when pinched. Reserving ½ cup of the soaking water, drain and set aside.

In a food processor, combine the jalapeños, garlic, onion, and lemongrass and pulse until a rough paste forms (scrape down the sides of the bowl if necessary). Add the sausage, dried shrimp, and dried cuttlefish and pulse until finely minced.

In a large wok or skillet, heat the neutral oil over medium-high heat until shimmering-hot. Add the onion/shrimp/sausage mixture and stir-fry until it's very fragrant and beginning to crisp, 4 to 5 minutes. Add the sambal, oyster sauce, brown sugar, fish sauce, Cognac, five-spice powder, and sesame oil and continue to stir-fry until the mixture starts to caramelize, 2 to 3 minutes.

Deglaze the pan by stirring in the reserved shrimp soaking water, scraping up any browned bits on the bottom of the pan. Continue cooking until the liquid has mostly evaporated, then remove from the heat. Transfer to a jar or sealable glass container and let cool. Once the mixture has cooled, cover and refrigerate. Store in the refrigerator for up to 1 month. Bring back to room temperature before using.

ROOF LEMONS

MAKES ABOUT 1 GALLON

Salt lemons or wet lemon peel are the preserved lemon of Hawai'i, a spinoff of the traditional Chinese or Japanese method for preserving citrus with boatloads of salt. In my family, we called them roof lemons because once the lemons (or calamansi) were packed with salt in a glass jar, the local *mama-sans* (Japanese grandmothers) would put the jar on their roof or carport to age and preserve in the sun. After six months to a year of exposure to the salt and heat, the lemons shrink into themselves and start to break down, turning a deep brown color as they oxidize. You know you've got a good roof lemon when that buggah is nice and dark and the lid is rusted, a sign it's been curing for a while and has concentrated in flavor. As little jerk kids, my cousins and I would cruise around my grandparents' neighborhood in Pepe'ekeo on our bikes trying to shoot roof lemon jars with slingshots we made from guava tree branches. Lucky for those lemons, we were such bad shots we never hit a single jar!

When making this style of lemon at home, a roof isn't essential. A spot with a good amount of sunlight will do fine. For the first week or so, you'll want to shake the salt and lemons so that they'll give up their juice. Once enough liquid has seeped out to submerge the fruit, you can leave it be. It will probably take a couple months in the sun before the liquid levels start to fall, but that's when you know your lemons are preserved. Brightly flavored and super fragrant (salty sunshine, they call them)—all those weeks of patience will be worth it. The cured lemons can be used in any recipe that benefits from salt and lemon juice: salads, vegetables, seafood, noodles, soups, dips. Just wash off the excess salt and finely chop—flesh, rind, and all.

Or, you can do as locals do and make candied "wet" lemon by adding some brown sugar and whiskey. After a few days the salty-sweet lemons will be ready to eat or use in Prune Mui (page 253). Great snack with cold beer and boiled peanuts.

14 to 16 lemons (about 4 pounds), or enough to fill a one-gallon jar
Boiling water
1 cup Diamond Crystal (or ⅔ cup Morton) kosher salt

Place the lemons in a large bowl and cover with boiling water. Once cooled, scrub them under warm running water and dry well. Slice the lemons in half through the equator; cut large lemons in quarters.

Sprinkle a few tablespoons of the salt in the bottom of a sterilized one-gallon glass jar (the kind with a screw-top lid). Pack the lemons into the jar, alternating with layers of salt, occasionally squishing them down with a wooden spoon or spatula. Sprinkle any remaining salt over the top.

If your jar has a metal lid, place a layer of wax paper or press-and-seal plastic wrap between the jar and the lid to keep it from rusting. Screw the lid on firmly and shake to distribute the salt.

Place the jar in an area with lots of exposure to the sun or natural light, if possible. Shake the jar vigorously a few times a day for the first week or so, until the lemons are nearly submerged in the salty liquid.

(recipe continues)

The lemons will be ready to eat after 1 to 2 months, once the liquid level in the jar starts to drop, but they will be at their peak after 4 to 6 months (or longer), when the lemons have shrunk and concentrated in flavor and the rind is tender to the bite. Depending on the level of sunlight, the lemons will also slowly turn a light brownish color. This is normal and good.

Once you're happy with how long the lemons have aged, they can be stored in a cool, dry place (out of the sunlight) indefinitely. To use, remove a piece of lemon and rinse it. Add the minced rind as a finishing touch when cooking or use raw; the pulp can be added to braises or simmering pots.

WET LEMONS

Roof Lemons (page 275)
2 cups packed light brown sugar
1 shot whiskey (optional)
Chinese five-spice powder (optional)

If you'd like to make salty-sour candied "wet" lemons, drain off the remaining salty liquid from the roof lemons. Rinse the lemons with warm water, drain thoroughly, and return to the jar. Cover the lemons with the brown sugar. If desired, add the whiskey or a few teaspoons of five-spice powder to taste. Shake the jar until the lemons are evenly coated. Let it sit for a week or so at room temperature until the sugar has dissolved into a thick glaze. Wet lemons will keep indefinitely in the fridge.

COOK REAL HAWAI'I

QUICK-SALTED LEMON PEEL

MAKES ABOUT 1 PACKED CUP

If you want salted preserved lemons (what locals refer to as wet lemon peel) without waiting months, this streamlined method made using just the zest will yield you a comparable product in a couple days. The amount of sugar and salt used can be adjusted to taste, but remember that it should taste balanced, like salty lemonade.

8 lemons
Boiling water
1¼ cups sugar
½ cup Diamond Crystal (or ⅓ cup Morton) kosher salt

Place the lemons in a large heatproof bowl and cover with boiling water. Once cooled, scrub them under warm running water and dry well. Using a vegetable peeler, remove the zest from the lemons, doing your best to avoid the bitter white pith. Set the lemon zest aside. Juice the lemons and scrape out the pulp with a spoon, then place the zest, juice, and pulp in a zip-top plastic bag along with the sugar and salt. Seal the bag, squeezing out as much air as you can. Mix thoroughly until the salt and sugar are dissolved. Place in the fridge for 2 to 3 days. When ready, the lemon peels will be salty-sweet and tender to the bite and the pulp can be used as well in dressings and sauces. No need to rinse before using.

LEMON OLIVE OIL

MAKES 2 CUPS

During an insane period in my life when I was working double shifts at two restaurants, I cooked at an Italian place on Maui called Vino's. It was there that I was introduced to Agrumato brand lemon olive oil, which is made by pressing lemon zest with olives so the citrus flavor infuses into the oil. The first time I tasted it my mind was blown—I was amazed you could add both brightness and richness to a dish at the same time.

Since then, lemon olive oil has always been in my pantry—I even brought a bottle with me during both seasons of *Top Chef*. Though it's worthwhile to pick up a bottle for $25 at a gourmet food store or online, you can also easily make lemon olive oil yourself using fresh peels. I'll use this stuff anywhere I would regular olive oil—in dressings, in sauces, or for a quick drizzle to finish a dish just before serving. Can't go wrong.

4 lemons, thoroughly scrubbed in hot water
2 cups extra-virgin olive oil

Peel the lemon zest in long strips with a vegetable peeler, making sure to avoid the bitter white pith. (Reserve the lemon flesh and juice for another use.) Combine the zest strips and olive oil in a saucepan and simmer over very low heat for 15 minutes, stirring occasionally. If any bubbles appear, even on the side of the pan, reduce the heat or briefly remove the pan from the heat. Let the oil cool to room temperature while the zest strips are left in to steep (about an hour will do). Strain out the zest and transfer the lemon oil to a clean jar or sealable container. Store in a cool, dark place. The oil will keep for about 1 month on the shelf, or for several months in the fridge (just be sure to bring it up to room temperature before using).

FINÁDENNÉ

MAKES ABOUT 1½ CUPS

This doctored-up shoyu condiment hails from Guam, an island country that has nearly as many cross-cultural influences shaping its food as Hawai'i does. The broad formula is saltiness balanced with sour and heat, with chopped onion thrown in for flavor. You can make it as spicy or as tangy as you prefer, using whatever type of chili and a blend of vinegar or citrus. The Chamorro, the native people of Guam, use finádenné in the same way we use chili pepper water (see page 264), splashed onto meat, poultry, fish, vegetables, and rice, or placed in a small bowl and used as a lovely dipping sauce throughout the meal.

½ cup apple cider vinegar
¼ cup shoyu (soy sauce)
2 tablespoons fish sauce
1 tablespoon Lemon Olive Oil (page 278)
1 small sweet onion, thinly sliced
3 Hawaiian chili peppers, thinly sliced, or 1 red Fresno chili, seeded and finely chopped
2 teaspoons minced garlic

In a small bowl, stir together all the ingredients. Let sit at room temperature for at least 1 hour before using.

COCONUT CANDY

MAKES ABOUT 4 CUPS

Sugar-glazed, oven-toasted coconut chips are now a trendy keto snack, so I've been told, but let the record show that gift shops on Maui have been charging tourists for an extremely similar item called coconut candy for years.

At Lineage, I sprinkled coconut candy over any dish that welcomed extra crunch and nutty sweetness, but just as often I ended up eating it by the handful. It's that good.

½ cup honey or agave syrup
1 tablespoon neutral oil
1 teaspoon vanilla extract
4 cups unsweetened coconut flakes
Kosher salt

Preheat the oven to 325°F. Line a sheet pan with parchment paper.

In a large bowl, whisk together the honey, oil, and vanilla. Add the coconut flakes and stir to coat. Spread the coconut mixture on the lined sheet pan. Sprinkle with a pinch or two of salt.

Bake until golden brown and crisp, 12 to 15 minutes, tossing and rotating the pan front to back halfway through. Remove from the oven and let cool completely. Store in a sealable container in a cool, dry place for up to 1 week.

FRIED GARLIC

MAKES ABOUT 1½ CUPS

Without the savory crunch of fried garlic, my kitchen wouldn't be the same. I use it on rice, noodles, soups, salads, vegetables, and anything else that benefits from a sprinkle of these magical golden flavor nuggets. For the Fried Garlic Noodles (page 196), I showed you how to make a quick version of fried garlic in the microwave. If you want to take your fried garlic game to the next level, though, you can fry it in large batches like we do at Tin Roof, since it will keep for several weeks. Though more labor-intensive, this cooking method produces a crispier, evenly browned fried garlic that packs a ridiculous amount of roasted garlickiness. Plus, you'll end up with an infused oil that can be used in other dishes.

8 ounces peeled garlic (about 1½ cups or 25 cloves)
Neutral oil, for frying
Kosher salt

Preheat the oven to 250°F. Line a baking sheet with paper towels.

In a food processor, pulse the garlic until finely minced.

Fill a medium-width, deep-sided pot halfway with water and bring to a boil, then turn off the heat. Fill a large bowl with ice water. Transfer the garlic to a sieve and submerge in the hot water, blanching for about 2 minutes. Remove and dunk the garlic in the ice water until cooled, then drain well and spread evenly onto the lined baking sheet. Bake until the garlic is dry to the touch, 12 to 15 minutes.

While the garlic is drying, empty out the pot and dry well. Fill the pot with at least 2 inches of oil, making sure to leave a few inches of clearance from the top of the pot. Heat the oil over medium-high until it reaches 350°F (use a thermometer).

Have the baking sheet lined with paper towels at the ready. Add the garlic and fry until the bubbles begin to subside and the garlic turns golden and rises to the surface, 3 to 4 minutes. Transfer the fried garlic back to the paper towels and let cool completely. Season generously with salt, then transfer to a sealable container and store in a cool, dry place for up to 3 weeks. Reserve the garlic-flavored frying oil for future use.

PORTUGUESE SAUSAGE

MAKES ABOUT 2 POUNDS

Just behind Spam on the seasoned meat depth chart, Portuguese sausage is one of those local foods that immediately says "Hawai'i" to those in the know.

As you might have guessed, this zesty style of sausage has roots in Portugal, where pork links spiced with vinegar, black pepper, garlic, and paprika are known as linguiça. Portuguese immigrants brought it with them to Hawai'i in the late nineteenth century, and like most things imported here, the sausage evolved over time, becoming plumper, sweeter, and softer in texture than its predecessor. These days, Portuguese sausage is so popular in Hawai'i that even McDonald's offers it with eggs and rice on their breakfast menu.

For recipes that call for it, Hawai'i-made Portuguese sausage can be found at well-stocked Asian markets (local brands always have the best names—look for Gouvea's, Redondo's, Uncle Louie, Rego's Purity, Aloha Brand, or Pacific Sausages). Otherwise you can substitute linguiça, or season your own ground pork, which is easier than you think. For the sake of simplicity, this recipe makes loose sausage for hand-shaping into patties. If you have a sausage maker at home, feel free to grab some casings and stuff the sausage into links.

2 pounds boneless pork butt, cut into ½-inch cubes
6 cloves garlic, minced
2 teaspoons Diamond Crystal (or 1½ teaspoons Morton) kosher salt
2 tablespoons white white vinegar
2 teaspoons sugar
2 teaspoons smoked paprika
1 teaspoon red chili flakes, or to taste
½ teaspoon freshly ground black pepper
½ teaspoon ground coriander
¼ teaspoon ground nutmeg
¼ teaspoon ground cloves
Neutral oil, for cooking

Place the pork on a baking sheet and chill in the freezer for 20 to 30 minutes, until the meat is firm on the edges but not frozen solid. Working in batches, fill the bowl of a food processor halfway with the pork and pulse until finely chopped, about 15 pulses. Transfer to a large mixing bowl.

Add all other ingredients (except the oil) and ¼ cup cold water to the pork. Mix thoroughly. Cover and marinate overnight in the fridge, or for up to 2 days, stirring occasionally. Shape into thin, 2-inch-wide patties (or stuff into sausage casings, if using).

To cook, heat a skillet over medium heat and slick it with oil. Add as many patties as will fit comfortably, sear for 3 to 4 minutes until browned, then flip and sear until browned and cooked through, another 3 to 4 minutes.

EASY CHAR SIU

MAKES ABOUT 2 POUNDS

If you've been to an American Chinatown, you know the joy of seeing a glistening hunk of deep-red char siu pork in a shop window. One of the original foods brought to the islands by Chinese immigrants, char siu takes many forms here in Hawai'i, from being stuffed into manapua (see Biscuit Manapua, page 74) to an essential topping on a bowl of Saimin (page 190).

For recipes that call for char siu, my first recommendation would be to pick up an order from your local Chinese deli or restaurant, or use the convenient frozen brands that some grocery stores carry. That said, you can also buy pork butt at the store and make your own simplified char siu at home, as many locals do. A basic combination of thick, salty hoisin sauce; Chinese five-spice; and honey creates a sticky, shiny glaze that will keep the pork tender and succulent as it roasts. Char siu *can do*.

2 pounds pork butt or shoulder steaks, about 1 inch thick, preferably boneless
⅓ cup shoyu (soy sauce)
3 tablespoons honey
2 tablespoons hoisin sauce
2 tablespoons whiskey
3 tablespoons sugar

1 teaspoon Diamond Crystal (or ½ teaspoon Morton) kosher salt
½ teaspoon Chinese five-spice powder
4 cloves garlic, minced
2 tablespoons minced fresh ginger
1 teaspoon red food coloring (optional)
Oil, for greasing

Cut the pork into long strips about 3 inches wide by 1 inch thick, cutting out the bones if needed. In a shallow pan or zip-top plastic bag, combine the shoyu, honey, hoisin, whiskey, sugar, salt, five-spice, garlic, ginger, and food coloring (if using). Add the pork strips, tossing to coat. Let marinate for at least 3 hours, or overnight, in the fridge, mixing occasionally.

Fill a roasting pan with ½ inch of water and place it on the lowest rack of the oven, then preheat the oven to 400°F.

Grease a wire rack and place it in a sheet pan. Remove the pork from the marinade and arrange it on the rack, reserving the leftover marinade for basting.

Roast on the top rack of the oven for 15 minutes. Remove the sheet pan and reduce the oven temperature to 350°F. Flip the pork and carefully baste with its drippings and the reserved marinade. Return to the oven to roast for another 20 minutes, or until a thermometer inserted into the pork reads at least 145°F.

Remove it from the oven and baste once more with only the pork drippings, then let rest for at least 15 minutes before slicing against the grain. If you're not using it immediately, store the char siu unsliced in a sealable container in the fridge for up to 5 days, or tightly wrapped in plastic in the freezer for up to 2 months.

ALCOHOL (NOT JUST FOR DRINKING!)

Beer

Although there are no recipes in this book where beer is an ingredient, there are many dishes that suggest drinking a cold one on the side. I find a light, crisp lager or pilsner usually pairs best.

Mirin

Mirin is a sweet Japanese cooking wine that is a little lower in alcohol and higher in sugar than sake. It's often used to add a particular mellow-sweet flavor to Japanese sauces, dressings, and marinades.

Sake

The original Japanese rice brew, sake is used in situations where a drier cooking wine is needed. Use a clear sake rather than unfiltered. Don't hesitate to pick the cheapest bottle rather than something meant for sipping.

Shaoxing wine

Shaoxing, sometimes called "shao hsing," is a Chinese cooking wine. It tends to be less sweet and more savory than sake. Dry sherry is the best substitute.

Whiskey/brandy

Many locals use brown liquor as a substitute for aged Chinese spirits or an Okinawan spirit called awamori. Use whatever brand you normally drink (in my family it's Crown Royal).

ARARE (RICE CRACKERS)

Also called *kakimochi* (mochi crunch), these soy-glazed rice crackers come in many different sizes, colors, and shapes. A popular snack that can be eaten by themselves, they can also be crushed and used as a topping for rice and vegetables.

BAGOÓNG (FERMENTED FISH PASTE)

Sometimes labeled salted fish paste, this funky fermented condiment is a crucial element in Filipino dishes that come from the Ilocos region, where my family is originally from. If you can't find it in an Asian market, you can substitute shrimp paste, which is commonly used in Southeast Asia, mixed with a little fish sauce.

BANANA KETCHUP

Made with mashed bananas instead of tomatoes, banana ketchup is a popular condiment in the Philippines. Like the regular kind, it's sweet, tangy, red, and delicious on anything fried. Look for the Jufran brand in Asian markets.

BLACK BEANS, SALTED OR FERMENTED

Chinese fermented or salted black beans are made from black soybeans. They usually come in vacuum-sealed bags or cans, but once opened will last for months in a cool, dark place. Most often salted black beans are used to make black bean sauce for Chinese stir-fries or other dishes. Soak them in hot water until soft, then roughly mash with a fork before using. If unavailable, prepared black bean sauce sold in jars can be substituted.

BROTH

When using canned or boxed broth, I prefer to use the low-sodium kind and season with salt later as needed. If you have regular broth, hold back a bit of the salt (or salty seasonings) in the recipe.

CHINESE FIVE-SPICE POWDER

This powdered seasoning blend is a classic ingredient in Chinese cooking. Ingredients can vary, but most contain: cinnamon, star anise, cloves, licorice or fennel seed, and white pepper. You can find it in any grocery store.

CHINESE HOT MUSTARD

Sold prepared or in powdered form, this zippy nasal-clearing mustard is a popular condiment in Hawai'i, often used in combination with shoyu (soy sauce) as a dip for noodles or sashimi. I prefer the powdered kind because it lasts longer and you can mix it with water to your own taste.

COCONUT

This book calls for three kinds of coconut products: coconut milk, shredded coconut, and coconut flakes. Canned coconut milk works great, just be sure to use the unsweetened full-fat kind that has only coconut milk and water as ingredients. Both shredded coconut and coconut flakes should be unsweetened.

CORNSTARCH/TAPIOCA STARCH/ ARROWROOT POWDER

These are my starches of choice, useful for thickening sauces, battering fried foods, or adding texture to baked goods. They are mostly interchangeable, though keep in mind that tapioca and arrowroot don't stand up as well to prolonged heat.

DRIED SEAFOOD

This book calls for dried shrimp and dried shredded fish. Dried shrimp is often used as a seasoning or topping and can be found at Asian or Latino markets, usually in the spice section. Dried shredded fish is a jerky-like snack usually made from pollack, cod, or cuttlefish. Find it in the snack section or seafood section of Asian markets.

FISH SAUCE

Many styles of funky, salty, umami-rich fish sauce can be found all over Southeast Asia. I mostly use Filipino patís, which tends to be a little sharper in saltiness. The differences in flavors are pretty minimal though, so if you only have Thai or Vietnamese fish sauce, they will work fine.

FLOURS
All-purpose flour

I don't use tons of flour in this book, but when I do it's regular all-purpose flour.

Mochiko (sweet rice flour)

An essential component for making mochi, mochiko is sometimes confusingly labeled "sweet rice flour," even though it's not sweet—it's just made from glutinous rice . . . which actually doesn't contain gluten. (Go figure.) Koda Farms is a good brand.

FRESH CHILIES

The most common local chili is known as 'nioi, commonly called Hawaiian chili pepper. Small, hot, and brightly flavored, it's similar to the Tabasco pepper, but is very hard to come by on the mainland. Instead, you can substitute Thai bird's eye chilies, which are much hotter (use less), or red Fresno chilies, red jalapeños, or red serranos, which are slightly milder (use a little more).

GARLIC SALT

Garlic salt is a wonderful seasoning, delivering a one-two punch of savoriness in one sprinkle. I'm a fan of Lawry's brand. You can also combine 1 part garlic powder with 3 parts kosher salt.

GREEN PAPAYA/GREEN MANGO

Green (unripe) papayas and mangoes are used in many local dishes for their crunch and tart flavor. They can easily be found at Asian markets, but you can also seek out the firmest and least ripe mangoes and papayas at grocery stores (ask them if they have green ones in the back).

GUAVA JELLY

Fresh guavas are great in season, but the thing you want stocked in your pantry is guava jelly, a sweet, sticky condiment that is beloved by locals. Goes great with toast or any baked good, as well as breakfast meats (sweet-n-salty gang).

HOISIN SAUCE

Hoisin is a thick brownish sauce made from preserved soybeans, garlic, ginger, and spices. The brand I use is Lee Kum Kee, the same one that makes my favorite premium oyster sauce.

INSTANT DASHI POWDER

Dashi, a deeply flavored stock made from dried fish and dried kelp, is a cornerstone of the Japanese kitchen. Think of instant dashi like a dashi bouillon powder. HonDashi is the most common brand. It's a powerful umami-bomb. Used as a seasoning, a pinch sprinkled over any dish will add a deep savoriness. I call it the flavor booster of all flavor boosters. In Hawai'i, it has long been a pantry secret among home cooks and chefs. Many use it to season fried rice or noodles, create time-saving saimin broth, poach vegetables or seafood, or amp up sauces, dips, and dressings. A small container should last the average household for a while.

KAMABOKO

Kamaboko is a style of Japanese fish cake that's usually sold in pink and white logs. Find them in the refrigerated section at Asian markets, or substitute other types of fish cake or imitation crab.

KOCHUGARU (GOCHUGARU)

Kochugaru (often spelled gochugaru) is a spicy, fragrant, earthy Korean chili flake that is a crucial seasoning for kim chee and other dishes requiring a boost of heat as well as flavor. The closest substitutes are Chinese red chili flakes, or in a pinch, crushed red pepper. Kochugaru has a bit finer texture than those, so you can break them down in a spice grinder before substituting.

KOCHUJANG (GOCHUJANG)

A quintessential part of the Korean pantry, kochujang (also spelled gochujang) is a thick fermented red chili and soybean paste that is spicy and a little sweet. It's concentrated and pungent in flavor. In this book, it's used for marinade and sauces, but it has a million other applications, too, like soups, braises, etc. A container will last in the fridge for a long time.

LAP CHEONG (CHINESE SAUSAGE)

Lap cheong is a semidried, cured Chinese pork sausage. Usually it's smoked, sweetened, and seasoned with soy and various spices. In Hawai'i it often shows up in classic Cantonese dishes, paired with seafood or rice.

LI HING MUI

Li hing mui is a style of dried salted sour plum that originated in China's Pearl River Delta and eventually found its way to Hawai'i, becoming a cult favorite snack-slash-treat that is broadly known as crack seed. Hawai'i is home to whole crack seed stores that sell dozens of flavors and varieties of sweet-salty-sour preserved fruits. Red li hing mui, which has a certain medicinal, sweet licorice flavor to it, is the perennial top seller at any crack seed establishment. It can be sold whole as dried leathery fruit, or crushed and turned into a powerful salty-sour powder used to coat anything from gummy bears to shave ice to fresh fruit. The best bet is to buy them online from one of the many Hawai'i goods stores. Look for dried sweet red li hing mui (sometimes just labeled sweet li hing mui) and li hing mui powder, which is li hing plums that have been seasoned with salt, and sugar, and sometimes licorice powder. Since the flavor profile of li hing mui powder can vary widely from brand to brand, it's best to use it in recipes according to taste.

MACADAMIA NUTS

Despite what you might think, mac nuts are native to Australia, not Hawai'i. They were first cultivated in the islands in the 1920s and through good advertising became one of the state's most popular exports. Buttery and rich but mild in flavor, they're a good substitute for the *kukui* (candlenut), which was eaten by the native Hawaiians. For recipes in this book, use salted dry-roasted mac nuts.

MANG TOMAS ALL-PURPOSE SAUCE

Mang Tomas is a Filipino brand of condiment that is usually eaten with lechon and other crispy meats. It's thick, sweet, and tangy with a mellow savory flavor. Look for it in yellow-labeled bottles at Asian markets.

MAYO

In Hawai'i it's gotta be Best Foods (or Hellmann's if you're east of the Rockies): creamy, rich, tangy, sweet, savory, well-balanced. Accept no substitutes.

MISO

Made from fermented soybeans, umami-rich miso paste is a must-have for any local pantry. There are many varieties, but the kind I use most is called shiro miso (white miso), also known as sweet or mellow miso. Shiro miso is fermented for a shorter time and is less salty than the darker kinds.

MUSHROOMS

For recipes in this book that call for fresh mushrooms, any mix of what you have will work. But when we talk about dried mushrooms, we're talking shiitakes. Not only do dried shiitakes last a long time in your pantry, they have a more concentrated flavor than the fresh ones. Soak them in hot water until rehydrated, then slice the caps and use as needed. And use the soaking water—it's got good flavor.

NOODLES

Saimin/ramen noodles

When using fresh noodles for Saimin (page 190) or Dry Mein (page 192), there is a hierarchy of preference involved: At the top is fresh or frozen saimin, which some Asian markets carry but might be hard to get on the mainland. Just below that is any kind of fresh or frozen ramen-style noodle.

"Faux-min"

If you can't find either of the above, you can make "faux-min": Boil spaghetti with 1 teaspoon kosher salt and 1 tablespoon baking soda per 1 quart of water. The water will fizz and foam when the baking soda goes in, so make sure your pot isn't too full (stirring will help keep the bubbles down). Cook the pasta as directed on the package, then remove from the heat and stir in 2 tablespoons distilled white vinegar per quart. Immediately drain and rinse the noodles thoroughly under cold water. The baking soda will help turn the pasta bouncy and chewy like ramen (or pretty close). If all else fails, you can use instant ramen noodles (my standard breakfast for most of my adolescence).

Chow mein/pancit Canton

These Cantonese-style egg noodles can usually come fresh or close to it, which means you don't have to cook them for more than a couple minutes before using in a stir-fry (follow package directions). Chinese brands will often label them chow mein noodles, but if you see a Filipino brand labeled pancit Canton, that's the same thing.

Cellophane (glass) noodles

Also known as bean threads, mung bean noodles, or long rice (what they're called in Hawai'i), these translucent noodles are usually made from various types of starches like mung bean, tapioca, or arrowroot. They need to be soaked in warm water before using, but not for very long—just long enough to untangle and soften a bit.

Dried chow fun or fettuccine

Chow fun are thick, wide rice noodles that can be tough to find fresh on the mainland. For certain dishes like Miki Noodles (page 183), dried chow fun works well because the noodles will hydrate in the soup broth and soak up extra flavor. If you can't find dried chow fun at an Asian market, use the thickest, widest dried fettuccine you can find instead.

OILS

Neutral oil

When a recipe calls for neutral oil, use any mild-flavored oil with a high smoke point: Canola, grapeseed, sunflower, or avocado are good choices.

Toasted sesame oil

Nutty and dark in color, a little amount of sesame oil delivers a lot of flavor.

Lemon olive oil

Brightly flavored Agrumato lemon olive oil is perfect for drizzling over finished dishes. If you can't find it (check gourmet grocery stores), you can easily make your own using lemon zest and a nice bottle of extra-virgin olive oil (see Lemon Olive Oil, page 278).

OYSTER SAUCE

Thick, salty, sweet, and deeply savory, oyster sauce is one of my favorite all-time condiments. It's made with caramelized oyster extract, which gives it a unique umami flavor that doesn't even taste like seafood. Good oyster sauce is worth tracking down, so look for brands labeled "premium oyster sauce" like Lee Kum Kee. Store opened bottles in the fridge.

RICE

The first appliance that any local kid learns to use is the rice cooker, which is an irreplaceable kitchen tool when you cook as much rice as we do in Hawai'i. So my first suggestion is to invest in a rice cooker. Zojirushi brand is the best, but even a cheap one will work fine. Always rinse the rice until the water runs clear before using, then drain it very well and add the recommended amount of water (most rice cookers come with their own measuring cups and water level markings, but in general my preferred rice-to-water ratio for short- or medium-grain white rice is 1:1). As for types of rice, Japanese short-grain or medium-grain white rice is what is most often used in Hawai'i. Calrose, Kokuho Rose, Nishiki, and Koshihikari are good varieties to look for in particular. If you want to experiment outside classic white rice, here are some variations to try:

Hapa rice

A Hawaiian word that means half, *hapa* in pidgin often refers to someone who is mixed race, usually half haole, half something else. Hapa rice is a cheeky play on that idea: half white rice, half brown rice. The story goes that in early plantation days when rice farming in Hawai'i became popular, low-quality rice husking equipment was often used, which resulted in grains that were only half-milled, somewhere between white and brown rice. Locals developed a taste for this hearty, textured style and soon began producing it even once their rice milling skills were on point. To make this healthyish blend, mix equal parts uncooked white rice with uncooked brown rice (same grain size); cook in the rice cooker as you would white rice.

Garlic rice

Mix cooked rice with fried garlic (see page 283) and garlic oil to taste.

Furikake rice

Mix cooked rice with furikake (see page 262) to taste.

SALT

Kosher salt

My preferred brand of kosher salt is Diamond Crystal, which has large, light flakes, is less salty by volume, and dissolves quickly. However, if you're using Morton kosher, I've included adjusted measurements for each recipe. As a general rule, 2 parts of Morton salt (by volume) is as salty as 3 parts Diamond Crystal.

Hawaiian sea salt

If you're wondering why Hawaiian sea salt, called *'alaea*, doesn't show up much in this book, there's a good reason. It's because most of the "Hawaiian" brands of 'alaea you'll see sold on the mainland are actually processed California sea salts colored with clay powder. Traditional 'alaea made by native Hawaiian artisans is very expensive to produce and rarely leaves the islands. That said, there are certain brands of commercially produced 'alaea brands that are very nostalgic for locals, like Hawaiian Pa'akai Inc., which is sold online. Feel free to use it when making traditional dishes like poke and laulau. Otherwise substitute kosher salt instead.

SAMBAL OELEK

This simple, flavorful, not-too-hot Indonesian chili paste is good to have on hand: It's basically crushed chilies, vinegar, and salt.

SEAWEED

Furikake

This Japanese seasoning is made with dried seaweed, sesame seeds, and salt, and is a great flavorful topping for rice or other things. You can also make it yourself (see page 262).

Nori

These large sheets of roasted dried seaweed are sold in stacks and are usually cut before using. They quickly become soggy when they come out of the package, so most people toast them by waving them over a flame or putting them in the oven briefly to turn them crispy.

Kombu

Kombu is a dried seaweed that usually comes in wide sheets. Most often it's simmered in water, stock, or broth as a seasoning agent, adding a deep umami flavor.

Shio kombu

Shio kombu are thin sheets of kelp that are seasoned with soy, salt, and sugar, then dried and cut into small pieces. I use them to season rice, salad, or pickles, as they lend a delicious savory saltiness.

Ogo

Ogo is a type of *limu* (Hawaiian seaweed) known by its brownish-red color and lacy appearance. It's most commonly added to poke or salads, but its fresh oceanic flavor and crisp texture make it great in sauces and pesto, too. Fresh or frozen ogo is rare on the mainland, so I would suggest ordering dried ogo (see nohfoods.com) and rehydrating it according to the package instructions. If you're unable to find ogo of any kind, the closest substitute would be dried wakame or hijiki seaweed, soaked in water until tender.

SESAME SEEDS

I use white sesame seeds, preferably ones that have already been roasted (or toasted), since it will save you a step when cooking. If you can only find raw sesame seeds, toast them over low heat in a dry pan until fragrant and lightly browned, 3 to 5 minutes, to bring out their nutty flavor before using.

SHOYU (SOY SAUCE)

Hawai'i calls soy sauce *shoyu*, which is the Japanese word for soy sauce. Aloha brand shoyu, which is brewed on Oahu, is a smooth and mild soy sauce that will work for all occasions. If you're unable to find Aloha, I recommend using Yamasa, or if you can't find that, Kikkoman, as they are both made in the mellower, rounder Japanese style. Some locals even mix Kikkoman with a tiny splash of sugar water to mimic the softer taste of Aloha, but I'll leave that to your discretion. If you're looking to make a dish gluten-free or gluten-reduced, use tamari soy sauce (which is made without wheat, just soybeans), a style of shoyu that is bolder in flavor.

SPAM

For my canned meats needs, I always use Spam 25% Less Sodium, because not only is it slightly healthier, I find it to be more balanced in flavor than the original.

STAR ANISE

Star anise is the fruit—yes, fruit—of an evergreen tree native to southern China. The spice's pungent aroma is similar to fennel and anise seed: sweet with hints of licorice. In Hawai'i, it's often added to Chinese soups or stewed dishes or boiled peanuts, providing a certain earthy and warming flavor.

TI LEAVES

Hawaiian ti leaves are classic tropical foliage, often used in Hawaiian flower arrangements or for wrapping laulau (see Deluxe Laulau, page 165). You might be able to find some at your local florist, but if not, use banana leaves instead, which can be found at Asian or Latino grocery stores.

TARO LEAVES

The tough-but-edible leaves of the taro plant are used to make traditional Hawaiian dishes like laulau (see page 165) and luau (page 163). Since quality taro leaves are tough to find on the mainland (and I'm not a fan of the precooked frozen kind), the best move is to substitute Swiss chard or other braising greens instead.

VINEGARS

Apple cider vinegar

Heinz brand apple cider vinegar was a pantry staple in our kitchen when I was growing up. It's tangy but mellow with a mild fruity taste.

Cane vinegar

Traditionally used in Filipino cuisine, cane vinegar is made from sugarcane syrup. It's not quite as potent as distilled white vinegar, but it's still sharp in flavor with a sweetish aftertaste. Look for the Datu Puti brand.

Rice vinegar

Smooth and gentle, its balanced flavor is great for dressings and pickles.

White vinegar

Classic distilled vinegar. Punchy and strong in acidity, because sometimes that's the effect you want.

MAHALOS

First and foremost, mahalo to the Lord above for all the blessings in my life. I have so much to be thankful for and I know it's because of Your doing.

To my amazing family, Janice, Chloe, Peyton, Quinn, and Asher. You've had to sacrifice so much, and I love all of you more than words can express. Janice, you are my rock and my biggest critic. Thank you for pushing me and making me a better person. I would never have tried to do this cookbook without your encouragement, and you always, always got my back.

To Mom and Dad, thank you for the life you gave me. Growing up, I always felt like we never had much, but the values and lessons you instilled in me proved to be priceless.

Mom, I miss you every day. Whenever I look at my girls, I see a bit of you smiling back at me.

Dad, with your deep love and respect for food, you've been the biggest influence in my life. I know our stubbornness sometimes gets in the way of our relationship and expressing our feelings, but know that I'm so grateful to have someone that's always encouraged and supported me to "Just go!"

To my brother, Jeremy, given our upbringing, I guess we were destined to become chefs. Thank you for always looking out for me and showing me the way.

To my Simeon 'ohana, I always look forward to our get-togethers. Our memories of cooking and eating together are the foundation of what my work is all about.

To Nolan, I couldn't ask for a better wingman. I've seen you grow from a bright-eyed cook into a confident, young chef of your own. You've been there and had my back for some of the highest highs in my career: nights in the trenches, long hours in the kitchen, laughing in the streets of NYC in the wee hours. The sky is the limit for you.

To Garrett, I don't know if there's another writer out there who would have been able to swallow a culture and digest it the way that you did, with full understanding and respect, writing it through my voice. I'm forever grateful.

To Kevin, you were such a pleasure to work with. You fit right in and felt like family. I'm so thankful that our paths crossed and you were able to lend your incredible eye to this book.

To Melissa, you went above and beyond in bringing the vibe I imagined to life—you're a true master at making things make sense, if that makes sense.

To the Tin Roof crew, you all keep me young with your energy and positivity. Mahalos for being a part of our community, and for keeping the fire alive when I couldn't.

To the Lineage crew, thank you for being patient with me as we brought this project to life. You totally grasped my vision to share the story of Hawai'i through food. Your curiosity and dedication is infectious.

To Kitty, thank you for keeping the faith. The idea of a cookbook seemed so far-fetched at first but you made it a reality.

To Nicole and the crew at Bolster Media, you nudged me out of the shadows and into brighter spotlights that have led to more opportunities than this local boy could have ever imagined, all while holding my hand along the way.

To my bruddahs Gooch, Isaac, Kelii, mahalos for reminding me to stay grounded in my Hawai'i roots and for doing big things that never cease to motivate me.

To Ryota, you always manage to make us look like we know what we're doing. Thank you for sharing your immense talent.

To Hilo, my hometown—I can always count on you to set my head straight and provide inspiration, whether it's a fresh catch for the grill or wild pig for the smoker, or just a late-night crew to knock back some beers with and reminisce in the Popolo Street garage. Mahalos for the love and support.

And last but not least, mahalos to all the people of Hawai'i working to protect the future of our islands—without you I would have no story to tell.

INDEX

Note: Page references in *italics* indicate photographs.

Library of Congress Cataloging-in-Publication Data
Names: Simeon, Sheldon, author. | Snyder, Garrett, author.
Title: Cook real Hawai'i / Sheldon Simeon with Garrett Snyder.
Description: New York: Clarkson Potter/Publishers, 2021. |
    Includes index.
Identifiers: LCCN 2020031835 (print) | LCCN 2020031836
    (ebook) | ISBN 9781984825834 (hardcover) |
    ISBN 9781984825841 (ebook)
Subjects: LCSH: Hawaiian cooking. | LCGFT: Cookbooks.
Classification: LCC TX724.5.H3 S55 2021 (print) |
    LCC TX724.5.H3 (ebook) | DDC 641.59969—dc23
LC record available at https://lccn.loc.gov/2020031835
LC ebook record available at https://lccn.loc.gov/2020031836

Printed in China

Photograph on page 8: Erin Kunkle

10 9 8 7 6 5 4

First Edition

PRODUCTION CREDITS

Photographer: Kevin J. Miyazaki
Food Stylists: Sheldon Simeon and Nolan Gonzales
Prop Stylist: Melissa Padilla
Recipe Tester: Nolan Gonzales
Editor: Francis Lam
Editorial Assistant: Lydia O'Brien
Designer: Marysarah Quinn
Production Editor: Christine Tanigawa
Production Manager: Philip Leung
Composition: Merri Ann Morrell and Hannah Hunt
Copy Editor: Kate Slate
Indexer: Elizabeth Parson